THE ART OF LIVING

BENJAMIN FRANKLIN

From the portrait by the Scottish painter David Martin (1737-98), commissioned by Franklin in London, in 1767, for his family, and bequeathed by him to the Executive Council of Pennsylvania.

F. L. LUCAS

Fellow of King's College, Cambridge
University Reader in English

THE ART OF
LIVING

FOUR EIGHTEENTH-CENTURY
MINDS

Hume

Horace Walpole

Burke

Benjamin Franklin

(Sequel to *The Search for Good Sense*)

THE MACMILLAN COMPANY
NEW YORK
1961

TO CHARLES, HUGH, AND CLARISSA HINSLEY

'A century had now passed since reason had begun to attain that ascendant in the affairs of the world, to conduct which it had been granted to man six thousand years ago. If religions and governments were still domineered by prejudices, if creeds that contradict logic, or tyrannies that enslave multitudes to the caprice of one, were not yet exploded, novel absurdities at least were not broached; or if propagated, produced neither persecutors nor martyrs. Methodism made fools, but they did not arrive to be saints; and the histories of past ages describing massacres and murders, public executions of violence, and the more private though not less horrid arts of poison and daggers, began to be regarded almost as romances. Caesar Borgia seemed little less fabulous than Orlando; and whimsical tenures of manors were not more in disuse, than sanguinary methods of preserving or acquiring empires. No prime ministers perished on a scaffold, no heretics in the flames: a Russian Princess spared her competitor; even in Turkey the bow-string had been relaxed.'

Horace Walpole, Memoires of the last ten Years of George II (*under the year* 1757)

'En tout, qu'on pense ce qu'on veut, il n'y a de sûr que le sens commun. Il me semble que toute autre sorte d'esprit n'est qu'un écart, une manière de déraisonner agréable pour le moment, mais suivie de regrets. Notre route nous est crayonnée, bornée, limitée. Il faut y marcher aussi doucement qu'il est possible; il ne tient pas à nous d'en tracer une nouvelle, sans rendre la seule que nous ayons plus difficile et quelquefois dangereuse. Si j'avais un enfant à élever, je serais tenté de ne lui dire que ce peu de mots: ne prenez de guide à votre conduite que le sens commun, qu'il soit votre confesseur, votre médecin et votre avocat.'

Horace Walpole to Mme du Deffand
(7/11/1771)

PREFACE

THIS book continues a previous volume, *The Search for Good Sense*. Together, they deal with eight outstanding figures of the later eighteenth century—Johnson, Boswell, Chesterfield, and Goldsmith; Hume, Horace Walpole, Burke, and Benjamin Franklin.

To many of us, theirs is a particularly interesting and attractive age. I feel no wish to have lived then—even if it would not involve being dead now (which I remain optimistic enough to think a disadvantage). But there are certain men and women of the period whom, were I a necromancer, I should especially like to recall to life; whom, had I a time-machine, I should love, as an unborn ghost, to overhear.

Travel has long seemed to me one of the most repaying of all extravagances. But one can travel in time as well as in space. And whereas the modern world of geography grows yearly smaller and more monotonously uniform, the world of past history becomes, on the contrary, ever wider and more strange to us, as time passes and distances increase.

Among the dominating figures of that age of sense, Johnson seemed to me almost indispensable. And from Johnson, Boswell seemed almost inseparable. He may not have found much good sense in himself; but at least he pursued it in others, with a passionate perseverance that won, in the end, a considerable immortality for both them and him. Johnson's old enemy Chesterfield provided, I thought, a striking example of 'good sense' carried, at times, to senseless excess. And Goldsmith, as warm as Chesterfield was chilly, but preserved by irony from over-sweetness, appeared to me in some ways, however feckless his own life, the wisest and most charming of them all.[1]

---

[1] Some of my critics seemed slightly to misunderstand the book's title, as if 'The Search for Good Sense' meant 'The Achievement of Good Sense'. Searches often fail. Chesterfield and Boswell, for example, seem to me to have failed here in certain vital respects; even Johnson and Burke in many respects; even Hume and Franklin in some. Inevitably. But failures can be as interesting as successes. The common factor was the effort.

The four characters dealt with in the present volume likewise include a Scot, an Irishman, and two of English stock. But they make a very different four. Hume and Franklin appealed to me as unusually rational, and unusually happy, types of their rational age. Hume, with a sceptical intelligence that yet never chilled his humanity and gaiety, remained as philosophical in death as in life; Franklin, beginning as a poor tallow-chandler's son, ended, by sheer good sense, energy, and good humour, as an international figure who lastingly changed the history of England, France, and the United States.

Horace Walpole and Burke are less purely rational, more imaginative characters. They show, like Boswell, certain traits of the coming Romanticism. But the much-maligned Walpole, for all his frivolity, attained a wisdom that seems to me too often forgotten, and a generosity forgotten more often still. It is worth contrasting him with an extremer Romantic like Beckford. Both men were sensitive, æsthetic sons of bluff, prosaic fathers; both tried their hands at fantastic building, and fantastic fiction. But Walpole kept much of the balance, measure, and realism of his classic age. His persevering pen has left a lasting monument. His life retains a certain artistic completeness—where Beckford's became a romantic chaos.

Finally, Burke. He does not give the impression of a happy man. He gave himself, rather, to study the happiness of nations. His real wisdom in that field is still violently disputed. To tax him as inconsistent for defending revolution in America, but denouncing it in France, seems unjust. One can see why he felt that the change lay in the situation, not in his own principles. Yet there *is*, I feel, a tragic change between the earlier and the later Burke—a change not so much logical as psychological. His earlier career, though it failed to avert the American War, appears to me a triumph of passionate good sense: but in his last phase the good sense is more and more swept away by a foaming spate of emotionalism. There is much interest and significance in the final fate of Burke.[1]

For those who think human nature the most interesting thing in

---

[1] I might well have also included Gibbon; and Gray, in the lectures on which this book is based, I did include; but excellent portraits of both, on a similar scale, have been done not long ago—Gibbon, by Mr Peter Quennell; Gray, by Lord David Cecil.

the world, these eight figures are fascinating enough in themselves, without drawing conclusions. Yet I have added a chapter of these. I can understand people who are content simply to observe the oddity of human existence, without trying to make head or tail of it. But if a thing is worth reading about, it is worth thinking about. If my readers dislike conclusions, let them shorten the chapter by not reading it. And if they find my conclusions false, let them find better. I believe in certain values which seem to me endangered, or deteriorating, in the modern world—much to the danger or deterioration of that world. If one thinks so, then it is one's business to say so. Indeed, though many disagree, I feel that any historian should have clear values (as even the detached Thucydides had, or the sedate Gibbon)—how else can he select?—and should stand by them.[1] Even though he well knows he may be wrong. (For if only those spoke who were sure of being right, nothing would be heard but the voices of imbeciles.) And even though he may prove no more effectual than the blind King of Bohemia who struck his stroke on Crecy field.

I should like to express my thanks for most helpful suggestions on Hume to Professor George Boas of Johns Hopkins University; and on Burke to Mr F. H. Hinsley of St John's College and Mr G. C. Morris of King's. I am also indebted to J. M. Dent and Sons for permission to quote part of the great speech of Achilles in *Iliad IX*, from my *Greek Poetry for Everyman*.

---

[1] This does not mean that historians and biographers should lavish rash, anachronistic moral judgements on figures of the past with quite different standards from their own. It is unjust, for example, to rail at Calvin or Philip II of Spain as abominable men. For often they made painful sacrifices to live according to their lights. Rather they are to be pitied. But it seems to me no less vital to condemn outspokenly many of their beliefs as abominable, many of their lights as 'darkness visible'. For cruelty, unreason, intolerance, and fanaticism are among the worst curses of mankind. The Devil too has his idealists.

It is all part of the larger principle that one should hate things, not people. Hate, like atomic power, can be devastating (when it is hate of people); or a vital source of energy (when it is hate of things).

Contents

DAVID HUME

*To sit down in a quiet ignorance of those
things which, upon examination, are found
to be beyond the range of our capacities.*

LOCKE

*Le vrai sage est celui qui fonde sur le sable,
Sachant que tout est vain dans le temps éternel
Et que même l'amour est aussi peu durable
Que le souffle du vent et la couleur du ciel.*

HENRI DE RÉGNIER

THE most congenial type of philosopher, to me, is the cannibal. That is to say, just as the best literary critics have often been those who destroyed the dictatorial dogmas of other literary critics (as Johnson did with the Unities), so the best philosophers may often be those who have sceptically questioned the theories of philosophers less sceptical.

Hume, in particular, is a very suitable philosopher for the Age of Reason. For both in theory and in practice he seems, for a philosopher, exceptionally reasonable. He belongs to the line of that Socrates whose chief claim to wisdom was the full knowledge of his own ignorance; not to the line of Plato, who put into the mouth of this same Socrates so many confident conclusions that to some appear highly questionable.

Philosophers have often been recluses; sometimes because they were unpractical, and could not cope with the world; sometimes because they were unworldly, and renounced the world; sometimes because they were timid, and hid from the world. But it seems to me far healthier to keep like Hume, a balance between abstruse meditation and practical activity. 'Reality' may be Maya—illusion; but it can become a very dull and tedious illusion if we try merely to elude it.

Philosophers ought to be wise; a 'lover of wisdom', who fails to show it, grows comical. And of wisdom it seems to me an important part to train oneself to act, as well as to think. Far better to alternate, like a skylark, between airy heights and solid earth, than to turn into an owl brooding blindly all one's days, and emerging only among the shadows to watch and prey—on mice.

Hume was a man with a minimum of beliefs, who refused to become a dreaming Buddha; loved laughter, intelligent women, and solid meals; and could turn his hand quite happily, serenely, and successfully to soldiering or diplomacy. Gayer than Locke, more practical than Berkeley, little ever ruffled him except the incorrigible arrogance of Englishmen and the incomprehensible frenzies of Rousseau. By conviction a Sceptic, 'le bon David' savoured life like a sensible Epicurean, and met death—much to the disappointment of bigots—as calmly as a Stoic; though with a humour and humanity that most Stoics have sadly lacked.

3

As a writer, too, he became wisely versatile. Philosophers have not always forgiven him for so often forsaking philosophy. But surely he gained far more from life, and gave more to it, by becoming also essayist, economist, historian, and critic—as well as a charming letter-writer.

Further, philosophic writers often cannot write. There is justice in the ironic comment of Schopenhauer (who *could*): 'Doubtless had Hume lived till our day he would have improved his style, and thrown aside terseness and lucidity to spread a mystery of darkness over his writings. With involved periods and self-coined words, he would have begun by puzzling his readers, making them feel that, the less they thought themselves, the more the author must have thought.'[1]

No doubt Hume's literary criticism often seems to us bizarre; and his history has grown obsolete, in a way that Gibbon's has not. Yet his criticism is not proved wrong, because a later age feels it odd; for him it *was* true. And his history did good service in his own day, both by bringing him fame and independence, and by setting an example of impartiality previously far from common in that age of political venom.

David Hume was born at Edinburgh on April 26, 1711 (old style), of a good, but poor Berwickshire family, which had owned since the early sixteenth century his paternal home at Ninewells, on a bluff eighty feet above the Whiteadder, only a few miles from the Border and in sight of that England which was often to irritate him as intensely as Scotland irritated Johnson.

An ancestor, Lord Home of Douglas, fell in 1424 at Verneuil: Hume's grandfather, John Home (1657?–95) was a vigorous person, who fought in 1688–9, as captain of dragoons, for King William; married thrice; and left seven children when he died, not yet forty. One of these, Joseph, the philosopher's father, was also, unlike the philosopher, a violent Whig—so much so that he is recorded to have once returned home shirtless and wigless, having tossed

[1] Cf. Voltaire's irony on Bayle: 'A-t-on jamais vu un plus abominable homme? Il expose les choses avec une fidélité si odieuse; il met sous les yeux le pour et le contre avec une impartialité si lâche; il est d'une clarté si intolérable, qu'il met les gens qui n'ont que le sens commun en état de juger et même de douter: on n'y peut pas tenir; et pour moi j'avoue que j'entre dans une sainte fureur quand on parle de cet homme-là et de ses semblables.' (*Entretien d'Ariste et d'Acrotal*, 1761.)

both appendages into a bonfire in celebration of the Protestant succession. But in 1713 Joseph too died young, at thirty-three, 'leaving me, with an elder Brother and Sister,[1] under the care of our Mother, a woman of singular Merit, who, though young and handsome, devoted herself entirely to the rearing and educating of her Children'.

At twelve David went, for two or three years, to Edinburgh University. Then, from fourteen or fifteen till twenty-three, the youth did little but read. At eighteen he made a half-hearted attempt on the law. But he preferred literature. He preferred thinking. 'The Law . . . appear'd nauseous to me.' Indeed he seems to have read and thought beyond his strength. From 1729 to 1734 he suffered from overstrain, ill-health, and 'spleen'. To his mother, a practical Scotswoman, all this may well have seemed a most unpromising start. What folly for a young man with an inheritance of probably less than fifty pounds a year, to sit book-worming and mooning at home in melancholy fits! Hence, perhaps, her recorded comment— 'Our Davie's a fine good-natured crater, but uncommon wake-minded.' In years to come, even his worst enemies could hardly echo *that*.

No doubt the young Goldsmith, the young Wordsworth, and many another gifted youth must have seemed to their respectable relatives no less unsatisfactory. Yet a man who has not given some years to wide and often random reading in his youth, may find it far from easy to store his mind amid the preoccupations of maturer years. My impression is that many intelligent persons subsist for most of their lives, camel-like, on a literary hump accumulated during their unnoticed nonage.

In 1734 Hume left for London. He wrote a letter, perhaps never sent, to a physician there, perhaps Dr Arbuthnot, describing his own maladies. But his cure was to come, perhaps, simply from change of scene, and contact with the world. After an unsatisfactory attempt to work for a Bristol sugar-merchant, he retired for three years to France to write his philosophy; spending 1734 at Paris and Rheims, 1735–7 at La Flèche in Anjou, where he could use the library of the Jesuits' college that had once educated Descartes. Then London; there, in January 1739, he published the first two

[1] John and Katherine.

volumes of his *Treatise of Human Nature*; for which, considering his own obscurity, and that of his subject, he was by no means unlucky to be paid fifty pounds.

Further, the publication was anonymous; and 'it fell', said Hume long after in his autobiography, '*dead-born from the Press*; without reaching such distinction as even to excite a Murmur among the Zealots'. But this seems overstatement. In November–December 1739, the *History of the Works of the Learned* devoted to the book a review of, in all, no less than fifty-two pages.[1] True, the body of this article, perhaps by Warburton,[2] was hostile and sardonic. It referred to the author under such ironical titles as 'this incomparable Arguer'; and complained of his 'egotism'. This, indeed, if the author *was* Warburton, forms a climax to the irony, though an unconscious one. Warburton complaining of egotism! But the conclusion of the whole notice, possibly added by the editor himself, was far friendlier. Hume's work showed, it said, 'incontestable Marks of a great Capacity, of a soaring Genius, but young, and not yet thoroughly practised'. 'We shall probably,' it concluded, 'have reason to consider this, compared with his later Productions, in the same light as we view the *Juvenile* Works of *Milton*, or the first Manner of a *Raphael*, or other celebrated Painter.'

Few modern authors would feel their literary products quite

[1] Further, 46 pages were devoted to the *Treatise* in 1740 by the *Nouvelle bibliothèque* (The Hague); 49 pages in 1740–1 by the *Bibliothèque raisonnée* (Amsterdam). Both reviews were without sympathy or understanding, but not without respect. There were also two hostile notices in German learned periodicals. (See Mossner's article in *Mind*, LVI (1947), 31–43.)

[2] William Warburton (1698–1779), 'dictator and tyrant of the world of literature' and heavy-weight champion of eighteenth-century Anglicanism, began as an attorney's clerk (1714), then took orders (1723). Though at first leagued with Pope's enemies, in 1739 he defended the *Essay on Man* against Crousaz. He paid compliments; and the compliments paid. He was introduced by the grateful Pope to the rich Ralph Allen (Fielding's 'Allworthy'); and in 1745 married Allen's niece. In 1747 he edited Shakespeare; in 1751, as literary executor, Pope. In 1759 he attained the see of Gloucester.

His great work was *The Divine Legation of Moses* (1738–41), paradoxically proving that, since Moses taught nothing of immortality, the Jewish community could only have been upheld by an 'extraordinary providence'. For twenty-five to thirty years he is said to have read fourteen to fifteen hours a day; being endowed, in Bentley's phrase, with 'monstrous appetite and bad digestion'. Johnson owned Warburton to be better read than himself; but neither of them could abide the other's style. 'Warburton,' said Johnson, 'by extending his abuse, rendered it ineffectual.' Yet he also conceded: 'Warburton may be absurd, but he will never be weak; he flounders well.' He has, however, long floundered into obscurity.

'dead-born' if hailed by reviewers with praises of their 'soaring Genius', or with comparisons to Milton and Raphael. But even philosophers, it seems, can be a little exacting at twenty-eight—and sometimes later. Still, Hume might argue that the honey of the last half-page, too clearly the kindly addition of another hand, could not neutralize the vitriol of the rest.

In the spring of 1740, he gave his book a further prod by publishing an anonymous 'Abstract' of it, which purports to come from another hand than the author's. This was announced in the *Daily Advertiser* as 'An Abstract of a late Philosophical Performance, entitled *A Treatise of Human Nature* etc. Wherein the chief Argument and Design of that Book, which has met with such Opposition, and been represented in so terrifying a Light, is further illustrated and explain'd'. Hume may either have exaggerated the public 'Opposition'; or he may in later life have exaggerated the public indifference; but it becomes hard to see how both can have been true. (It is of some interest that in the three extant copies of the Abstract itself, the relative clause from 'which' to 'so terrifying a Light', is omitted.)

In November 1740 the *Treatise* was completed by a third volume —*Of Morals*. But this roused less—or still less—attention.

Very sensibly, Hume (who, after all, had somehow to live) now transferred his energies to topics less abstruse. His two volumes of *Essays Moral and Political* (published late in 1741 and early in 1742), turned to criticism, philosophy, and politics. They also included a character of Sir Robert Walpole, which had the luck to acquire topical interest—for in February 1742 Sir Robert fell from power. That same year, the *Essays* reached a second edition.

But literary success, though much more exciting, is much less secure than academic position. In 1744–5 Hume stood for the Edinburgh chair of Ethics and Pneumatical Philosophy. 'Pneumatical', to us, suggests tyres rather than chairs; but, after all, the Greek *pneuma* means 'spirit' as well as 'breath'. In May 1745, however, at a meeting of the Edinburgh Ministers, still a formidable body, the name of Hume was denounced. The *Treatise*, after all, was unlikely to be of a sweet savour to the orthodox. And so at the beginning of June 1745 the professorship was given to one William Cleghorn, now an empty name.

But if 1745 proved no more fortunate for the pretensions of David Hume than for those of Charles Stuart, that is hardly surprising. If this academic election was decided less on academic than on theological grounds, the same thing, after all, happened to Henry Sidgwick, for example, in the nineteenth century, and is not unheard-of in the twentieth. It was natural enough, and need cause no great moral indignation. After all, it remains uncertain that free-thinkers would always show themselves more liberal, or tolerant, in such matters than the devout. And, in the end, Hume probably gained rather than lost by his rejection. An academic chair might well have proved cramping; even if he had not quickly made it too hot to hold him.

This likelihood he seems, after his defeat, to have admitted himself; but that did not prevent him from making a second attempt, ending in a second defeat, at Glasgow six years later. Even if his *Treatise* had dropped 'dead-born', its ghost proved lively enough at haunting him.

But meanwhile he found a very different occupation, arising from the success of his *Essays*. These had 'charmed' the young Marquess of Annandale; and in January 1745 Hume was invited to become his tutor. By April he was installed at St Albans, with a salary of £300 a year; very welcome to a thrifty Scots philosopher with none of Diogenes' passion for poverty. But this pleasant arrangement had one drawback—the Marquess was mad.

By September 1745 he had become difficult to handle; further this unfortunate fool had a cousin, a naval Captain Vincent, who was a knave. On April 16, 1746, the day of Culloden, Hume quitted the Marquess's roof; but a lawsuit for his last quarter's salary dragged on for years, though the funds of the Annandale estate accumulated to over £400,000. Still Hume had earned £400. And now something better turned up.

From keeper of a lunatic, Hume found himself transformed to the secretary of a general—but in an enterprise that turned out not much saner than the poor Marquess. In London that May General James St Clair,[1] a distant kinsman, came on Hume; like most people,

---

[1] Scots soldier and M.P. (d. 1762). His only military command of importance was this expedition against Lorient; his conduct of which was later warmly defended by Hume in a written narrative.

was at once charmed by him; and invited him to become his secretary, at ten shillings a day besides perquisites. For, in prosecution of one of our more futile wars with France, General St Clair was to invade Canada. For Hume this was not only employment. He had already turned his thoughts to writing history; and it is good for one who would make a history, to see, with his own eyes, some history being made. We may recall Edward Gibbon, captain of Hampshire Grenadiers and member of parliament.

Unfortunately the English Cabinet was at sixes and sevens. The Duke of Newcastle was no Chatham; and fiasco now followed fiasco. On June 27, 1746, the enterprise was countermanded; three weeks later it was ordered again; throughout the summer, winds and ministers continued to veer. In August Hume was appointed Judge Advocate to the expedition—his nodding acquaintance with the law proved of service after all. Finally in September it was decided, as a diversion to the French campaign in Flanders, to attack either Normandy or the French west coast; and on September 15 from fifty to sixty sail left Plymouth to besiege Lorient—though, it is said, without so much as a map of that coast, except for one small-scale map of all France picked up by the General's A.D.C. in a Plymouth shop.

By a feint the English got ashore; but it was found, when the siege-guns had been dragged into position, that most of the ammunition, and the furnace to heat the shot, had been left on board; and when these at last were landed, that the bellows for the furnace had been forgotten. On September 26 the siege was abandoned. Even so this comic opera was not yet complete; at nine the very same evening the French commander sent a flag of truce to surrender. But the flag of truce found only four spiked British cannon, and a forsaken mortar, to surrender to. By late October Hume was back in Cork; by March, 1747, at Spithead. He had seen war in all its bungling absurdity, as Stendhal and Tolstoy were to see it after him; which was no doubt useful. And he had, as always, made friends; which was more useful still. All the same, when he returned to Ninewells in that summer of 1747, Hume was still without settled occupation. And he was now thirty-six.

Again, however, something turned up. At the beginning of 1748 General St Clair was sent on a military mission to Vienna and

Turin, to try to rouse our somewhat sluggish Austrian and Savoy-ard allies. He chose Hume for his secretary and A.D.C. In February 1748, they left Harwich, where fifteen years later Johnson was to toss his majestic figure while he watched Boswell tossing away across the North Sea towards Holland. In April at Vienna the mission was received by Maria Theresa, who graciously excused them from walking backwards after their audience. 'We esteemd our-selves,' wrote Hume, 'very much oblig'd to her for this Attention, especially my Companions, who were desperately afraid of my fall-ing on them & crushing them.' For already Hume was become as solid as his reasoning, and had put in practice that maxim of Lorenzi— 'la vera filosofia è quella d'ingrassare.'[1]

At the end of April they left for Italy; and, reaching Mantua, Hume kissed the soil that once gave birth to Virgil—one more example of the fatuity of supposing Hume the rationalist, or his Age of Reason, to have lacked emotion. One may suspect Sterne, when he knelt before the statue of Henri IV on the Pont Neuf, of some affectation; but not Hume.

At Turin, Hume's heart was touched in a different way—by a playfully flirtatious Countess; but Turin proved, it seems, no more indulgent to Hume's romantic side than later to Boswell's. Nor is that altogether surprising, if one may trust James Caulfield, the future Lord Charlemont, who once watched the philosopher's woo-ing from behind a curtain. Hume, he says, was 'better fitted to com-municate the Idea of a Turtle-eating Alderman than of a refined Philosopher'. Nor was he, according to Caulfield, more engaging to the ear than to the eye, with 'the broadest and most vulgar Scot-tish accent'. But, after all, a Scottish accent is only 'vulgar' to Eng-lish prejudice. And Caulfield himself was won over, like almost everyone that ever met him, by Hume's unfailing good nature.

But the military mission had now lost its purpose; a few weeks later peace preliminaries were signed at Aix-la-Chapelle. In Novem-ber 1748 Hume set out from Turin, by way of Paris, for England. By the summer of 1749 he was back in his native land. 'I was now Master of near a thousand Pound.' That, at least, for a thrifty Scot, however sceptical, had some show of material reality.

Meanwhile Hume's reputation was also solidifying. In 1748, des-

[1] 'The true philosophy is to grow plump.'

pite his absence abroad, his publications had multiplied. There was a third edition of *Essays Moral and Political*. These were also supplemented by a third volume—*Three Essays, Moral and Political* (one on 'the Original Contract', directed against the Whigs; one on Passive Obedience, directed against the Tories; and one on national characters). There was also a volume of *Philosophical Essays concerning Human Understanding*, which included the famous, or infamous, 'Of Miracles'. This last book, which changed its title in 1758 to the now familiar form—*An Enquiry concerning Human Understanding*, was meant to replace, in more readable shape, Hume's earlier *Treatise of Human Nature*. But, though easier reading, it has since come to be judged less original in thought, and inferior in value. Hume himself considered it 'at first little more successful than the *Treatise of Human Nature*'. However, it reached three editions in three years; though the 1750 issue of so impious a work was delayed by the prudent Andrew Millar on account of that year's earthquake in London.[1]

To-day Hume's reputation rests on his philosophy; but it was not by his philosophy that he won it. In 1751, *An Enquiry concerning the Principles of Morals*, intended to replace Volume III of the *Treatise of Human Nature*, was again not much noticed; though its author thought it 'of all my writings . . . incomparably the best' (a view that few share to-day).

It was as a political and economic essayist that Hume really made his name. His *Political Discourses* (1752) proved 'the only work of mine that was successful on the first publication'. It ran through two editions in two years. It had also two French editions, and 'sold like a novel'. For Hume was at last becoming known abroad. After reading the 1748 Essays, Montesquieu had sent him his own *Esprit des Lois*. By 1754, at forty-three, this persevering Scot was a name in Europe.

[1] Hume did not allow this slight annoyance to depress his spirits. Writing to his friend Dr Clephane in London, he typically adds: 'I wish you may not also be a Loser by the same common Calamity. For I am told the Ladies were so frightened that they took the Rattling of every Coach for an Earthquake, & therefore wou'd employ no Physicians but from amongst the Infantry. . . . But this may only be Waggery & Banter, which I abhor.'

For other effects of this earthquake, cf. the Pastoral Letter of Sherlock, Bishop of London, denouncing lewd books as a cause of the divine displeasure; and *Old England's* demand that *Tom Jones* be suppressed by Act of Parliament.

Meanwhile he had been making himself more at home in his own country. In 1751 he moved into an Edinburgh house; and though he was that year rejected as successor to Adam Smith in the Glasgow Professorship of Logic (Glasgow preferred the safe and obscure Mr Clow, as Edinburgh had preferred the safe and obscure Mr Cleghorn), in the next year, 1752, Hume at last gained official position in the Scottish capital as Keeper of the Advocates' Library. True, this was not without a struggle that became a miniature civil war; but that may not have made his victory any less pleasant.

'What is more extraordinary,' Hume wrote on February 4, 1752, 'the cry of religion could not hinder the ladies from being violently my partisans, and I owe my success in a great measure to their solicitations. One has broke off all commerce with her lover, because he voted against me! and Mr Lockhart, in a speech to the Faculty, said there was no walking the streets, nor even enjoying one's own fireside, on account of their unfortunate zeal. The town says that not even his bed was safe for him, though his wife was cousin-german to my antagonist.

' 'Twas vulgarly given out, that the contest was betwixt Deists and Christians; and when the news of my success came to the playhouse, the whisper ran that the Christians were defeated. . . .

'The whole body of ladies brought flambeaux, and made illuminations to mark their pleasure at my success; and next morning I had the drums and town music at my door, to express their joy, as they said, of my being made a great man.'

But Hume's official position had not only to be won; it had to be kept. In 1754 the unco' guid raised an outcry because he had bought for the Library La Fontaine's *Contes*, Crébillon's *L'Ecumoire*, and Bussy Rabutin's *Histoire Amoureuse des Gaules*. The shocked Curators ordered that these be removed as indecent, and no books bought in future without their authority.[1] Now if Hume resigned, he lost useful access to thirty thousand volumes; if he did not resign, he was humiliated. Ingeniously he compromised. His stipend of

[1] Hume's comment to Robert Dundas is frank: 'By the bye, Bussi Rabutin contains no bawdy at all, though if it did, I see not that it would be a whit the worse. For I know not a more agreeable subject both for books and conversation, if executed with decency and ingenuity. . . . And even some of these reverend gentlemen I have seen not to dislike the subject.'

£40 he made over to poor Blacklock[1], the blind poet; and kept his office. Not till three years later (1757) did he finally give up the post; probably to provide an employment for his friend Adam Ferguson.

The next two years, 1755–6, brought more serious attacks from the Scottish church militant, on both Hume and Lord Kames.[2] The Highflyers endeavoured to have Hume called to account before a committee of the General Assembly. The intellectual level of eighteenth-century orthodoxy may often have been insignificant; but its power, even in Britain, was not. In 1697 the nineteen-year-old Thomas Aikenhead had been hanged at Edinburgh for making jokes about the Bible.[3] A statute of 1698 ordained that attacks on the Trinity, Christianity, or the Bible should be punished by debarment from public service and, on a second offence, by three years' imprisonment. Defoe's *Shortest-Way with The Dissenters* (1702) ended in the pillory, prison, and bankruptcy. Thomas Woolston, Fellow of Sidney Sussex, for his comments on New Testament miracles (1727–30) was fined and thrown into prison, where he died. Even in 1763 Peter Annet's *Free Enquirer* brought its author, a deistic ex-schoolmaster of seventy, to the pillory and a year's hard labour.[4]

Hume, however, was not unduly ruffled.

'Meanwhile,' he wrote to Allan Ramsay in Rome (June 1755), 'I am preparing for the Day of Wrath, and have already bespoken a number of discreet families, who have promised to admit me after I shall be excommunicated. . . . You may tell that reverend gentleman the

[1] Thomas Blacklock (1721–91), son of a Cumberland bricklayer, lost his sight by smallpox in infancy, and began writing verse at twelve. But for his shyness, he might have been made Greek Professor at Aberdeen. In 1762 he became minister at Kircudbright; but his flock objected, and after two years he resigned. His poems do not seem to me remarkable except as the work of a man blind almost from birth.

[2] Henry Home, Lord Kames (1696–1782), an eminent Scottish judge, now chiefly remembered for his *Elements of Criticism* (1762). He seems to have been a rugged character. At Ayr in 1780, when an acquaintance, Matthew Hay, with whom he had often played chess, was found guilty before him on a charge of murder, the old judge, having passed sentence of death, is said to have chuckled, 'That's checkmate for ye, Mat!' At the beginning of the Christmas vacation of 1782 he took an affectionate farewell of his legal colleagues and, leaving the court, cried in familiar tones, 'Fare ye a' weel, ye bitches!' Two days after that Christmas he was dead.

[3] See an eloquent passage in Macaulay's *History of England*, ch. XXII.

[4] Peter Annet (1693–1769) published in 1761 nine numbers of the *Free Enquirer*, with attacks on Moses.

Pope, that there are many here who rail at him, and yet would be much greater persecutors had they equal power. The last Assembly sat on me. They did not propose to burn me, because they cannot. But they intend to give me over to Satan, which they think they have the power of doing. My friends, however, prevailed, and my damnation is postponed for a twelvemonth. '

In the end the Highflyers were foiled by Robertson, Wedderburn, and the Moderates. But in 1757 the conflict shifted, oddly enough, to the theatre. Hume's namesake, John Home or Hume,[1] though a minister of the Kirk, had been so shameless as to dabble in the black art of the drama. In 1754 Hume read Home's *Douglas* with enthusiasm; in 1755 Garrick rejected it; in December 1756, patriotic Edinburgh wept and cheered over it; and in January 1757 the Highflyers opened their attack on the backsliding minister (whose odium was deepened by the dedication to him of Hume's *Four Dissertations*). The general tone of this controversy may be gathered from the title of a pamphlet contributed to it by a Cameronian upholsterer, John Haldane—'The Player's Scourge: Or a Detection of the ranting prophanity and regnant impiety of stage plays, and their wicked encouragers and frequenters: and especially against the nine prophane Pagan Priests who countenanced the thrice cursed tragedy called Douglas'. Haldane wanted the English and Irish actors of the play sent back to their own countries with faces branded and tongues cut out. But John Home made good his retreat. In March 1757 his *Douglas* was successfully, though less successfully, acted again, at Covent Garden;[2] and in June he preached a farewell

---

[1] John Home (1722–1808); captured by Jacobites at Falkirk, 1746; succeeded Blair, author of *The Grave*, as minister at Athelstaneford, 1747. Of *Douglas*, now forgotten except for the couplet beginning 'My name is Norval', Wesley said that it was 'one of the finest tragedies I ever read'; Gray, that it 'retrieved the true language of the stage . . . lost for 200 years'; Scott, that it was a 'masterpiece' and 'one of the best acting plays going'. Johnson, on the other hand, denied 'that foolish play' to contain ten good lines. My sympathies are with Johnson.

In 1770 Home married an unattractive wife; of whom, when Hume asked how he could think of such a woman, the simple husband could only say 'Ah, David, if I had not, who would have had her?' But Home should be honoured for the devotion with which he rushed up from London to see Hume in his last illness and, meeting him southward-bound at Morpeth, accompanied him back to London, then to Bath, and home. It is extraordinary how little Hume's scepticism interfered with his warm clerical friendships.

[2] Described in Thackeray, *The Virginians*, ch. 59.

sermon to his weeping flock at Athelstaneford, before leaving Scotland and the Kirk to become Secretary to Lord Bute, and tutor to the Prince of Wales. The fanatics had successfully cut off the offending member; but they had made themselves ridiculous. They were never to give much trouble to Hume again.

Yet plenty of hostility remained in other quarters. In 1754 appeared the first volume of his *History*, dealing with the Stuarts. But it was not well received; and its sale was at first effectively choked by a ring of London booksellers, leagued against the invasion of their market by Hume's Edinburgh publisher, Hamilton. The year 1757 brought a second volume on the Stuarts and, more contentious still, *Four Dissertations* ('The Natural History of Religion', 'A Dissertation on the Passions', 'Of Tragedy', and 'Of the Standard of Taste'). Hume had originally intended to include 'Of Suicide' and 'Of the Immortality of the Soul'. But the publisher, Millar, appears to have been frightened with threats of prosecution, engineered by the pugnacious Warburton. 'From my abundant Prudence' Hume agreed to omit these two perilous pieces. Even so, the book was jointly attacked by Warburton and his henchman Hurd.[1] In 1761 Hume's works were also placed on the Papal Index.

However, his *History* steadily continued to appear—in 1759, the two Tudor volumes; in 1762, the two on the period from Caesar's invasion to Henry VII. It might have been thought, at fifty-one, that Hume's active life was now over. For fourteen years he had been merely a writer; and merely a writer he might well have remained. But, in fact, his real public life was only about to begin.

In 1763 was signed the Peace of Paris. As ambassador in Paris was appointed Lord Hertford, Horace Walpole's cousin and Seymour Conway's brother, a not brilliant, but highly respectable and religious English peer—in an age when English peers were often neither. For Secretary, at £1000 a year, Lord Hertford was given

---

[1] See Mossner, *Hume's Four Dissertations, Mod. Philol.* XLVIII, 37–57. The two suppressed essays, on Suicide and on Immortality, later crept into print without Hume's authorization—first in French (1770), then in English (1777). They seem to me common-sense, but not striking; though of course Hume's view of suicide remains still, after two centuries, in advance of English law. It is, indeed, a curious thought that in this, as in some other respects, our civilization has not even yet, after two thousand years, wholly climbed back to the sanity of Antiquity from the abysses of unreason into which men slid with Rome's decline.

Charles Bunbury. But Charles Bunbury was a rake. Hertford 'was resolved never to see, or do business' with such a Secretary. But an assistant he must have, in the Secretary's place. He invited Hume; and obtained for him from the King a pension of £200 a year for life.

Now Hume was an 'infidel'. To Lord Hertford he was 'totally unknown'. The choice, therefore, was thought then, and remains still, a mystery and a riddle. To exchange Bunbury for Hume seemed running from the devil to the deep sea. People asked, laughing, if Hume would have to attend prayers; and if Lord Hertford had lost his religion, or never really had any.

Horace Walpole attributed Hume's appointment to the influence of Scots friends; but it has been suggested by Greig and Mossner, not ur.plausibly, that the real influence was French, and feminine. Marie-Charlotte-Hippolyte, Comtesse de Boufflers, (1724–1800) was mistress of the dashing Prince de Conti,[1] a patroness of Rousseau, and the aversion of Mme du Deffand (who called her 'the Idol', with allusion to the Prince de Conti's Paris residence in the Temple). On the other hand, for the exiled Jacobite, Alexander Murray, she was 'the most amiable and accomplished Lady in this kingdom, or indeed any other'. In 1761[2] she wrote Hume a letter full of passionate admiration for his works, especially for his *History of the Stuarts*. The correspondence continued. She invited him to Paris. Two months after the Peace of Paris, in April 1763, she invited herself to England; confiding to her cousin, Lord Elibank, that, really, 'her only errand' was the hope of meeting Hume. In London she was extravagantly fêted; for a moment rivalling even Wilkes in the public eye. She was shown the wonders of England— Walpole's Strawberry Hill, with French horns and clarinets for breakfast; the Duke of Bedford's Woburn; even Dr Johnson in the Temple—a very different Temple from her own in Paris. That sage, indeed, would hardly have clattered so thunderously down his stairs in his old shoes to hand her to her carriage, had he known that she was really here on a pilgrimage to the 'Great Infidel' of Scotland.

---

[1] The Prince de Conti (1717–76) distinguished himself in the Alpine campaign of 1744 against the King of Sardinia. In disfavour with Mme de Pompadour, he remained unemployed during the Seven Years' War.

[2] England and France were at war; but the eighteenth century was in some ways civilized. War was not allowed to interfere too much with private life.

There is a charming study of the Comtesse by Sainte-Beuve (*Nouveaux Lundis*, IV).

But Hume remained coy in the north. He disliked anti-Scottish London; he may also have viewed this huntress with some alarm. That she was merely lion-hunting seems to me unlikely; for there were plenty of other lions in the social and literary jungles; but, to Hume, the passionate personal admiration of a *grande dame* may have seemed still more alarming. When, after three months, the Comtesse recrossed the Channel in July 1763, she had still not seen her Hume. But it appears not impossible, from certain cryptic remarks in a letter of hers, that Lord Hertford's offer in June owed something to strings pulled by this determined lady.

Anyway, in the following October, 1763, whether it was the result of chance, faith, or works, the mountain duly came to Mahomet—though unfortunately the Comtesse had measles and could not welcome the miracle on its arrival in Paris. But it must have been a strange experience for Hume. At the age of fifty-two, he found himself suddenly 'arrived' in another sense also—a celebrity. To the Parisians the secretary seemed far more important than the ambassador. Hume had long endured the fate of prophets in their own country; but here in France he appeared a prophet indeed. 'I eat,' he wrote, 'nothing but Ambrosia, drink nothing but Nectar, breathe nothing but Incense, and tread on nothing but Flowers.' 'I am convinced that Louis XIV never, in any three weeks of his life, suffered so much flattery.' 'Je crois qu'il est mort,' observed the sardonic Chamfort; 'je ne l'ai rencontré que trois fois aujourd'hui!' Indeed Hume grew oppressed by 'so much lusciousness'; and longed to be back in his easy chair in James's Court, Edinburgh. What was even more extraordinary, he proved no mere nine days' wonder; throughout the twenty-six months of his stay, though *gauche*, simple, and halting in his French, by his wisdom, goodness, and gaiety he yet retained the admiration and affection of that fickle and fastidious society.

It was, of course, natural enough that he should be welcomed by *philosophes* and intellectuals like d'Alembert,[1] Buffon, Marmontel,

---

[1] In this connection Horne Tooke records a typical instance of Hume's kindness. Horne Tooke called on d'Alembert in fashionable dress; and drew from the philosopher only a little perfunctory talk of operas and suppers. Withdrawing in humiliation, he was followed by a plainly clad stranger, who said, 'I beg your pardon, Sir, but M. d'Alembert mistakes you for a petit-maître'(fop). Horne Tooke changed his finery.

Helvétius, d'Holbach, Turgot, or Diderot (who likened him to 'un gros Bernardin bien nourri'); and by those ladies who mustered *philosophes* in their *salons*, such as Mlle de Lespinasse, Mme Geoffrin (for whom he became 'mon gros Drôle'), or Mme du Deffand (who called him 'le Paysan' after La Fontaine's Peasant of the Danube; but described him to Voltaire as 'gay, simple, and good').[1] Yet he was hailed also in circles far more exalted, and far less congenial. He was presented to Louis XV, to Madame de Pompadour, to the Dauphin, and to the Dauphin's children—the Duc de Berry, aged ten; the Comte de Provence, aged eight; the Comte d'Artois, aged five. It was not every man's lot to be solemnly complimented by four kings of France, present or future. And it has to be remembered that for the bored Louis XV the great writers of his own France were merely 'tout ça'; while it is still stranger that his son, the pious Dauphin, only a few months before he died, should have lain in bed reading this infidel.

Similarly, Hume's own superior, the pious Lord Hertford, could not do enough for him. 'He hoped,' he told Hume in 1765, 'that I woud embrace no Scheme of Life, which wou'd ever separate him and me; He now lovd me as much as ever he esteemd me; and wished we might pass our Lives together.' At the beginning of 1764 Hertford tried to have Hume appointed Embassy Secretary; it took him sixteen months of importunity; but after 'a very hard Pull' he got his way, and Hume found himself, in July 1765, with £1200 a year, £300 for his equipage, and three hundred ounces of plate for his table.

Then again there is the tribute of Sterne, who encountered him in Paris in May 1764—'In all my life, did I never meet with a being of a more placid and gentle nature.'

No doubt Hume's prestige in France was helped by the general *Anglomanie* of the time. In three-quarters of a century England had risen from being the hired satellite of France to perhaps the first place in Europe. She was envied for her victories; for her growing wealth; for her freedom, constitutional and individual. Such success

---

[1] True, he later lost her favour ('je n'estime guère le Paysan'), as anyone was bound to do, by frequenting the Comtesse de Boufflers, whom she disliked, and Julie de Lespinasse, whom she detested; but not the favour of Mme Geoffrin. Even after his return to England she wrote: 'I wish I could forget you; but I cannot.'

might well seem miraculous. The next quarter of a century, under the deplorable George III, was sadly to dim all that. But for the moment we were dazzling.

Yet men are not lastingly liked just for reasons of national prestige. Mme du Deffand, I believe, hit on the true explanation—Hume *was* 'gay, simple, and good'. With his good sense and good nature, he did not provoke distrust like the sometimes malicious and irresponsible Voltaire, or the cantankerous and pretentious Rousseau; he was not a rough bear like Johnson, nor a whimsical squirrel like Sterne. He was, indeed, far more like his friend Franklin, who twenty years later succeeded him as the idol of Paris. The truth is that genius, goodness, and gaiety are, in any period, an extremely rare combination. When they do occur together, they may prove irresistible, even to men who themselves lack all three.

And the Comtesse de Boufflers? It was she, perhaps, that had been the prime cause of Hume's coming to France. She was now thirty-eight; and he fifty-two. It is clear that, once they had met, he felt her attractiveness. They talked, they corresponded, constantly. But in October 1764, her husband died and thus left her free to marry the Prince de Conti—if only the Prince were willing. True, it would have been for him a misalliance; and would have cost him the 50,000 livres a year which he enjoyed as Grand Prieur of Malta. Further, for some time the Comtesse had been his mistress only in name. Yet her ambition was set upon this social ascent; and Hume's situation, as confidant of both, demanded all his tact. His letters of advice to her are admirable. In the end her hopes failed. Were she and Hume lovers? No one knows; nor does it matter much now. She seems to me a somewhat artificial, though clever and kindly person. Indeed, the chief gap in Hume's life, I feel, is that he appears never to have found a woman good enough to make him happy. One cannot be positive, since, fortunately, even the ferrets of modern biography are not omniscient; but it seems highly unlikely.

Still there can be no doubt that Hume's feelings for Marie de Boufflers were real. 'You have saved me,' he wrote at the time, 'from a total indifference towards everything in human life.'[1] And perhaps the best thing recorded of her is that she could inspire the

[1] Cf. Mme de Verdelin to Rousseau (27/4/1766): 'On le dit amoureux fou de Mme de Boufflers.' But it would be rash to trust 'on dit'.

letter he wrote her from the harsh reality of his deathbed, ten years after they had parted for ever.[1]

In August, 1765, Lord Hertford, on leave in London, accepted the Lord Lieutenancy of Ireland. There, too, he wanted his beloved Hume for Secretary; an apartment was even fitted up for that purpose in Dublin Castle. But Irish Protestantism was outraged at the prospect of a free-thinker, a Scot, and a supposedly Jacobite historian. The suggestion also made 'a great Fray' in London; though the Princess Amelia gaily suggested that all difficulties might be met if Lord Hertford would simply appoint Hume an Irish Bishop. Reluctantly Hume's faithful patron dropped the scheme; but at least secured him a life-pension of £400 from the King. Meanwhile, from July to November 1765, Hume was left alone in Paris to bear successfully the important responsibilities of chargé d'affaires.

But now approached a much less pleasant interlude—tragi-comedy to us, but painful enough at the time—the famous affair of Rousseau. To-day that clash seems not only dramatic, but prophetic. Here one may symbolically see the sanity of the Enlightenment attacked, bewildered, and baffled by that romantic, neurotic, fanatic frenzy which was to erupt in French Revolution and Romantic Revival;[2] to be checked awhile by the material solidity of the nineteenth century; and to devastate with yet wilder irrationalism the first half of the twentieth.

At the end of 1765, released from public duty, Hume was wondering whether to settle in Paris or Edinburgh. 'I have taken,' he wrote, with his charming self-mockery, 'a house at Paris; but I will have one also in Edinburgh; and shall deliberate in London which of them I shall occupy.' On December 16 there arrived in Paris Rousseau and his dog Sultan.

In 1762, after publishing *Emile*, Rousseau had fled to Môtiers in Neuchâtel, where Boswell visited him in December 1764. Next autumn (1765) Rousseau's house was stoned;[3] and he fled to the Ile

[1] See p. 29. The end of her life was sombre. Imprisoned under the Terror, she died obscure in 1800.

[2] This is not said with the least intention of disparaging the great Romantics; but, especially on the Continent, the movement produced also the most grotesque extravagances in many of its minor figures. (See my *Decline and Fall of the Romantic Ideal*, ch. ii.)

[3] Frederick Hervey, later notorious as Bishop of Derry and Earl of Bristol (the endless Hotel Bristols of the continent go back to him) told Hume that he had visited

St. Pierre, only to be expelled by the Senate of Berne. He then turned towards Berlin, but at Strasbourg received a letter from Hume suggesting a refuge in England. In December 1765, urged by his friend the Marquise de Verdelin (who, like so many others, lost her original prejudice against Hume as soon as she came to know him), Rousseau accepted.

Unfortunately, Rousseau was one of the many distinguished eighteenth-century figures with more than a streak of craziness. For many of his admirers, that only added, and still adds—as the way is —to the charm of his genius; but he seems to have been not only a most unpleasant person, but also a very dangerous one. One characteristic, in particular, Rousseau shared with Pope's Atossa—

Oblige her, and she'll hate you while you live.

Now Hume had already been warned by d'Holbach—'Je vous le dis franchement, vous allez rechauffer un serpent dans votre sein.' But though one of Hume's great qualities is that he realized, in theory, the vast importance of psychology, none the less his practical knowledge of it seems to have been far from adequate. (In that, too, he is typical of the Age of Reason, which owed some of its most fatal mistakes to bad psychology.) So now he tossed aside d'Holbach's warning. 'The Philosophers of Paris fortold to me, that I coud not conduct him to Calais without a Quarrel: but I think I cou'd live with him all my Life, in mutual Friendship and Esteem.' That 'lifetime' was to last six months.

On January 4, 1766, the pair left Paris. At Senlis, unknown to Hume, there already occurred the first jolt. As they lay in the same inn-bedroom, Hume, according to Rousseau, cried out several times in his sleep, 'Je tiens Jean-Jacques Rousseau.' It does not seem a very plausible story; and over any point of fact it would be rash to risk sixpence on the word of Rousseau. But even fantasies must be caused by something; and it seems to me not impossible that there was running in Rousseau's head a complacent parallel between the banishment of Themistocles from Athens to Persia and his own banishment from France to England. Now in Plutarch the Great King is related to have cried out thrice in his sleep, delighted by the acquisition of so distinguished a refugee, 'I hold Themistocles the

Neuchâtel and been assured by the local magistrates that this lapidation was a mere invention of Rousseau's. (Hume to Davenport, 9/5/1767.)

Athenian.' From this memory the Plutarch-reading Rousseau could conceivably have evolved the auditory hallucination—'Je tiens Jean-Jacques Rousseau.' Classical self-dramatization was quite in his style. Taking refuge at Môtiers in Neuchâtel (which then belonged to Prussia), he reflected: 'When Jean-Jacques uplifts himself beside Coriolanus, will Frederick fall below the general of the Volscians?' (*Confessions*, II, 12.)

I should not dream of suggesting this explanation as more than a possibility. But it seems to me at least less improbable than the too picturesque little anecdote told by Rousseau himself.

On January 13, 1766, they reached London. The King wished to see the wild philosopher. So Hume produced him at Drury Lane (with some difficulty, as he was loth to leave his dog Sultan alone) in a box opposite King and Queen; whence Rousseau craned forward so perilously (whether to see or to be seen) that Mrs Garrick had to cling on to his coat-tails. There was, naturally, a vast concourse, for it was not only the King that was curious—'a number of Gentlemen lost their hats and wigs'.

But already Rousseau began to feel like an owl mobbed in a July noon, and had to be removed to the seclusion of Chiswick. There in mid-February he was rejoined by his houri, Thérèse Levasseur, dearer even than his Sultan. She had been escorted across the Channel by James Boswell and, as Hume had feared beforehand, duly seduced by him on the way[1]—though his triumph in this illiterate conquest was outweighed by the humiliating comparisons she drew between Rousseau, as lover, and himself.

Various hermitages were now considered—in Scotland, in Surrey, and elsewhere. Finally, it was decided to accept the generous offer from a Mr Davenport of a house at Wootton in Staffordshire. But this only led to more trouble. A kindly stratagem to save Rousseau expense on his post-chaise woke fresh suspicions of Hume in that distorted and distorting mind. He further suspected Hume of trying to get hold of one of his letters; he even suspected the horrid way Hume looked at him—'son regard, sec, ardent, moqueur, et prolongé'.[2] And so he sulked; then with a sudden revulsion, perched

[1] See *The Search for Good Sense*, pp. 222–3.
[2] We gather from d'Alembert that Hume, no doubt when lost in thought, had a fixed and disconcerting stare.

himself on Hume's knee, embraced him, kissed him, wept over him
—'No, David Hume is not a traitor; that is impossible.' The bewildered, but soft-hearted Hume patted the neurotic reassuringly on
the back, weeping also. 'I think no Scene in my Life was ever more
affecting.' But this good nature only stabbed Rousseau with fresh
suspicions. Why did Hume not *ask* what reason could have made
Rousseau think him a traitor? How sinister! How incriminating!
Next morning, in mid-March 1766, Rousseau departed for Wootton. It was the last that Hume was ever to see of him; but not the
las t he was to hear.

At Wootton, Rousseau botanized, and worked on his *Confessions*.
But, having almost ceased to read, he had only too much time to
think. The spring sun might shine on Dovedale; but the clouds only
gathered thicker and blacker in that haunted brain. At the end of
1765 the mischievous Horace Walpole had concocted in Paris a
supposed letter from Frederick of Prussia to Rousseau, ridiculing
his persecution-mania and his mania for being persecuted. This was
reprinted in the English press, along with other articles on Rousseau,[1] not always flattering, and sometimes satirical. The victim
became convinced that the 'King of Prussia's letter' was really the
work of his enemy and Hume's friend, d'Alembert. In May he refused the pension of £100 which Hume had been at pains to get
him, in a mysteriously-worded letter addressed, not to Hume, but
to Conway. Hume in his simple kindness, supposing that Rousseau
might be piqued by the secrecy which George III had wished attached to the pension, wrote to ask his difficult *protégé* if he would
accept a pension publicly announced. Rousseau replied in June with
a frantic accusation that Hume had only brought him to England 'to
dishonour me'. When the bewildered Hume asked for explanations,
he received in July an indictment of no less than eighteen folio pages
in small handwriting. Hume, it raved, was leagued with Walpole
and d'Alembert to ruin him; Hume had talked in his sleep at Senlis;
Hume had stared at Rousseau; Hume's landlady had looked coldly

---

[1] See F. A. Pottle, in *Phil. Quart.* IV (1925), 351–63. Boswell seems to have cham-
pioned Rousseau against Walpole and Hume in a letter published by *The St James's
Chronicle*, 16–8/12/1766; it is signed merely 'A Friend to Rousseau', but the stilted
foolishness of its style seems typically Boswellian. As Boswell also ridiculed Rousseau,
both in prose and in illiterate French verse, one suspects that his main motive for
intervening may have been simply an itch to meddle.

at him in the passage; Hume or Walpole had suborned attacks on him in the English press.[1]

At last—rather belatedly, I feel—Hume realized that the author of this amiable effusion was not, as he had at first thought, 'the Blackest and most atrocious Villain that Ever disgraced human nature', but, quite simply, mad.[2] But Hume was also seriously alarmed. Rousseau might be mad; but the world did not suspect that; and, like some other neurotic geniuses, Rousseau had a large public of neurotics and noodles (unable to distinguish between the genius in him and the neuroses) for whom Rousseau's word was gospel. Hume had never minded being attacked for dangerous thoughts; but he was all the more sensitive about imputations on his honesty. He feared that this eighteen-page letter might shortly appear in print,[3] and pillory him before all Europe as a treacherous cad. So he produced, in three copies, a narrative of the truth—one for himself, one for Lord Hertford, one for d'Alembert. It was even read by the King and Queen. But should he publish? His British friends were divided; but finally those in Paris urged that the general gossip and excitement had already reached a pitch where, in self-defence, publication became imperative. And so in October 1766 a French version of Hume's narrative was issued in Paris by d'Alembert and Suard; followed in November by an English translation.

In March, 1767, with Hume's full approval (though Rousseau had made it a condition that the perfidious Hume should have nothing to do with it), Rousseau's English pension was finally granted. But in the following May he suddenly bolted with Thérèse from Wootton, leaving an abusive letter for his landlord, Davenport; and mysteriously turned up at Spalding,[4] whence he wrote to

---

[1] A similar persecution-mania tortured Strindberg, leading him likewise to the most fantastic misrepresentations.

[2] The Comtesse de Boufflers here showed herself at her best and wisest. She wrote to Rousseau, remonstrating against his folly; and to Hume, regretting his perturbation and his hasty publicity. 'J'ose croire que si vous eussiez été auprès de moi lorsque cette cruelle offense vous a été faite, elle vous eût inspiré plus de compassion que de colère.'

[3] 'The whole is wrote with great Care, and I fancy he intends it for the Press.' (Hume to la Présidente de Meinières, 25/7/1766.)

[4] Why Spalding, is hard to conceive—unless he was making for King's Lynn, as the nearest seaport? Hume, however, mentions (to Davenport, 9/5/1767) that Rousseau had written 'to a gentleman in Lincolnshire', asking to live with him; and had been refused.

the Chancellor, saying he dared not quit the house for fear of his enemies, and asking for escort out of England. He also wrote in penitent tones to Davenport that he would return to Wootton. Then he dashed off again, in two days, to Dover; and thence wrote to Conway that he supposed himself to be, at Hume's suggestion, a state-prisoner; but that it would be dangerous to assassinate him. If only he were allowed to sail, he would promise never to write against England, or against Hume.

Naturally there was not the slightest official obstacle to his sailing anywhere. So Rousseau recrossed the Channel, and passed out of Hume's story—to die, or kill himself, eleven years later at Ermenonville. By his own goodness and generosity Hume had been trapped in what was perhaps the most unpleasant incident of his whole life. But, as Philippe de Commines has well said, it is only odious characters that are never duped. One of the last infirmities of noble minds is often blindness to the infirmities of minds less noble. No sensible person thought the worse of Hume at the time; and he had himself too much sense to brood over it afterwards.

Meanwhile he was back in public office. In February 1767, Hertford's brother, Conway, became Secretary of State for the Northern Department (responsible for foreign relations with countries north of France, including Russia, and for the home affairs of Scotland). Hertford, and Lady Hertford, at once pressed Hume to become Conway's Under-Secretary. He accepted. For he felt deep obligations to the Hertfords; he liked Conway; it was 'a place of great credit and confidence'; and he did not expect his tenure to be long. Actually, he held his post only till Conway's resignation in January 1768. Then, in August 1769, after revising his *History* for a new edition, he returned to Scotland with a further pension of £200, but 'done with all Ambition'.

For some restless souls that would mean being done with all happiness also. But Hume knew when to make his exit, and how to enjoy tranquillity off the stage. Seven quiet years were left him (1769–1776); and towards their end he commented, 'were I to name the Period of my Life which I shoud most[1] choose to pass over again I might be tempted to point to this later Period'.

[1] Note 'most'; compare Franklin's willingness to repeat his life; and contrast Johnson's horror at the idea.

For forty years he had served truth and his country; he had well earned his rest. He occupied himself at Edinburgh with a new house and old friends; with light-hearted jests and solid good cheer. On the wall of that new house, Nancy Orde, daughter of Chief Baron Orde of the Scottish Exchequer, gaily chalked 'St. David's Street'. Hume's autocratic serving-woman, Peggy Irvine, was angry— 'Never mind, lassie,' smiled the philosopher, 'many a better man has been made a saint of before.' 'St. David Street' it still remains. But it seems that Hume felt, on his side, a more serious temptation to change the young lady's name to 'Mrs Hume'. Yet he was sixty; she in her twenties. Once again philosophic prudence prevailed.

True, his peace was not wholly unbroken. In 1770 he was assailed, in *An Essay on the Nature and Immutability of Truth*, by James Beattie,[1] author of *The Minstrel; or the Progress of Genius*, and Professor of Moral Philosophy at Aberdeen. This ran through five editions in as many years; brought a pension of £200 from the King; and was commemorated by Reynolds in 'The Triumph of Truth', where Beattie, his volume under his arm, watches Truth push into the abyss three demons, one of them admittedly meant for Voltaire, one supposedly intended for Hume. But Goldsmith was a better prophet, when he rebuked Reynolds for flattering a nonentity like Beattie who would be forgotten in ten years. True, 'ten years' was a slight underestimate; yet to-day the memory of Beattie's essay hardly exists outside biographies of Hume.

But now approached a more serious enemy than Beattie. In 1772 Hume's health began to fail—apparently from a kind of dysentery, leading to colitis. In 1776 he was persuaded to see Sir John Pringle in London, and by him was sent to Bath.[2] But though Hume's spirits were unbroken, the medical 'science' of the day could do nothing for his illness, nor even agree what it was—one physician

---

[1] Beattie (1735–1803), son of a shopkeeper and farmer, became a master at Aberdeen Grammar School in 1758, Professor of Moral Philosophy at Marischal College in 1760. He is best remembered for his Spenserian *Minstrel* (1771–4). George III said the *Essay on Truth* was the only book he ever stole—he stole it from the Queen to give it to Lord Hertford to read. Johnson approved it; and told Boswell, 'Mrs Thrale says, if ever she has another husband, she'll have Beattie'. (Johnson must have winced later, if he recalled that jest.)

[2] On the way he had the strange experience of finding that, while the fate of the British Empire trembled in the balance, Lord Sandwich, First Lord of the Admiralty, was spending three indolent weeks trouting near Newbury.

diagnosed 'hemorrhage'; another, 'sphincter in colon'. 'This Disorder,' wrote the sceptic, wasted, but still humorous, 'as it both contained two Greek Appellations and was remediable, I was much inclined to prefer.' On the day of the Declaration of American Independence, July 4, 1776, Hume, now back in Edinburgh, gave a farewell dinner. During it Adam Smith complained of the world's spitefulness. But Hume refused to take so sombre a view—'No, no. Here am I, who have written on all sorts of subjects that are calculated to excite hostility. But *I* have no enemies—except all the Whigs, all the Tories, and all the Christians.'[1]

Three days later, on July 7, 1776, enter Boswell. He found the once plump philosopher now 'lean, ghastly, and quite of an earthy appearance'. But it did not matter that Hume was seriously ill— Boswell, tormented by that passionate sense of his personal identity which made him chronicle himself as if he had been an empire, plunged into anguished cross-questionings about the after-life. Would Hume not admit that the soul might be immortal? 'He answered It was possible that a piece of coal put upon the fire would not burn'—but it was 'a most unreasonable fancy'.[2] Yet was Hume not disquieted by the idea of annihilation? 'He said not the least'; and cited Lucretius. 'The truth is that Mr. Hume's pleasantry was such that there was no solemnity in the scene; and Death for the time did not seem dismal.' 'He said he never had entertained any belief in Religion since he began to read Locke and Clarke.'

Such appalling composure in such desperate circumstances threw poor Boswell into 'a degree of horrour'. He was seized by a strange compulsion to visit the Advocates' Library and pore over Hume's 'worst Essays'; then fled for refuge to his usual drugs—wine and women.

Towards other visitors Hume was equally gay, though with no illusions about his chance of recovery. To Dr Dundas expressing hopes of it, he replied—'Doctor, as I believe you would not choose

---

[1] Actually one of the strangest, and pleasantest, features of Hume's career is his lasting friendship with several moderates of the Kirk, such as John Home, Hugh Blair, Alexander Carlyle, and William Robertson.

[2] Not, perhaps, a very good analogy from Hume's point of view. The modern householder knows to his cost, when a piece of coal is put upon the fire, how much slate or stone may survive unburnt. A piece of wood or paper might have served Hume's purpose better.

to tell anything but the truth, you had better tell him' (Colonel Edmonstoune) 'that I am dying as fast as my enemies, if I have any, could wish, and as easily and cheerfully as my best friends could desire.' It was not that Hume was indifferent—'poor Edmonstoune and I parted to-day with a plentiful effusion of tears'. But what use, after all, in tears? Better, laughter.

> Lusisti satis, edisti satis atque bibisti,
> Tempus abire tibi est.[1]

To Adam Smith he humorously imagined the answers Charon might make to any pleas of his for longer life. If he asked for time to see how the public took his corrected works,[2] the grim ferryman might well retort, 'When you have seen the effect of these, you will be for making other alterations. There will be no end of such excuses; so, honest friend, please step into the boat.' Or if he pleaded to continue his work of freeing his countrymen from 'the Christian superstition', Charon would lose all temper—'You loitering rogue, that will not happen these many hundred years.'

At the beginning of Hume's last illness, a tallow-chandler's wife presented herself to convert him. But he gently evaded her. 'This is a very important matter, madam, we must take it with deliberation —perhaps you had better get a little temporal refreshment before you begin. Lassie, bring this good lady a glass of wine.' After which the 'good lady' was sent away comforted by an order for two stone of candles—light in one form, if not in another.

A typical last codicil was added to his will—'I leave to my Friend, Mr John Home of Kilduff,[3] ten dozen of my old Claret at his Choice; and one single Bottle of that other Liquor called Port. I also leave him six dozen of Port, provided that he attests under his hand, signed *John Hume*, that he has himself alone finished that

---

[1] Enough now you have dallied, enough you have eat and drunk;
Time now to get you gone.
(Horace, *Epistles*, II, 2, 214–15.)

[2] Even on July 27, 1776, writing to Strahan, he laughs at himself for still sending in corrections for his *History*—'You may compare me to the modern Greeks, who, while Constantinople was besieged by the Turks and they themselves were threatened with total Destruction, occupied themselves entirely in Disputes concerning the Procession of the holy Ghost. Such is the effect of long Habit.'

[3] The author of *Douglas*. See p. 14.

Bottle at two Sittings: By this Concession, he will at once terminate the only two Differences,[1] that ever arose between us, concerning temporal Matters.'

And now, for a last time, he wrote to Marie de Boufflers, condoling on the recent decease of the Prince de Conti, and concluding —'I see Death approach gradually, without any Anxiety or Regret. I salute you, with great Affection and Regard, for the last time.'[2]

That was on August 20, 1776. Five days later he was dead. He had directed that he should be buried 'in a private manner' in Calton Churchyard, with a monument not costing over a hundred pounds, and inscribed only with his name and the years of his birth and death, 'leaving it to Posterity to add the Rest'. Gibbon, in *his* will, perhaps did even better—'Shall I be accused of vanity if I add that a monument is superfluous?' Hume might perhaps have been wiser to think the same.[3] But neither of them trusted posterity in vain.

For the moment, however, posterity added kicks as well as caresses. To Boswell who, with morbid fascination, had peered into the open grave, and then lurked behind a wall during the interment, Johnson passionately pooh-poohed in 1777 the idea that Hume had really died in calm of mind—'He lied. He had a vanity in being thought easy. . . . And you are to consider that upon his own principle of Annihilation he had no motive not to lie.' The logic seems Irish. If Hume really felt no motive not to lie, one might have supposed it to follow logically that Hume's disbelief was real, and therefore that he was *not* lying. But this was a topic on which Johnson felt too intensely for logic. Early in the same year 1777 was published Hume's brief autobiographical sketch, *My own Life*, with a letter from Adam Smith to Strahan—'Upon the whole, I have always considered him, both in his lifetime, and since his death, as approaching as nearly to the idea of a perfectly wise and virtuous man, as perhaps the nature of human frailty will admit.' This naturally roused fresh fury. Boswell exhorted Johnson to 'knock Hume's and Smith's

[1] One difference was Hume's preference for port and Home's for claret; the other difference lay in the way they chose to spell their names.

[2] Even the bitter and cynical Mme du Deffand was moved by it. 'Cette lettre', she wrote to Walpole, 'm'a paru de la plus grande beauté'. She asked the Comtesse for a copy.

[3] Cf. Adam Smith's comment on the monument in question—'it is the greatest piece of vanity I ever saw in my friend Hume'.

heads together, and make vain and ostentatious infidelity exceed-
ingly ridiculous. Would it not be worth your while to crush such
noxious weeds in the moral garden?' But to Boswell's impassioned
plea for moral gardening Johnson did not respond. Johnson's genius
did not lie in the field of metaphysics; and here were nettles that,
perhaps, even he shrank from grasping.

On the other hand, Hume's own voice made itself heard again
from beyond the grave. In 1777 appeared his two suppressed essays
on Suicide and on Immortality; in 1779, his *Dialogues concerning
Natural Religion*, which friends had dissuaded him from publishing.
These, indeed, were easy to abuse: less easy to answer.

Wesley, too, was outraged by the jesting talk with Charon.
Fourteen years after, in 1790, he thundered exultantly—'Did Mr.
David Hume . . . know the heart of man? No more than a worm or
a beetle does. After "playing so idly with the darts of death", do
you now find it a laughing matter? What think you now of Charon?
At length he has taught you to know a little of your own heart! At
length you know it is a fearful thing to fall into the hands of the
living God!' Little wonder that the Enlightenment distrusted 'enthusiasm'. Curious into what bitterness some minds can twist
Christianity. But had not the Covenanters made their war-cry
against Montrose at Tippermuir, 'Jesus and no quarter'?

I am here concerned not so much with Hume the philosopher, as
with Hume the sage, the writer, and the man. Of the profounder
intricacies of his thought it would be impossible here (even were I
qualified) to tell anything like the whole truth; I can only try to tell
nothing but the truth.

The best course may be first to outline Hume's general attitudes
in philosophy, æsthetics, politics, and history; then to illustrate his
thought and style by a detailed summary of one of his liveliest and
most characteristic works—the posthumous *Dialogues on Religion*.

First, then, Hume's view of existence. Imagine Dr Johnson kick-
ing a large, grey stone to refute Berkeley.[1] He has a *feeling*, an impression of what he calls his foot coming in contact with what he

---

[1] For Berkeley, it will be remembered, matter had no independent existence. The
phenomenal universe, one might say, was a kind of television, broadcast by the mind of

calls a stone—a thing appearing to have certain qualities such as size, greyness, and hardness. Such impressions Hume calls 'impressions of sensation'.

Suppose Dr Johnson *thinks* of the episode in bed that night. The 'impressions of sensation' are no longer present to him; but, from them, he still has 'ideas' of the situation. Suppose he also has a *feeling* that he would rather not do it again, because it hurt his toe; this, in Hume's terminology, would be an 'impression of reflexion'.

But both 'ideas', and 'impressions of reflexion', follow on original 'impressions of sensation'. For Hume, this sequence is invariable.

True, one may have an 'idea' of the Heavenly Jerusalem, paved with gold and walled with precious stones, without ever having had any such 'impression of sensation'; but this imaginary vision is compounded from actual impressions, in past experience, of cities, gold, and precious stones. Without having seen a horse one could never conceive a centaur. Even the Deity of many popular conceptions is a compound concept, anthropomorphic in mind, and often in body too, with certain valued human qualities magnified *ad infinitum*.

In short, Hume does not believe in innate ideas.

But even the evidence of the senses about any external reality remains inadequate and contradictory. Seeing is *not* believing. Locke had maintained that bodies really possessed in themselves 'primary qualities'—solidity, extension, figure, motion, or rest; although 'secondary qualities'—'colours, tastes, smells, sounds, etc.'—were only in the percipient.[1]

But Hume, following Berkeley, argued that we had no more logical grounds for belief in the objective existence of primary qualities than of secondary. Dr Johnson was merely *seeming* to kick what *seemed* a solid stone with what *seemed* a solid foot. For aught we

God, and received by the minds of men,—
> no other than a moving row
> Of Magic Shadow-shapes that come and go
> Round with the Sun-illumined Lantern held
> In Midnight by the Master of the Show.

An attempt has been made to read philosophical profundities into Johnson's rather petulant piece of footwork (H. F. Hallett, *Mind*, LVI (1947, 132–47). I remain sceptical.

[1] *E.g.* colours differ for a man with jaundice; for a colour-blind person; for a bee, which cannot see red and would see a poppy black, but for the fact, apparently, that it sees some ultra-violet rays, and may see poppies some ultra-violet colour unknown to man.

know, all our perceptions are insubstantial pageants, as shadowy as Satan's vision of Death—

What seem'd his head
The likeness of a Kingly Crown had on.

Further, the term 'impression' suggests something that presses. But we can never know what it is that causes our 'impressions of sensation'. What, indeed, do we mean by 'cause'? Dr Johnson, if the stone hurt his toe, thought that the impact 'caused' the pain. But all he really knew was that (A) the impression of impact was followed by (B) the impression of pain. We can never see any intrinsic reason why A should 'cause' B—why, for example, violent impacts are usually painful. That belief is simply based on custom or experience. Adam could acquire it only by experience; and every infant does acquire it only by experience.

And, again, if we expect that A, having always 'caused' B, will continue to 'cause' it, this too is only because custom or experience is followed by a belief in the uniformity of natural laws. Yet why should natural laws be assumed *always* uniform? No doubt, we have always observed unimpeded apples to fall downwards; but we cannot *know* for certain that the next apple we see will not rocket upwards. 'Let the course of things be allowed hitherto ever so regular, that alone, without some new argument or inference, proves not that for the future it will continue so.'[1]

But if causation is not established as a certainty, then we can be absolutely sure of nothing except arithmetic and algebra (and, to a lesser degree, of geometry; for geometry involves certain axioms).[2] 'All the objects of human reason or inquiry may naturally be divided into two kinds, to wit, *Relations of Ideas*, and *Matters of Fact*. Of the first kind are the sciences of Geometry, Algebra, and Arithmetic.' But 'all reasonings concerning matters of fact seem to be founded on the relation of *Cause and Effect*.'

[1] In accordance with this a Cambridge philosopher once assured me that, whenever he put his kettle on the gas, he was always prepared for it to freeze. Hume's reasoning may seem to some merely fantastic; in the light of modern physics with its 'indeterminacy', it may seem less fantastic after all.

[2] *Treatise of Human Nature*, Book I, Part III, Section I. In the simplified *Enquiry concerning Human Understanding*, Section IV, Part I, Hume drops this distinction between the demonstrative certainty of geometry, and that of arithmetic and algebra.

We only believe, for example, in the existence of Julius Cæsar because we believe that he caused certain impressions and ideas in his contemporaries, which caused them to make certain records in writing and sculpture; which caused others in turn to copy them; which, by a long chain of similar causation, causes certain impressions and ideas in ourselves. Indeed we can only believe in the objective existence of the pikestaff plain before our noses if we believe that there is some external object there which *causes* our impression of it.

I will to move my little finger; and I believe this *causes* it to move. But if I have had a stroke, it may not move. And even if it does move, I can only say that certain changes in my nerves and muscles appear to follow my volition, and to be followed in turn by the appearance of movement in what appears to be my finger.

One cannot even be certain of the existence of what is called one's 'self'. 'For my part, when I enter most intimately into what I call *myself*, I always stumble on some particular perception or other, of heat or cold, light or shade, love or hatred, pain or pleasure. I never can catch *myself* at any time without a perception, and never can observe anything but the perception.'[1] In fact, we seem to be 'nothing but a bundle or collection of different perceptions, which succeed each other with an inconceivable rapidity'.

> We are such stuffe
> As dreames are made on.

Dr Johnson, in fine, is now reduced to saying, if he would speak with certainty—(though he would doubtless have perished sooner

---

[1] *Treatise*, Book I, Part IV, Section VI. Hume would have been interested by modern psychology with its case-histories of lost personality; or of multiple personality, as in Moreton Prince's 'Sally Beauchamp', who developed half a dozen selves —some aware of their fellow-selves, some not. Even a normal individual, re-reading old letters or journals, may find his past self almost unrecognizably strange. Even nine centuries ago Lady Murasaki could make an unfaithful mistress reply to her lover's reproaches: 'What in waking hours I may have promised, I know not; but now I wander in the mazes of a dream; or someone wanders, for I scarce think it can be I.' 'Je suis une autre personne,' wrote Anatole France of his childhood, 'que l'enfant dont je parle. Maintenant qu'il m'est devenu tout étranger, je puis en sa compagnie me distraire de la mienne.' And the most bewildering fluctuations of identity became a staple of the plays of Pirandello. A personality of this kind may be visualized as a column of midges, keeping a certain unity as it dances in the summer air, yet ceaselessly and restlessly changing shape.

than agree)—'What *seemed* myself *seemed* to kick what *seemed* a stone with what *seemed* my foot.'

Having thus undermined the certainty of external reality, of causation, and even of the self, leaving nothing but 'impressions' and 'ideas', and pure mathematics, Hume had reached a position of considerable scepticism.[1] And yet, in the words of Russell, these sceptical conclusions, 'are equally difficult to refute and to accept. The result was a challenge to philosophers, which, in my opinion, has still not been adequately met.' This seems a sufficiently remarkable achievement for a young man only in his twenties, over two hundred years ago.

So, by laborious reasoning, Hume has reached a complete doubt not unlike what Montaigne had arrived at by nonchalant common-sense. One may picture them together in that tower at Montaigne whose rafters were crowded with inscribed mottoes of the sceptics— οὐδὲν ὁρίζω (I take no definite view); ἐπέχω (I suspend judgement); ἀρρεπῶς (with even balance either way); ἐνδέχεται καὶ οὐκ ἐνδέχεται (it is possible, yet impossible); οὐ μᾶλλον οὕτως ἔχει ἢ ἐκείνως ἢ οὐδετέρως (it is not more this way than that way, or neither way).

Yet at times, for all his natural calm, Hume's head does not repose on the pillow of doubt with Montaigne's smiling insouciance; at times he almost recalls Pascal's dismay before the infinite silences, Pascal's vertigo before the bottomless abyss.

> 'I am first affrighted and confounded with that forelorn solitude, in which I am plac'd in my philosophy, and fancy myself some strange uncouth monster, who not being able to mingle and unite in society, has been expell'd all human commerce, and left utterly abandon'd

---

[1] Descartes had found, at one point, that he could doubt everything—except 'cogito, ergo sum'. But even this does not seem to me sceptical enough. Latin masks the difficulty by omitting the personal pronoun. But instead of saying 'I think, therefore I exist', Descartes could strictly say only—'There is thinking', since the meaning of 'I' is questionable.

Even Hume was, in a way, not sceptical enough. As Bertrand Russell has pointed out (*History of Western Philosophy*, pp. 692–3), though Hume questions causation, he yet uses the term himself in speaking of mental processes—*e.g.* 'Our impressions are the causes of our ideas, not our ideas of our impressions.' He should merely have said—'It has been frequently observed that changes in our impressions have been followed by changes in our ideas.' On his view, there is no ground for stating, even if this has happened hitherto, that it will continue to happen.

and disconsolate. . . . I have expos'd myself to the enmity of all metaphysicians, logicians, mathematicians, and even theologians. . . . When I look abroad, I foresee on every side, dispute, contradiction, anger, calumny and detraction. When I turn my eye inward, I find nothing but doubt and ignorance. All the world conspires to oppose and contradict me. . . . Every step I take is with hesitation, and every new reflection makes me dread an error and absurdity in my reasoning. . . . The understanding, when it acts alone, and according to its most general principles, entirely subverts itself, and leaves not the lowest degree of evidence in any proposition, either in philosophy or common life. . . . The *intense* view of these manifold contradictions and imperfections in human reason has so wrought upon me, and heated my brain, that I am ready to reject all belief and reasoning, and can look upon no opinion even as more probable or likely than another. Where am I, or what? From what causes do I derive my existence, and to what condition shall I return?'[1]

In such a predicament many men would have lost their nerve, and sought some mental anaesthetic or intoxicant. But Hume, whether right or wrong, soon recovered his cool head. If the wisdom of Prospero might seem to have failed him, he did not therefore collapse in the hairy arms of Caliban. Cheerfulness broke in. And honesty confesses it.

'I dine, I play a game of back-gammon, I converse, and am merry with my friends; and when after three or four hours' amusement, I wou'd return to these speculations, they appear so cold, and strain'd, and ridiculous, that I cannot find in my heart to enter into them any farther. . . . In all the incidents of life we ought still to preserve our scepticism.[2] If we believe, that fire warms, or water refreshes, 'tis only because it costs us too much pains to think otherwise.'

[1] This passage, which I take to be sincere, does not square very well with a comment on Hume in the *Times Literary Supplement* of 22/6/51: 'In spite of his admirable qualities, there is a suspicion of fat complacency in Hume's happy abandonment of the problems of metaphysics, which is sometimes irritating. He has, one feels, chosen too easy a way out.' 'Fat complacency' appears to be a sideblow at the philosopher's physique. But the metaphysician who thus exploits physical infirmities has himself, one may feel, 'chosen too easy a way out'.

[2] Cf. the great line of Epicharmus, partly quoted by Hume in his memoranda—
Νᾶφε καὶ μέμνασ' ἀπιστεῖν · ἄρθρα ταῦτα τᾶν φρενῶν.
'Still be sober, still be doubting.
Such the sinews of the mind.'

'A fine conclusion,' some Squire Western might growl, 'to years of sleepless midnights chopping logic! "Fire warms." "Water refreshes." I knew that much before I was breech'd. If I want a headache, I prefer to find it at the bottom of a bottle of port.'

But Hume, I think, would have answered, first, that he found philosophy amusing. So much laborious reasoning would be idle, 'were it not that, to some tempers. this occupation is one of the most amusing in which life could possibly be employed'. Or, as Professor Broad has put it, 'to try to understand in outline what one solves *ambulando* in detail is quite good fun for those people who like that sort of thing'. Secondly, the sceptic who has once established his scepticism escapes from various mental tyrannies. He escapes from the tyranny of philosophy itself. Metaphysics is a cure for metaphysics. It reduces itself to absurdity.

For a moment, curiously enough, Hume is at one with his opposite, Pascal, that true philosophy lies in making mock of philosophy.

> 'The only method of freeing learning at once from these abstruse questions, is to enquire seriously into the nature of the human understanding, and show, from an exact analysis of its powers, and capacity, that it is by no means fitted for such remote and abstruse subjects. We must submit to this fatigue, in order to live at ease ever after; and must cultivate true metaphysics with some care, in order to destroy the false and adulterated.'[1]

For example, if causation is suspect, arguments from the apparent design of the universe in favour of a First Cause collapse. Again, if it is doubtful that a 'self' exists at all, it becomes still more doubtful that it exists for ever.

> 'When we run over libraries, persuaded of these principles, what havoc must we make! If we take in our hand any volume; of divinity or school metaphysics, for instance; let us ask, *Does it contain any abstract reasoning concerning quantity or number?* No. *Does it contain any experimental reasoning concerning matter of fact and existence?* No. Commit it then to the flames: for it can contain nothing but sophistry and illusion.'[2]

[1] *Enquiry concerning Human Understanding*, Section I.
[2] *Ibid.* Section XII.

In fact, as Hume put it at the close of his *Natural History of Religion*,

> 'The whole is a riddle, an enigma, an inexplicable mystery. Doubt, uncertainty, suspense of judgment, appear the only result of our most accurate scrutiny concerning this subject. But such is the frailty of human reason, and such the irresistible contagion of opinion, that even this deliberate doubt could scarcely be upheld; did we not enlarge our view, and opposing one species of superstition to another, set them a-quarrelling; while we ourselves, during their fury and contention, happily make our escape into the calm, though obscure, regions of philosophy.'

Further, when the sceptic turns, as, being human, he must, to the practical world, he can still carry with him a 'mitigated' scepticism, which fortifies him as the moly of Hermes preserved Odysseus from the enchantments of Circe, against the dogmatism, 'enthusiasm', fanaticism, and superstition of the world. He escapes the illusions of 'men of bright fancies', who may, says Hume, 'in this respect be compar'd to those angels, whom the scripture represents as covering their eyes with their wings'.[1]

The consistent sceptic will even escape that last infirmity of philosophic minds—too confident belief in oneself after ceasing to believe in anyone, or anything, else.

> 'On such an occasion we are apt not only to forget our scepticism, but even our modesty too; and make use of such terms as these, *'tis evident, 'tis certain, 'tis undeniable.* . . . I may have fallen into this fault after the example of others; but I here enter a *caveat* against any objections, which may be offer'd on that head; and declare that such expressions were extorted from me by the present view of the object, and imply no dogmatical spirit, nor conceited idea of my own judgment, which are sentiments that I am sensible can become no body, and a sceptic still less than any other.'

Having thus reduced most philosophers to absurdity, and most metaphysics to dust, Hume turns back to the phenomenal world. A man cannot live in an ivory cloud. He must act as well as think; and

---

[1] I suspect that Hume's irony twinkled as he chose this image and saw himself, in the eyes of the devout, as the devil quoting scripture for his purpose.

think about practice as well as theory. Let us, then (since our minds are constituted and conditioned to work in this way) *suppose* causation to exist, scientific induction to be possible; and proceed on the hypothesis that phenomena *are* real, and *can* to some extent be judged, and predicted. In fine, Hume has, I take it, two quite different standpoints; first, in logical theory, an extreme scepticism; second, for practice, a 'mitigated' scepticism, which provisionally assumes, as a working hypothesis, the truth of causation and natural laws, though these cannot be proved.

And why not? It works very well to act *as if* such things were true; and it does not work at all well to act *as if* they were not. I do not see why Hume should be accused of inconsistency, because, having suspended his judgement on the ultimate facts, he refused to suspend all thought and action in the practical world of appearances.[1]

'Strictly logical reasoning,' he might have answered, 'leads us only into chaos—into Cimmerian darkness and Serbonian bogs. Vain to build metaphysical structures on that quaking mire. Doubt swallows the phenomenal world—causation and natural law—even the human self. Uncertainty of uncertainties, all is uncertainty. Man finds himself like an osprey that has clawed a fish too large for it, and is dragged down by its quarry to sunless and suffocating abysses; perforce he must let go and return to the surface. Superficial it may

---

[1] Failure to recognize this double standpoint seems to me to make much of Professor A. E. Taylor's *David Hume and the Miraculous* a beating of the air. No doubt, in his essay *Of Miracles* Hume seems setting out to be naughty rather than profound. But with his conclusion, that one should not believe in the occurrence of a prodigy unless it would be still more prodigious that the witnesses for it should be wrong, I still see no reason to disagree. St Bonaventura, I have read, found it easier to believe that an ox could fly than that his brother could lie. If St Bonaventura was right in this genial estimate of his brother's reliability, he was right to believe (though still, I trust, with some reserves) in flying oxen. Being, however, less trustful than St Bonaventura, I do not believe Professor Taylor, when he proceeds to cast doubt even on Hume's sincerity. 'We can all,' he says, 'make it our purpose that our philosophy, if we have one, shall be no mere affair of surface opinion, but the genuine expression of a whole personality. Because I can never feel that Hume's own philosophy was that, I have to own to a haunting uncertainty whether Hume was really a great philosopher, or only a "very clever man".' I do not see what justification is provided by Hume's life, and death, for doubting that his philosophy was a 'genuine expression of his whole personality'. It is, indeed, an ancient tactic in philosophical or religious controversy to imply dark hints about one's opponent's morals; but it is hardly a very admirable tactic, even for mediocre philosophers. However 'le bon David' might merely have smiled. And that, indeed, seems the best comment.

be: but there only can he breathe. To demand total certainty, I have argued, is to find total scepticism. You may think my arguments a mere battle with shadows. But in *my* day men thought they could *prove* things like the existence of God. It was against such dogmatisms that I fought; not, it seems, wholly in vain.

'And so in this world of Maya—of illusion—let us go our ways content with the flickering lantern of "mitigated scepticism". Let us provisionally assume causation to be true, things and people to be real. We shall find that even this "mitigated scepticism" leads us to new scepticisms about such matters as ethics or aesthetics; but also to some probabilities.'

Thus, having accepted the existence of causes as a working hypothesis, Hume now proceeds to work it hard. And so, paradoxically enough, this thinker who had previously questioned all causation, now argues from it against the freedom of the will. A man is, of course, often free to do what he wills; but he is not free to will what his will shall be; his impulses are as much determined as the colour of his eyes. So Freud also was to conclude. Try as one may even to think of a number at random, one's choice seems determined by subconscious causes.

Similarly, if causation be supposed to exist, miracles become as dubious as the freedom of the will. A miracle is an infraction of the seeming uniformity of natural laws. Belief in this uniformity is based on infinite numbers of observations. But that men should deceive, or be deceived, in their testimony is certainly not contrary to natural law—indeed it is constantly occurring. Therefore it is not reasonable to believe any testimony that a miracle occurred, unless the falsehood of that testimony would be a miracle greater still.

So too with the idea of a perfectly wise and just Providence. It has often been argued that the Universe is so like an artefact as to imply an artificer. But, first, says Hume, this analogy is weak. We have small experience of creations of Universes. Secondly, even if the analogy be admitted, it is still not reasonable to attribute to any cause more qualities than are implied by its effect. Now the world seems far from perfect in its working, or in its justice; there is therefore no rational ground for arguing greater perfections in its First Cause, than would suffice to produce so imperfect a work. A faulty product suggests a faulty workman.

Similar doubts attend the immortality of the soul; Hume's essay on which, as already mentioned, had no English edition till 1777, the year after his death. He argues, for a number of reasons, against the soul's survival; though, as so often, he ends with the ironic profession that reason must bow to faith and revelation. 'Nothing could set in a fuller light the infinite obligations which mankind have to Divine revelation; since we find that no other medium could ascertain this great and important truth.'

I own that I find these perfunctory genuflexions of Hume's, like Voltaire's, a little tedious. I do not see that they could shield him much from the fury of the orthodox; especially as he elsewhere expresses himself with what, for that period, seems shattering audacity.[1] If, on the other hand, all this art had not a precautionary purpose, I do not much like it for its own sake.[2]

Having grown, however, this formidable hedge of sceptical thistles for the bafflement of metaphysicians and theologians, Hume turned to cultivate a harvest of his own in fields less rocky and forbidding—ethics, politics, literature, history. It seems to me part of his shrewdness that, two centuries ago, he already realized the paramount importance of psychology. 'Human nature is the only science of man; and yet has been hitherto the most neglected.' Even in his philosophical titles this sound preoccupation appears—'*A Treatise of Human Nature*'—'*An Enquiry concerning Human Understanding*'.[3] Unluckily for him, psychology was, as yet, hardly born.

---

[1] *E.g.* in *Of Miracles* where he imagines how one would react if historians averred that Queen Elizabeth died in January 1600; rose again after a month's interment; and governed England for three years more.

[2] One may, too, be a little shocked by Hume's advice (April 1764) to an unbelieving young clergyman not to quit orders and wreck his career: 'It is putting too great a Respect on the Vulgar, and on their Superstitions, to pique one'self on Sincerity with regard to them. Did ever one make it a point of Honour to speak Truth to Children or Madmen? If the thing were worth being treated gravely, I shoud tell him, that the Pythian Oracle, with the approbation of Xenophon, advisd every one to worship the Gods νόμῳ πόλεως.* I wish it were still in my Power to be a Hypocrite in this particular: The common Duties of Society usually require it; and the ecclesiastical Profession only adds a little more to an innocent Dissimulation or rather Simulation, without which it is impossible to pass thro the World.'

* According to the custom of his own city.

[3] Cf. the Introduction to the *Treatise of Human Nature*: 'Here then is the only expedient from which we can hope for success in our philosophical researches, to

Indeed, psychology without an understanding of the Unconscious was foredoomed to be as limited as geography before Copernicus, Columbus, and Magellan. Hume had indeed shown that reason played a far smaller part than supposed, in our notions of the external world; but even he could not realize, also, how much less than supposed was the part played by conscious reason in our own internal world of sensation, emotion, and thought.[1]

True, he saw through the common idea of the eighteenth century (which still remains a too common idea of ours about the eighteenth century) that reason conquers passion. When, he argues, such a conquest seems to occur, what really happens is that, aided by reason, a *calmer*, but more steadfast desire overcomes a more violent one. The real conflict within us is a civil war between antagonistic *desires*.

Take, for example, this poem by Walsh (1663–1708) on a lover who for a moment considers ending his anguish, like the legendary Sappho, by leaping into an abyss (a composition very typical of its time in its anti-romantic irony).

> When in a rage he came there,
>   Beholding how steep
> The sides did appear,
>   And the bottom how deep,
> His torments projecting,
>   And sadly reflecting

leave the tedious lingring method, which we have hitherto followed, and instead of taking now and then a castle or village on the frontier, to march up to the capital or center of those sciences, to human nature itself.'

[1] How naïve at times was his psychology, can be seen from such a remark as that in the *Dissertation on the Passions*—'Love is always followed by a desire of happiness to the person beloved, and an aversion to his misery.' Always! Contrast D. H. Lawrence—

> Against the haystack a girl stands laughing at me,
>   Cherries hung round her ears,
> Offers me her scarlet fruit: I will see
>   If she has any tears.

Cf. too Hume's statement in his *Principles of Morals*: 'Absolute, unprovoked, disinterested malice, has never, perhaps, place in any human breast.' When Hume died, the Marquis de Sade was already thirty-six. (Hume feels some doubts, however; for he continues: 'or if it had, must there pervert all the sentiments of morals, as well as the feelings of humanity'.)

That a lover forsaken
A new love may get,
But a neck when once broken
Can never be set,
And that he could die
Whenever he would,
Whereas he could live
But as long as he could—

why, then, this sensible man 'calmly returned To his cottage again'. This, Hume would say, was because the disconsolate lover now realized that his violent desire to end his torments might only bring worse torments, or at least a frustration of all other desires whatever. And so it was not simply reason, but his *calmer* desires for self-preservation, and for a chance of future pleasures, that prevailed. Or again, if a young lover heeds Nietzsche's advice to ask himself 'Can I stand the conversation of this woman till seventy?', he is counteracting the violent passions of the moment by the *calmer*, more steadfast desire for comradeship rather than boredom. But reason alone, if coupled with total emotional indifference, cannot make us take a single step in any direction. We should end with the immobile apathy of cabbages.

No doubt, in current speech, we *call* desires 'unreasonable'.[1] But, for Hume, a desire is 'unreasonable' only if its object is non-existent; or if the means it proposes are not such as to attain the end desired, because it is misjudging causes and effects.[2] Still I think it might be safer *never* to call desires 'unreasonable'.

In fine, one might say that reason is in some ways like an organist who can direct the wind in his instrument, but does not make it; or

[1] By 'an unreasonable desire' the ordinary man seems to mean either (1) a desire that reasonable men do not have; or (2) a desire that reasonable men overcome, by seeing its impossibility or its undesirable consequences. But both seem very loose language.

[2] When, however, Hume expresses this by saying what must have seemed most odd to the eighteenth-century reader—'Reason is, and ought only to be, the slave of the passions,' he seems rather misleadingly paradoxical; though it remains true that the reason of even the iciest mathematician is serving his *desire* to do mathematics.

All the same, I think Hume tends to underestimate the power of excessive reasoning and introspection, as with Amiel, to crumble away the vital emotions. It can *undermine* the passions, as well as serve them.

like an agriculturist, who can irrigate his fields, but not generate the water; or like a magician who can conjure, to some extent, with spirits from the vasty deep, but not create them. Plato's rational charioteer of the soul makes shift to control the horses of the passions; but *they* pull the chariot, not he.[1]

But although Hume, not knowing the Unconscious, could not fully realize how fantastically our desires, impulses, and emotions may fool our reason, and even our senses, still one should recall his comment on popular religions through the ages: 'You will scarcely be persuaded that they are anything but sick men's dreams: Or perhaps will regard them more as the playsome whimsies of monkeys in human shape, than the serious positive dogmatical asseverations of a being who dignifies himself with the name of rational.' Anyway, if in ethics Hume tended, perhaps, to be a little *too* rational, he was to receive a shrewd lesson from Rousseau, when that sick mind distorted his warmest kindness into the blackest treachery.

What, then, of ethics?[2] What makes actions or qualities seem to us meritorious or the reverse? Hume, as one would expect, does not believe in absolute moral goods and evils. Ethics is based, for him, partly on reason, which judges consequences; partly on feeling— above all, the feeling of *sympathy*. Men, one might put it, are moral because they are gregarious. A herd of cattle that spent all their days in butting and trampling one another would have an existence both nasty and short.

What we regard as personal merits, says Hume, are qualities agreeable or useful to their possessor, or else agreeable or useful to those associated with him. These are the qualities that win our approbation. And the ultimate *sanctions* of ethics, though not always the conscious motives or ends, are pleasure and pain.

There was a general tendency in the eighteenth century— Montesquieu and Herder are wise exceptions—to underestimate the diversities of human thought and feeling from age to age, and from land to land. This, for example, is one of the defects of Hume's or

---

[1] Ultimately all these processes, both impressions and ideas, are of course bound to the adamantine chain of causation (if causation exists). But such ultimates can be ignored for the nonce while discussing practical morals. Driving a car through London traffic, one is not concerned to remember that the earth, though it looks flat, is really round.

[2] Over which, said Robert Hall, Hume poured 'a more than Egyptian darkness'.

Gibbon's history then, as of Shaw's historic plays since; they are too prone to picture the people of the past as differing from us merely in their clothes and their superficial conventions. Hume himself, as we shall see, tends to underestimate the diversity and relativity of aesthetic tastes. But in ethics at least he is clear enough about the relativity of morals. *A Dialogue* amusingly and convincingly brings out how an honest and respectable citizen of fifth-century Athens would seem in eighteenth-century Paris an absurd and criminal monster; and how an *honnête homme* from eighteenth-century Paris would have seemed no less odious to fifth-century Athens.[1] All the same, he continues, these ethical differences can be largely explained by different social conditions and needs; whereas such fundamentally valuable qualities as wisdom, courage, kindness were honoured then as now.

On the other hand, medieval morals bring from our philosopher a burst of passion that in him is rare.

> 'Celibacy, fasting, penance, mortification, self-denial, humility, silence, solitude, and the whole train of monkish virtues; for what reason are they everywhere rejected by men of sense, but because they serve to no manner of purpose? . . . A gloomy, hare-brained enthusiast, after his death, may have a place in the calendar; but will scarcely ever be admitted when alive into intimacy and society, except by those who are as delirious and dismal as himself.'

No doubt this may seem narrow—typical 'eighteenth-century

---

[1] Cf. the more outspoken passage on the relativity of ethics (*Treatise*, Book III, Part I, Section I), about which Hume hesitated whether he should dare print it: 'So that when you pronounce any action or character to be vicious, you mean nothing, but that from the constitution of your nature you have a feeling or sentiment of blame from the contemplation of it. Vice and virtue, therefore, may be compar'd to sounds, colours, heat and cold, which, according to modern philosophy, are not qualities in objects, but perceptions in the mind: And this discovery in morals, like that other in physics, is to be regarded as a considerable advancement of the speculative sciences; tho', like that too, it has little or no influence on practice.' (It has, I think, a good deal of practical influence on tolerance. An action, like a work of art, strikes one observer as fine, another as ugly. About such feelings, argument is vain; argument can usefully debate only the probable consequences of a given action, or a given type of action.)

Hume would have been amused by Malinowski's savages for whom the supreme sexual abomination was to have a meal with a person one was not married to. Cf. the Indians in Herodotus who ate their dead parents instead of burning them, and were outraged at the Greek custom of burning instead of eating them.

prejudice' towards the Middle Ages. But if prejudice it is, then I must own that I partly share it. Naturally to many medieval minds such 'monkish virtues' were far from serving 'no manner of purpose'; they were pleasing to an eccentric deity, and would be rewarded. But if one regards such ideas as the product of an irrational sense of guilt, one of the commonest and most deplorable of mental diseases (which was unfortunately endemic, and encouraged, in the Middle Ages), then one is likely to agree with Hume. No doubt 'Middle Ages' is a deplorably vague term; but it still seems to me true that, from the sixth century to the fourteenth, a terrible mass of misery was caused in Europe by this neurotically cultivated sense of guilt, and by calling in a nightmare next world to upset the balance of this.

One of Hume's most recent expounders has objected to his dispraise of humility. But by humility Hume meant a sense of inferiority towards those one meets. He does not mean Newton's sense of human insignificance before the Universe. Now if a man really feels constantly inferior to those he meets, his state seems to me unpleasant and unhealthy;[1] and, if he does not really feel so, why pretend? Modesty forms part of courtesy; but that is quite another story. The tale of the pious Jesuit Barcena whose humility was such that he gave up his chair even to the devil, when that personage honoured his cell with a visit, is, I admit, charming; but, for me, it is the charm of a quaint absurdity. If one took it seriously, I suspect that the holy man was guilty both of heresy, and of a kind of inverted arrogance, in supposing that his iniquity surpassed even Satan's. But, of course, if he had given up his chair on the principle —'All possible politeness even to the worst of enemies', in that case the holy man would have my full admiration.

For Hume, then, the motive force of moral action springs from a sense of human sympathy; which it is socially desirable, and often

---

[1] When I say it seems unpleasant, I am, of course, only expressing a *feeling*. This is merely personal and subjective. Others feel the opposite. When I say it seems unhealthy, I am suggesting a proposition. It could, I think, be supported by *argument* from experience and observation. And it can further be *argued* that the *consequences* of unhealthy and neurotic states of mind are often such as few would find pleasant or desirable. Disagreements over ethics are often based on the difference between a short-term and a long-term view. It is hard to be far-sighted enough. Here lies one of the finest and most frequent themes of Ibsen.

pleasant, to obey. (Perhaps it would be truer to say that it often proves painful to disobey. The pains of a bad conscience are, I think, a much more frequent and cogent influence than the pleasures of a good one—except for prigs.) Hume also recognizes the reinforcing effect, here, of moral training in early years. But, living when he did, he could not know the full importance of that early environment— how it can build up, from the influence of those respected, admired, or revered in childhood, a kind of shadowy monitor, the superego; not wholly conscious and, indeed, partly unconscious;[1] a power that can punish transgressions not only by mental conflicts and self-frustrations, but even by physical maladies; so that, for example, young women who flout their upbringing by setting out to imitate Ninon de l'Enclos, can thwart themselves by frigidity; or men who have gained forbidden successes, can punish themselves by illness or 'accidents'. Nemesis and the Erinyes dwell often within ourselves.[2]

But, with these provisos, Hume's ethics seem to me sound.

Next, aesthetics: Hume is not, to most modern eyes, very happy as a practical critic. But in theory he at least sees, like Montesquieu,[3] that first principle of all criticism, which the vast majority of critics cannot, or will not, see (whence a great deal of criticism remains fundamentally irrational)—the relativity and subjectivity of taste. Even to-day the average piece of criticism uncritically presupposes that there exists one right view of the work in question; that the critic knows it; and that anyone who does not like what the critic likes, and dislike what he dislikes, is wrong, and 'ought' to think and feel otherwise. Most criticism is, in fact, a false religion which idolizes an absolute Beauty as mythical as Diana of the Ephesians.

'You have not even,' says Hume in *The Sceptic*, 'any single argument beyond your own taste, which you can employ in your behalf: And to your antagonist his particular taste will always appear a more convincing argument to the contrary. If you be wise, each of you

---

[1] Hence, as Freud pointed out, the superego can become at times, not a just judge, but an irrational tyrant. It needs close watching.

[2] I have tried to follow this further, from the psychological side, in *Literature and Psychology*, ch. XV, 'Values'

[3] 'Les termes de beau, de bon, de noble, de grand, de parfait sont des attributs des objets, lesquels sont relatifs aux êtres qui les considèrent.

will allow that the other may be in the right[1]: and having many other instances of this diversity of taste, you will both confess, that beauty and worth are merely of a relative nature, and consist in an agreeable sentiment, produced by an object in a particular mind, according to the peculiar structure and constitution of that mind.'[2]

Thus the fond mother is in raptures with her infant, 'though in every other eye it appears a despicable and a miserable creature'; the fond lover sees his mistress as goddess and angel—'you can infer nothing, however, from all this discourse, but that the poor man is in love'. All the same, says Hume, 'there is something approaching to principles in mental taste; and critics can reason and dispute more plausibly than cooks or perfumers.' (Sometimes, perhaps.) But even so, he admits, 'you will never convince a man, who is not accustomed to Italian music, and has not an ear to follow its intricacies, that a Scots tune is not preferable.'

Hume's aesthetic relativism seems to me a vast advance on the dogmatic certainties of most critics. But I doubt if even Hume goes quite far enough. He underestimates here too, I think, the endless variety of human temperament; even among the cultivated. In his essay *Of the Standard of Taste* he brings examples to indicate at least a certain uniformity and stability in aesthetic judgements; but one of his instances has become, ironically enough, an instance of exactly the contrary.

'Whoever,' he says, 'would assert an equality of genius and elegance between Ogilby and Milton, or Bunyan and Addison,[3] would be thought to defend no less an extravagance, than if he had maintained a mole-hill to be as high as Teneriffe, or a pond as extensive as the ocean. Though there may be found persons, who give the preference to the former authors; no one pays attention to such a taste; and we pronounce, without scruple the sentiment of these pretended critics to be absurd and ridiculous.'

Now it is possible enough that there survive to-day no very pas-

---

[1] Why not both in the right, if taste is relative? Perhaps Hume meant this; but if so one would expect him to say '*is* in the right'.

[2] Cf. the passage on the relativity of ethics, in the footnote to p. 44. And Montesquieu's dictum on such relativity—'Il est l'éponge de tous les préjugés.'

[3] Cf. Burke, *Sublime and Beautiful*: 'the refined language of the Aeneid... if it was degraded into the style of the Pilgrim's Progress.'

sionate admirers of Ogilby[1] (though Ogilby's *Homer* apparently gave exquisite delight to Pope at school); but there have been reputable judges, not only in our own day, who were by no means prepared to parallel Milton with Teneriffe. As for Bunyan being in 'genius' an obvious molehill compared with Addison, a mere pond beside Addison's ocean, so far has taste now veered, that many critics now prefer Bunyan. (Which does not mean that taste could not conceivably veer again.) Hume was not fortunate here in his illustrations.

Belief in the subjectivity of taste does not, of course, mean simply that any man's opinion is as good a guide to aesthetic values as any other. Some men are too ignorant. Some men are too insensitive. One cannot adequately pass judgement if one does not know, or cannot perceive, half the evidence. Hume well illustrates such subtlety of perception by Sancho Panza's story of his two kinsmen who complained that a certain otherwise excellent wine had a tang —according to one, of leather; according to the other, of iron. And sure enough at the bottom of the barrel was found an old key with a leathern thong.

But even this proves less, I think, than Hume supposes. A critic may sometimes suffer from too much sensitiveness, as well as from too little. I once heard a misogynist remark that women were capable of having one hanged for making a noise with one's soup. Now, supposing this trenchant generalization to be true of *some* women, one would hardly trust them as judges of character. Again, Snimdirides the Sybarite, who was blistered by sitting on a crumpled roseleaf, would not, for ordinary men, be a good guide in the choice of chairs. Those who dwell too much on little things, may miss bigger. In short, as Blake growled, one can be 'connoisseured out of one's senses'.

No doubt, as Hume rightly says, a critic needs to be, not only sensitive, but well-informed. He cannot produce opinions of any value on what he has not really studied; he cannot compare a work with its rivals, unless he knows them too. For to assert that a work is 'beautiful' must always imply such comparisons. To say 'few women are beautiful' is merely tautologous; for 'beautiful' means '*unusually* good-looking'.

[1] Scottish translator of Homer, Aesop, and Virgil (1600–76).

48

But here again there are dangers that Hume ignores. Sophistication, too, can be overdone. Erudite aesthetes are not always admirable human types. Wordsworth, or Tolstoy, preferred the spontaneous judgements of minds simple and uncorrupted. And there is something in the comment of Mark Rutherford on Byron—'He has awakened in the *people* lofty emotions which, without him, would have slept. The cultivated critics, and the refined persons who have *schrecklich viel gelesen*, are not competent to estimate the debt we owe to Byron.'

Even if we consider only the views of keen and cultivated judges, an irreconcilable subjectivity of taste remains. Goethe was disgusted by Dante; Tolstoy, by Shakespeare. Conrad had a special loathing for Dostoievsky. To Macaulay or George Eliot, the works of Jane Austen seemed perfect; to Charlotte Brontë or Alice Meynell, they seemed trivial and insensitive. Different natures have different needs. Literary rank, in practice, is roughly established by counting noses —noses of a certain sharpness. But the differing preferences of the minority remain just as true—for the minority. In a few generations a minority may become a majority. Aesthetic wranglings, then, are utterly futile. Anyone who tries to argue that any sincere and experienced aesthetic judgement is 'wrong', merely proves, I believe, that he is himself fundamentally wrong about aesthetics. Nearly a thousand years ago Lady Murasaki already observed that it was common, yet wholly useless, to argue whether spring or autumn is lovelier—'it is a question of temperament'. And also of fashion. Beauty stands poised on a weathercock; only ephemeral creatures could suppose that she always looks the same way. To the witchery of Herrick men became indifferent for a hundred years; to the heartbreaking poignancy of Ronsard, for two hundred years; to the dark magnificence of Aeschylus, for nearly two thousand.

Hume, however, having overstated his case, I think, with remarks about the principles of taste being 'universal', and nearly, if not entirely, the same in all men, then proceeds to give ground again. For he admits that men do show 'blameless' divergences due to age, or 'humour'; so that a reader may, for instance, prefer Ovid at twenty, Horace at forty, Tacitus at fifty; or one man may value copiousness where another likes conciseness; one man may prefer tragedy and another, comedy. Such judgements, he owns, 'can never reasonably be the object of dispute, because there is no standard by which they can be decided'.

Again, Hume suggests, we should not blame an author for portraying customs differing from our own; even though it may be upsetting to 'behold princesses carrying water from the spring'. (To-day most of us find this, not upsetting, but delightful; however, the eighteenth century was at times strangely formal.) On the other hand, moral blemishes remain, for him, 'eternal blemishes'. Thus *Polyeucte* and *Athalie* are permanently lessened in value by their bigotry.[1]

Those who believe, with Wilde, that books cannot be moral or immoral, only well or badly written, will, of course, find this ethical attitude of Hume's absurd. Yet it seems to me true.

Youth tends to look only at the flowers of art; Age may learn to consider their fruits also; to realize that here, too, are found Deadly Nightshade and hemlock. Unfortunately, many critics never grow up.

The value of literary work, I think, is both aesthetic and ethical. It has what I have called 'pleasure-value' and 'influence-value'. If, for example, it is decadent, like Wilde's *Salome*, or brutal, like some of D. H. Lawrence, it is, *to that extent*, less to be valued. And, whereas one cannot sensibly argue about 'pleasure-values', about 'influence-values' or 'consequence-values', one *can* argue (though with extreme circumspection). And one should.[2]

We tend, I think, often unconsciously, to make a somewhat similar distinction in our ethical judgements. When we say 'That was a *fine* action', we imply that it gives immediate pleasure, largely aesthetic, to contemplate: when we say 'That was a *good* action', we stress rather that it is the type of action that leads to laudable con-

---

[1] Here in this essay *Of the Standard of Taste*, written for a more popular audience. Hume seems a little forgetful of his own view that ethical feelings too are relative, (Though he admits that the bigotries of *Polyeucte* or *Athalie*, repugnant to English feeling, are yet 'received with great applause on the theatre of Paris'.)

One can only argue, I take it, that though some *feel* in favour of bigotry, and others against it, there remains a probability of truth in the view that bigotry tends to *long-term* consequences which even bigots would feel disagreeable; and tolerance to *long-term* consequences which work far better. But the honest liberal will, I think, own that here he advances through a twilight of probabilities which will tax all his resolution.

[2] More fully discussed in my *Literature and Psychology*, ch. XI.

sequences. Here there is a like contrast between immediate reactions and long-term results.

At all events, Hume's views on criticism, though healthily sceptical in comparison with those of most critics, seem to me still not quite sceptical enough. Aesthetic values, I believe, are even more subjective than he thought. One should be content to say, like the seventeenth-century Abbé de Saint-Pierre, 'Ceci est bon, *pour moi, quant à présent.*' For next year it may not be.

Certainly some of Hume's own judgements on individual authors provide curious examples of the relativity and subjectivity of taste. He could enjoy Homer, Sophocles, Milton, Racine. Indeed this man who kissed the earth of Virgil's Mantua, had more passion for poetry than one might have supposed. But his poetic tastes seem sometimes odd. Shakespeare he sees as a 'rude genius' with 'total ignorance of all theatrical art and conduct'—'a reasonable propriety of thought he cannot for any time uphold'. 'There may even remain a suspicion, that we over-rate, if possible, the greatness of his genius; in the same manner as bodies often appear more gigantic, on account of their being disproportioned and misshapen.' Wilkie's *Epigoniad*,[1] on the other hand, is classed by Hume with Homer and Milton; Home's *Douglas* praised as showing 'the true theatric genius of Shakespear and Otway, refined from the unhappy barbarism of the one, and licentiousness of the other'. As Wilkie and Home were Scots ministers, perhaps Hume was swayed by patriotism; like the Aberdeen man who cried from the Covent Garden gallery on the first night of Home's *Douglas*—'Ou fie, lads! Fat think ye o' yir Willy Shakespeare noo?' Yet Chesterfield too, thought Wilkie a great poet.

On the other hand not even patriotism could make Hume admire *Ossian*. He was no pre-Romantic. This becomes evident even from his taste in scenery—'A barren or desolate country always seems ugly and disagreeable, and commonly inspires us with contempt for the inhabitants.' Always! When Hume died, not far away there was a little lame boy of five hobbling about George Square who was

---

[1] William Wilkie, 'the Scottish Homer' (1721–72), was a successful farmer, then a minister, then Professor of Natural Philosophy at St Andrew's; and so eccentric that Charles Townshend said he knew no man 'so near the two extremes of a god and a brute'. His *Epigoniad* dealt, rather in the style of Pope's *Homer*, with the sack of Thebes by the sons (Epigoni) of the seven champions slain in the earlier siege.

to change all that. 'Contempt' for Loch Katrine, or Rob Roy!

About wit in poetry Hume felt like Johnson; not like Donne. 'If the merit of the composition lie in a point of wit, it may strike at first; but the mind anticipates the thought in the second perusal, and is no longer affected by it.' (This, I think, depends on the quality of the wit.) 'When I read an epigram of Martial, the first line recalls the whole; and I have no pleasure in repeating to myself what I know already. But each line, each word in Catullus has its merit, and I am never tired with the perusal of him.' (And yet do most of us easily grow tired of wit as good as Marvell's *Coy Mistress*, or Pope's *Rape of the Lock*?) 'It is sufficient to run over Cowley once; but Parnell, after the fiftieth reading, is as fresh as at the first.' (Fifty readings of Parnell?)

Some, again, will find it a strange view to put Prior's delightful *Alma* and his dreary *Solomon*[1] on the same level—'that admirable poet has succeeded perfectly well in the gaiety of the one, as well as in the melancholy of the other.' *Alma* seems to me delightful; but *Solomon*! Even Prior's friends groaned at his fondness for reading it aloud.

Among poets, in short, Virgil and Racine are Hume's ideal. In drama he thinks that the French 'excelled even the Greeks, who far excelled the English'. With him, as with Chesterfield, the pendulum of poetic taste swings too far, for most of us, towards good sense and clarity—almost as far as it has swung to-day in the opposite direction. Of the two extremes, little though I like either, I feel that Hume's was at least the less barbarous or decadent.

In prose, Hume's taste again leans to the rational, the plain, and the clear. 'The first polite prose we have' is Swift's. 'The prose of Bacon, Harrington, and Milton is altogether stiff and pedantic, though their sense be excellent.' In fine, Hume, as one might expect, admires the prosaic kind of prose, not the poetic. That is natural enough, in a man who so much preferred in life the calm emotions to the violent. Yet how much he missed!

---

[1] As *Solomon* has now few admirers, the reader may like a specimen. (Solomon is puzzled by the dispersion of species. For how can one attribute this to navigators?)

> Would they on board or bears or lynxes take,
> Feed the she-adder, and the brooding snake?
> Or could they think the new-discovered isle
> Pleased to receive a pregnant crocodile?

If he praised *Tristram Shandy* as the best book written by an Englishman for thirty years, he added 'bad as it is'. He admired Gibbon's *Decline and Fall*; but with a curious astonishment that any Englishman could still write so well.

On the other hand, Hume seems to me on firmer ground when he admits the happy mean in literature, between too much naiveté and too much elaboration, to cover wide limits; but adds that we should, of the two, be more on our guard against over-elaboration —the fault into which established literatures and sophisticated ages tend more to fall. Wordsworth, who thought Hume the worst critic produced by Scotland, 'a soil to which this sort of weed seems natural', here at least would have agreed.

In short, Hume's own aesthetic judgements exemplify, I think, far more than he realized himself, his 'Sceptic's' view of the subjectivity of all aesthetic judgements.

In politics, as one would expect, Hume remained a man of the centre, and was attacked by both sides accordingly; just as Montaigne became, in his own phrase, a Guelf for the Ghibellines, and a Ghibelline for the Guelfs. True to his family tradition, Hume regarded the revolution of 1688 as justified,[1] and the Hanoverian succession as a blessing. 'So long and so glorious a period no nation almost can boast of. Nor is there another instance in the whole history of mankind, that so many millions of people have, during such a space of time, been held together, in a manner so free, so rational, and so suitable to the dignity of human nature.' The difference between sensible men of both parties has really, he thinks, been far slighter than it seemed.

> 'A Tory, therefore, since the Revolution, may be defined in a few words, to be *a lover of monarchy, though without abandoning liberty; and a partisan of the family of Stuart:* As a Whig may be defined to be *a lover of liberty, though without renouncing monarchy; and a friend to the settlement in the Protestant line.*'

This sounds sane enough.

Tory though Hume might be called, there is no nonsense in him about St Charles the Martyr, or the beauties of passive obedience.

---

[1] Cf. Lord Acton's verdict—'the greatest thing done by the English nation. It established the State upon a contract.'

On the other hand, he rejected as mythical the Whig theory of an original social contract; he disliked the 'fanaticism' of the Puritans, if possible, even more than the 'superstition' of Laud. And he was no democrat; he cared far more for freedom of thought and speech than for the 'liberty' of John Wilkes and his 'factious Barbarians'. 'So much Liberty,' Hume thought in 1769, 'is incompatible with human society. And it will be happy, if we can escape from it without falling into a military Government, such as Algiers or Tunis.'

In fine, he seems to me a practical and utilitarian psychologist, opposed both to political legalism and to political mysticism; too sceptical to be impressed by talk either of the natural rights of men, or of the divine right of kings; sharing Burke's distrust of 'violent innovations', but without the later Burke's tendency to vapour about 'divine tactics'.

Hume would have liked the British constitution (did not age overtake everything) to remain as free as it then was; but, if it must decay, then absolute monarchy would be a better *euthanasia* than anarchy leading only to a military absolutism. To-day this notion of military absolutism in England seems rather fantastic. Yet, when Hume wrote, the absolutism of Napoleon in France was only a quarter of a century distant. And our own time has seen just such dictatorships arise in Italy, Germany, Russia, and elsewhere.

As things were, the English Crown seemed to Hume (sometimes at least) to be tending, thanks to its revenues, to recover power. Here he mistook the reflux of a wave for the turn of the tide. But at least he was not alone in *that*.[1]

On the other hand, he was far wiser than many of his contemporaries in regarding the American war as sheer folly. He would simply evacuate.

> 'I should have said,' he shrewdly writes on October 26, 1775, 'that this Measure only anticipates the necessary Course of Events a few Years; that a forced and every day more precarious Monopoly of about 6 or 700,000 Pounds a year of Manufactures, was not worth contending for; that we should preserve the greater part of this Trade even if the Ports of America were open to all Nations.'

[1] Here Pitt proved a truer prophet. Asked by an Abbé at Rheims in 1783 which part of the British Constitution would first decay, he replied, 'The prerogative of the King, and the authority of the House of Peers'.

Besides, how could the colonies, even if conquered, be held down? Who could pay for the necessary army of more than thirty thousand men? 'Let us, therefore, lay aside all Anger; shake hands, and part Friends.' Here are good sense and good humour worthy of the friend of Franklin and Adam Smith.

Indeed there are moments when America inspires Hume with strikingly prophetic wisdom. He dissuades Gibbon (October 24, 1767) from writing in French—'Let the French, therefore, triumph in the present diffusion of their tongue. Our solid and increasing establishments in America, where we need less dread the inundation of Barbarians, promise a superior stability and duration to the English language.' Similarly his *History*, in a passage later expunged, foresees in America 'an asylum secured in that solitary world for liberty and science, if ever the spreading of unlimited empire, or the inroad of barbarian nations, should again extinguish them in this turbulent and restless hemisphere'. That was very nearly fulfilled in 1940; nor is the menace even yet removed.

Some—especially philosophers—have regretted that Hume gave so much time and effort to produce a history that fills between two and three thousand large pages of small print, but is no longer read. Yet this regret may be exaggerated. Books can be useful without being immortal; and particularly a book that so lucidly, and impartially, interested men for generations in the history of their country. It brought Hume happy activity, fame, and financial independence. One cannot have everything. Nor, as I have said, do those seem to me the wisest philosophers who can do nothing all their lives but philosophize.

No doubt Hume's history has failed to endure monumentally like Gibbon's. It is rare for the brilliant to remain laborious, or for the laborious to remain brilliant. Razors are bad for cutting rocks. The plump Scots philosopher was probably too indolent, too unwilling to stir from his sofa for a piece of research, too philosophically inclined to doubt whether such minutiae as torment modern scholars, really matter. In Hume, for example, one is somewhat startled to read, of fourteenth-century France and England, that 'the government of the two kingdoms was at that time pretty much alike'. Again, as already noted, both Hume and Gibbon suffered from that strange eighteenth-century obsession with human uniformity from

China to Peru. 'Nor are the earth, water, and other elements, examined by Aristotle and Hippocrates, more like those which at present lie under our observation, than the men, described by Polybius and Tacitus, are to those who now govern the world.' With the classical world that seems not wholly untrue. But this tendency of Hume's grew more distorting the further he went back into the medieval twilight.[1] Actually, the men described by Gregory of Tours or Matthew of Paris seem to me often as incomprehensibly different from ourselves, as if they came from another planet.

None the less, it is only since his death that Hume the historian has been almost totally eclipsed by Hume the philosopher. In the catalogue of the Cambridge University Library his name still stands as 'David Hume, Historian'. His history struck intelligent contemporaries because it was so rational and so impartial. Voltaire (himself no mean figure in the history of history) thought it 'perhaps the best ever written in any language'. Which is interesting, though so fantastic—indeed, because so fantastic. Wiser and more penetrating, I think, is another comment of Voltaire's on Hume as historian— 'un esprit supérieur à sa matière, qui parle des faiblesses, des erreurs, et des barbaries comme un médecin parle des épidémiques'. That seems to me as it should be. The modern historian, especially since Marx, needs often to be an economist; but still more he needs to be a psychologist. Men are moulded by things; but in the end it is not things that matter, but men. Hume was, no doubt, accused of Toryism—but that was because his age was so violent in its politics, rather than because *he* was. 'It is called Jacobite,' wrote that convinced Whig, Horace Walpole, of the *History of the Stuarts*, 'but, in my opinion is only not *George-abite*; where others abuse the Stuarts, he laughs at them.'[2]

[1] Cf. Kirkpatrick's savage phrase to Bruce, doubting if John Comyn were really dead in the Dumfries church—'Ye doubt! *I* mak siccar'—with its tame and wholly unmedieval paraphrase in Hume—'And is that a matter to be left to conjecture? I will secure him.'

[2] It is a curious tribute to Hume's influence that in 1816 the Rev. G. B. Mitchell thought it worth while to expurgate his *History*, as Thomas Bowdler (1754–1825) expurgated Shakespeare (1807) and Gibbon (1826). Mitchell's eight-volume edition 'revised for family use; with such omissions and alterations as may render it salutary to the young, and unexceptionable to the Christian' is prefaced with a hope for 'the thanks and encouragement of an enlightened age, which has received with much marked favour a *Family Shakespeare*, in presenting them also with a FAMILY HUME'. Victorianism began very long before Victoria.

True, as Hume grew older, he did make alterations towards the Tory side. But not exclusively towards that side. Even in its final form his account of the seventeenth century, the most contentious period he treated, seems to me very fairly balanced. If Hume grew somewhat more Tory, that tendency is natural enough with age; and this is not simply because men grow more timid, and enfeebled swimmers welcome with less exhilaration the prospects of a deluge. There is also the factor that an observant person tends, the longer he lives, to grow more and more convinced of the folly and hysteria of men, the obscurity and complexity of things. Most revolutionaries are minds not fully adult. A few revolutions have been both necessary and beneficial, like the English Revolution of 1688. Some have been beneficial, though not really necessary, like the American Revolution of 1775. (Only a minority wanted it, and it could have been won without any war by merely waiting a generation or two.) But most revolutions seem to me to have cost an extortionate amount of needless suffering. Well might Hume distrust them.

Perhaps the wisest summary of the whole matter comes from a letter by Hume himself (1756?; *Letters*, I, 237): 'My views of *things* are more conformable to Whig principles; my representations of *persons* to Tory prejudices. Nothing can so much prove that men commonly regard more persons than things, as to find that I am commonly numbered among the Tories.'

Of Hume's essays in political economy this is not the place to speak, nor am I competent. Enough to say that he paved the way for his friend Adam Smith and *The Wealth of Nations* (1776).[1] Nor does it seem worth dealing here in detail with his general essays; which are always readable, and sometimes interesting, but without the charm of Montaigne, the point of Bacon, or the literary quality of Hazlitt and Lamb.

It is Hume the philosopher—and the man—that really matters. And, to see his mind at work, it is worth returning, in some detail, to one of his most characteristic pieces of philosophy—those *Dialogues on Religion*, which he spent the last days of his life revising, and which, says Professor Broad (who is not prone to facile praise), 'so far as the present writer can see, leave little further to be said on the subject'. For these *Dialogues* illustrate not only Hume's philoso-

[1] See E. Rotwein, *D. Hume, Writings on Economics*, 1955.

phical attitude, but also his gaiety, his whimsicality, his irony—and also a certain elusiveness, partly prudent, but perhaps also partly mischievous.

The framework is simple. Pamphilus reports a discussion between his master Cleanthes (a deist), Demea (a mystical believer), and Philo (a sceptic, though a somewhat mysterious one).

Demea begins by outlining the right course of education for a youth like Pamphilus—simple piety, then logic, ethics, natural theology. For the young must learn to distrust the absurd fallibility of human minds, and so to accept the mysteries of faith.

The sceptical Philo agrees. Having learnt how little we can understand of anything, we realize that our reason cannot even begin to grasp the universe.

This gratifies Demea (who is an owl). But Cleanthes sees the sceptic snake lurking in the grass; and he objects that, in practice, even Sceptics, like Stoics, throw aside their own principles as soon as they quit their studies. For example, when this very party breaks up, 'we shall then see, whether you go out at the door or the window'. Who can doubt that even the doubting Philo will then turn out to retain a prudent belief in gravity?

Philo admits that in ordinary life the sceptic is forced to behave like ordinary men. Nevertheless, he argues, his scepticism about reason does lastingly affect him in other fields also. In religious questions he realizes that 'we are like foreigners in a strange country, to whom everything must seem suspicious, and who are in danger every moment of transgressing against the laws'.

And yet, retorts Cleanthes, sceptics really believe Copernicus and Newton. Why, then, should they reject natural theology? They are, in fact, mere jesters. The Christian Fathers and the Reformers, it is true, stressed our human blindness. But the 'judicious' Locke saw, more wisely, that '*faith* was nothing but a species of *reason*, that religion was only a branch of philosophy'.

But, for this change in religious attitudes, the mischievous Philo offers an explanation. In early ages of faith the priests had most to fear from freedom of thought; so they then stressed human imbecility. To-day the world at large reasons freely; so the priests have now been driven to turn reasoners too.

The mystically devout Demea, however, is seriously shocked by what seems to him the too philosophic, too rational, tone of Clean-thes. God, he argues, must remain a mystery. As Malebranche said, we should shun all anthropomorphic errors of crediting God with a human shape, or with human ideas, or even with a spirit bearing '*any* resemblance to our spirit'.

Again Philo readily agrees. We have no experience of divine attributes. Reason and piety 'establish the adorably mysterious and incomprehensible nature of the supreme Being'.

In answer, Cleanthes trots out the familiar argument from design. The world is like a marvellous machine; by analogy we must infer a marvellous engineer. But Demea snorts at such appeals to mere human experience, mere human notions of probability.

Philo, of course, supports him. We may say, he argues, that the Universe is rather like a house. We can say a house implies a builder, for we have ourselves seen houses built. But we have never watched the building of a Universe. So the analogy fails.

And yet, Cleanthes objects, we know stairs are designed for mounting. We see legs are designed for walking.[1] Therefore there *must* be a designer of the Universe.

Again Demea is shocked; and Philo urges that we know too little to rely on this sort of argument. Other agencies, as well as intelligence, mould the visible world. 'What peculiar privilege has this little agitation of the brain which we call thought, that we must thus make it the model of the whole universe?' It is just like a peasant forming notions of imperial government from the housekeeping of his own little cottage.

---

[1] Teleology on these lines was later carried to far sublimer flights than those of Cleanthes or Paley—such as theories that trees were made green to rest our eyes; melons ribbed to aid their division among families; alligators created to prevent rivers being choked with fish; and fleas coloured black to help us catch them. See Heine's ironic *Zur Teleologie*:

'... Gott gab uns nur einen Mund,
Weil zwei Mäuler ungesund.
Mit dem einen Maule schon
Schwätzt zu viel der Erdensohn;
Wenn er doppelmäulig wär',
Fräß und lög'er auch noch mehr.
Hat er jetzt das Maul voll Brei,
Muß er schweigen unterdessen,
Hätt' er aber Mäuler zwei,
Löge er sogar beim Fressen. . . .'

'... Only *one* mouth God gave man—
Two would be an *un*sound plan.
Even with one the son of earth
Says too much, of little worth:
Double-mouthed were he created,
Still more he'd have stuffed and prated.
Supping soup, he must remain
Silent, while his jaws are plying;
But if human mouths were twain,
Even eating he'd be lying. . . .'

Then, retorts Cleanthes, you might as well object to the theory of the earth's motion because you have never seen other earths move.

But we *have*, retorts Philo—there are the sun, moon, and planets. That is why we believe Copernicus and Galileo.

Cleanthes counters this with a curious fantasy. Suppose there were books that lived and propagated themselves. Would one deny that such books had authors? Yet even the finest book remains an organism less complex than even the simplest animal.

But Demea, as resolute as the author of *Job* to preserve the impenetrable mystery of God, will not admit this odd analogy either. A book reveals the author's mind[1]; but God remains inscrutable. Plotinus even denied the Deity to possess intellect or understanding.

But, complains Cleanthes, if you are going to make God so utterly remote and unintelligible, as well be an atheist as such a mystic.

But again the mischievous Philo supports the obscurantist Demea. If, he urges, you make the Divine mind like a human one, which is delicately influenced by all sorts of causes, then what causes govern this Divine mind? Or, if God's thoughts fall into order uncaused, why may not matter equally well fall into order uncaused? We do not in the least understand how a tree orders its own growth; on the other hand, in lunatics, we see that mind itself may fall into disorder. Why then attribute order to mind, especially, rather than to matter?

Cleanthes, of course, remains unconvinced. He is satisfied, he says, to take the single step from creation to Creator. 'You ask me, what is the cause of this cause? I know not; I care not; that concerns not me.'

But in that case Philo can see no point in taking any step at all— especially such a long one—if we are only to be left as ignorant after it as before.

Besides, if it is argued by Cleanthes that 'like effects prove like causes', the vaster and more microscopic the world of science comes to seem, the more unlike to man its Creator too must become.

Further, if you argue from effect to cause, since the world does not appear to be infinite, you cannot claim the Deity Himself to be

[1] Demea had not the advantage of knowing some modern literature.

infinite. Likewise, since the world is full of imperfections, you cannot claim the Deity Himself to be perfect.

Again, the argument from design might equally well suggest that, as a house is built by a *number* of men, the world was made by a *number* of Gods.

And since men propagate sexually, why may not their Creators do the same?

> 'In a word, Cleanthes, a man who follows your hypothesis, is able, perhaps, to assert, or conjecture, that the universe, sometime, arose from something like design: But beyond that position he cannot ascertain one single circumstance. . . . This world, for aught he knows, is very faulty and imperfect, compared to a superior standard; and was only the first rude essay of some infant Deity, who afterwards abandoned it, ashamed of his lame performance; it is the work only of some dependent, inferior Deity; and is the object of derision to his superiors; it is the production of old age and dotage in some superannuated Deity; and ever since his death, has run on at adventures. . . .'[1]

Cleanthes remains unperturbed, though he does not accept Philo's fantasies; for at least this jester cannot get rid of the hypothesis of design in the universe. But Demea is outraged.

Philo, however, pursues his ironic whimsies. If we argue, he continues, that like effects have like causes, then the whole universe might be one vast animal, with God for its soul. (After all we have no experience of minds existing without bodies.)

Cleanthes rejoins that, if it comes to that, the Universe, lacking sense-organs or a local seat of reason, is more like a vast vegetable. But Philo, he objects, seems picturing an eternal world. Now the world shows, on the contrary, signs of *not* being immeasurably old.[2] The cherry-tree was only brought from Asia by Lucullus; vines were only introduced into Gaul less than two thousand years ago. Why were they not there before? And if they had been, only a general convulsion could have removed them.

Philo retorts by asking—And why not a general convulsion?

---

[1] Here Hume for a moment gives full rein to his impishness, in a way that would have amused Anatole France.

[2] Compare the views of some modern scientists about the age of the universe.

Why not many revolutions from one world-order to another?[1] 'Were I obliged to defend any particular system of this nature (which I never willingly should do), I esteem none more plausible than that which ascribes an eternal, inherent principle of order to the world.'[2]

Further, if the world suggests more resemblance to an animal or vegetable than to an artefact, analogy would also suggest it to have been generated like an animal or vegetable, not fabricated by a Creator. 'A comet, for instance, is the seed of a world'; or a comet is an egg—'in like manner as an ostrich lays its egg in the sand, which, without any farther care, hatches the egg . . .'

'In this little corner of the world alone', we see four principles which all cause similar effects—reason, instinct, animal generation, vegetable propagation. But elsewhere there may exist hundreds of other such principles. Any of these might equally well originate a world-order; as a tree bestows order and organization on another tree.

Then Philo grows impish again. 'The Brahmins assert that the world arose from an infinite spider, who spun this whole compli-cated mass from his bowels.' We may think that grotesque. But, 'were there a planet wholly inhabited by spiders (which is very possible), this inference would there appear as natural and irre-fragable'.[3]

Again, one could without absurdity adopt the theory of Epicurus, provided one supposed, unlike him, the number of particles in the Universe to be finite. For then, if they are constantly shuffled by perpetual motion, in infinite time every possible arrangement of those particles must necessarily occur, including our world as it is.

[1] Hume would have been interested to hear of Ice Ages.
[2] A significant pointer to Hume's real view, however tentative.
[3] Cf. Xenophanes (c. 565–470 BC)—

If oxen, or lions, or horses had hands like men, they too,
If they could fashion pictures, or statues they could hew,
They would shape in their own image each face and form divine—
Horses' gods like horses, like kine the gods of kine;

Montesquieu—'On dit fort bien que si les triangles faisaient un Dieu, ils lui don-neraient trois côtés'; Yeats—

I passed a little further on and heard a peacock say:
Who made the grass and made the worms and made my feathers gay,
He is a monstrous peacock, and He waveth all the night
His languid tail above us, lit with myriad spots of light;

and the infinite Fish of Rupert Brooke's *Heaven*.

Consider, too, that, in our own experience, ideas are copied from real objects; not objects from ideas, as on Cleanthes' theory.

In fine, for Philo, all philosophic or religious systems involve hopeless difficulties; all 'prepare a complete triumph for the sceptic; who tells them, that no system ought ever to be embraced with regard to such subjects'.

Demea intervenes. He agrees with Philo that arguments *a posteriori*, such as the argument from design, are merely futile. But why not, rather, argue *a priori*?

Everything in existence has a cause. The infinite succession of causes that we see, must have been caused by some 'necessarily existent Being, who carries the REASON of his existence in himself.'

It is left for Cleanthes to demolish this piece of metaphysics. Nothing, he argues, can be demonstrable *a priori* 'unless the contrary imples a contradiction', and is therefore impossible to conceive. But we *can* conceive the non-existence of any such Being; therefore its existence is not logically demonstrated. Besides, why might not the material Universe itself be the said necessarily existent Being?

To this Philo adds that, if you sum the figures of any product containing 9, they make either 9 or a multiple of 9. This extraordinary fact might well seem miraculous; yet a skilful algebraist can show it to be mathematically inevitable. The order of the universe might be similarly inevitable.

In reply, Demea shifts his ground to the general misery of life. 'The whole earth, believe me, Philo, is cursed and polluted.' Therefore man *must* have a divinity to cry to.

He adduces examples such as Charles V, by his own confession never happy in power, yet regretting that power as soon as he had abdicated it; or Cicero's Cato protesting that he would not live his life again. And he cites that favourite eighteenth-century quotation, beloved by both Johnson and Chesterfield, from Dryden's *Aurengzebe*, about the folly with which men cling to existence—

> And, from the dregs of life, hope to receive
> What the first sprightly running could not give.

Philo, to confound Cleanthes, gladly joins Demea in heaping up the miseries of mortality. In fact, he says, no one has ever answered the argument of Epicurus—has God the wish, but not the power, to prevent evil? Then He must be impotent. Has He the power, but not the wish? Then He must be malevolent. Therefore the only explanation of God is—that His nature is utterly inexplicable.

Cleanthes, however, denies this pessimism; and makes the astounding statement—'If you can prove mankind to be unhappy or corrupted, there is an end at once of all religion.'

But Demea will not have this. For him, the only solution lies in faith that this world is merely a confused prelude; God has eternity to reveal His ultimate benevolence.

But this, objects Cleanthes, is pure hypothesis; which may indeed be possible, but lacks any evidence to make it probable.

Philo, as well he may, now feels the debate swinging in his favour.

> 'Here, Cleanthes, I find myself at ease in my argument. Here I triumph.... There is no view of human life ... from which, without the greatest violence, we can infer the moral attributes, or learn that infinite benevolence, conjoined with infinite power and infinite wisdom, which we must discover by the eyes of faith alone. It is your turn now to tug the labouring oar.'

Cleanthes, however, persists that unless God is to some degree anthropomorphic, He is quite useless to man. Religion vanishes. It would be at least less intolerable to suppose God benevolent, but only finitely perfect, and limited by necessity.

Philo, however, still maintains that a stranger visiting our world would feel like a man viewing some building full of discomfort, darkness, heat, cold, and confusion—and so would condemn the architect.

There are, Philo continues, four particular sources of the world's misery. First, if creatures must needs be impelled to action, this could have been effected more by pleasures and less by pains, more by the carrot and less by the stick.[1] Secondly, the world seems governed by ruthlessly inflexible laws, which no divine hand ever intervenes to soften. 'Some small touches, given to Caligula's brain in his infancy, might have converted him into a Trajan.' Thirdly, human beings are only grudgingly endowed, like maltreated chil-

---

[1] Compare modern methods of education.

dren, with the qualities they need for coping with so difficult a life. Fourthly, the great machine of nature is so crankily constructed that men are constantly tormented by droughts and by deluges, by passions too strong and by bodies too frail. 'The whole presents nothing but the idea of a blind nature, impregnated by a great vivifying principle, and pouring forth from her lap, without discernment or parental care, her maimed and abortive children.'[1]

All this, says Philo, may not disprove God's goodness; but assuredly such a state of things cannot be used to prove it.

It might indeed seem that the answer could be found in the Manichaean idea of good and evil powers at war. Yet the perfect uniformity of the natural universe shows no signs of any such conflict.

There are, for Philo, only four possible hypotheses:

(1) the first causes of the universe are perfectly good;

(2) they are perfectly malignant;

(3) 'they are opposite and have both goodness and malice';[2]

(4) they have neither goodness nor malice.

Now the mixed good and evil of the world is against the first two views; the uniform working of natural law is against the third, Manichaean hypothesis; 'the fourth, therefore, seems by far the most probable'.[3]

Indeed, Philo concludes, human wickedness is a still greater problem for the hopeful anthropomorphite, than human unhappiness.

But at this point Demea can contain himself no longer. 'Are you secretly, then, a more dangerous enemy than Cleanthes himself?'

With justified irony Cleanthes comments that Demea has taken a very long time to perceive that Philo 'has been amusing himself at both our expence'.

Hereupon the scandalized Demea, 'on some pretence or other', withdraws.

Philo now makes some most curious statements. Despite his own seeming 'flippancy', he says, Cleanthes must know that 'no one has a deeper sense of religion impressed on his mind, or pays more pro-

[1] Surely another key-utterance.

[2] Hume does not seem (though his wording remains a little obscure) to consider a fifth possibility—that the deity, or deities, might, like human beings, be in character a mixture of good and bad.

[3] Again a particularly significant utterance.

found adoration to the divine Being, as he discovers himself to reason, in the inexplicable contrivance and artifice of nature'.[1] Then he re-erects that argument from design which he has himself been so successfully trampling to fragments. For example, Galen enumerates over six hundred human muscles, each adapted to its purpose in at least ten ways.[2]

Naturally Cleanthes agrees; and adds that, though men may talk of suspending judgement on these points, such neutrality becomes in practice impossible to maintain or defend.

Yes, answers Philo, and anyway the dispute is largely verbal. 'God', 'Mind', 'Thought'—how can it matter which term we use? No doubt, 'we have reason to infer that the natural attributes of the Deity have a greater resemblance to those of a man, than his moral have to human virtues'. But from this we can only conclude that men are still more defective morally than mentally.[3]

Then the two proceed to argue about the actual benefits of religion. Cleanthes thinks even the worst religion better than none at all. Morality depends on a belief in eternal rewards and punishments. Philo, however, now resumes his ironic scepticism. 'The smallest grain', he urges, 'of natural honesty and benevolence has more effect on men's conduct, than the most pompous views suggested by theological theories and systems.' The eternity of the life to come is cancelled, for human short-sightedness, by its comparative remoteness. Again, the vulgar always debase religion and corrupt its ethics; so that some creeds[4] have even decried mere morality, and represented God as angry with those who trusted to good works. Religion can breed hypocrisy, fanaticism, superstition, or selfish concern with

---

[1] One would have thought that not much 'discovery' could be made from 'the inexplicable'; and the divine Being sketched by Philo had hardly been very 'adorable'.

[2] This change of front is very odd. In dialogues no character need wholly represent the author; yet here one is puzzled because Philo seems to contradict, not only Hume, but himself. I can only attribute it to that extreme circumspection which was so strangely combined in Hume with extreme audacity. With a mixture of timidity and mischief, he seems to dance in and out of his own smoke-screen. Even here he is about to re-emerge, in a moment, with devastating destructiveness. Yet, if the orthodox grew too furious, he (or his literary executor) could always safeguard themselves by quoting this sort of edifying profession of faith.

[3] I find it hard to believe that this was Hume's own view. Experience of life seems to me to teach that men are, in general, more stupid, but nicer than one had thought— their hearts are often better than their heads.

[4] Doubtless Hume is thinking of predestination and the gift of grace.

one's own salvation. And experience shows that, so far from clerical influence being good, wise statesmen have repeatedly been compelled to curb it.

Cleanthes replies that, all the same, religion is life's chief comfort. Philo retorts that, on the contrary, it often adds more to life's terrors than to its joys. Hence Cerberus and the Furies; or the belief that the damned far outnumber the saved. Even the joy of the religious tends to a hysteria that may lead to new melancholy and dejection.

And yet, Philo continues, how idle are such terrors! As if God had a vulgar passion for applause, or could be stupid enough 'to be offended at the vices and follies of silly mortals, who are his own workmanship!' If anyone deserves God's favour, surely it must be the philosophical theist, who seeks to see truly His divine perfections; if anyone deserves God's indulgence, surely it must be the philosophical sceptic, who modestly tries to suspend judgement.

So to Philo's conclusion. (All this mental labour ends with a grotesquely, but deliberately minute mouse.) 'The cause or causes of order in the universe probably bear some remote analogy to human intelligence.' There is no more to say than simply this. In fine, Hume remains a very vague deist.

> 'If it afford no inference that affects human life, or can be the source of any action or forbearance. . . . Some astonishment indeed will naturally arise from the greatness of the object: Some melancholy from its obscurity: Some contempt of human reason, that it can give no solution more satisfactory with regard to so extraordinary and magnificent a question.'[1]

Then, with a demure countenance, but subtly twinkling eye, Philo steps back into his smoke-cloud. 'To be a philosophic sceptic is, in a man of letters, the first and most essential step towards being a sound, believing Christian.'

And now the shadowy Pamphilus who, Boswell-like, records the whole dialogue, adds his own final puff of confusing smoke—'I cannot but think, that Philo's principles are more probable than

---

[1] This very eighteenth-century passage, with its significant reiteration of the studiously moderate 'some', always reminds me of the style of Hume's great fellow-sceptic, Gibbon—e.g. (on the choice of a profession) 'the law requires some abilities: the church imposes some restraints'.

Demea's; but those of Cleanthes approach still nearer to the truth.'

Yet the real conclusion seems an acceptance of the same fundamental scepticism in theory ('mitigated' in practice by an acceptance of probabilities in dealing with ordinary life) as appears elsewhere in Hume. The already quoted close of the *Natural History of Religion* had spoken of 'opposing one species of superstition to another . . . while we ourselves, during their fury and contention, happily make our escape into the calm, though obscure, regions of philosophy'. This is just what Philo has done with his two interlocutors.

In March 1751 Hume had regretted that he did not live near enough to Gilbert Elliot of Minto, for Elliot to write the part of Cleanthes, while 'I shou'd have taken on me the Character of Philo'. 'By this Means, that vulgar Error woud be avoided, of putting nothing but Nonsense into the Mouth of the Adversary.' And so Hume asked Elliot at least to suggest arguments for use by Cleanthes; who is therefore, for Hume, clearly an 'Adversary'.

If Philo is at least largely Hume (he has two thirds of the talk—more than thrice Cleanthes' share, more than five times Demea's), then who are the other two? Professor Mossner[1] has given what seem convincing reasons for supposing Demea a thinker of the type of Samuel Clarke,[2] who took 'the high Priori' road to the mystical mathematics of the Kingdom of Heaven; while Cleanthes would represent a mind like Bishop Butler[3] preferring *a posteriori* arguments from experience and analogy.

And yet, astonishingly enough, Hume has been at times identified, not with Philo, but with Cleanthes.[4] That a view so strange should have been taken by at least eight philosophic authorities suggests that one can become distinguished in philosophy without much sense of psychology—or, indeed, of humour.

True, in his letter to Elliot of March 1751 Hume had said, 'You

---

[1] '*The Enigma of Hume*' in *Mind*, XLV (1936).

[2] Samuel Clarke (1675–1729), classicist, Newtonian, and divine, called by Voltaire 'un moulin à raisonnement', and attacked by the orthodox as a deist or Arian, by the deists for keeping too much to orthodox language.

[3] Joseph Butler (1692–1752), 'the Bacon of theology' and author of *The Analogy of Religion* (1736); clerk of the closet to Queen Caroline (1736), Bishop of Bristol (1738), of Durham (1750). It was he who told Wesley that to claim special gifts of the Spirit was 'a horrid thing, Sir, a very horrid thing'.

[4] This, to me quite fantastic, notion has been effectively dealt with by Professor Kemp Smith in his edition of the *Dialogues* (2nd ed. 1947), pp. 57–75.

wou'd perceive by the sample I have given you, that I make Clean-thes the Hero of the Dialogue.' But this not wholly unambiguous remark seems merely for the benefit of Elliot. Again, on June 8, 1776, Hume wrote to his publisher Strahan, 'I there introduce a Sceptic, who is indeed refuted, and at last gives up the Argument, nay confesses that he was only amusing himself by all his Cavils.' But here it is a question of encouraging a timid publisher to publish.

True, Philo ends with pious sentiments; and Pamphilus assigns the victory to Cleanthes. But it seems a little naive, in view of Hume's persistent habit of scattering his impious pages with occa-sional drops of holy water, to be duped by that. Gilbert Elliot and Adam Smith were *not* duped—they opposed publication. Hugh Blair was not duped either—on September 29, 1763 he wrote to Hume that the French *philosophes* might consider the British philo-sopher 'somewhat bigotted'[1]—though, had he gone a step farther, they might, Blair hears, have honoured him with statues. 'If you will show them the MSS of certain Dialogues perhaps this honour may still be done you. But for Gods sake let that be a posthumous work, if ever it shall see the light: Tho' I really think it had better not.' And again the critic of *The Monthly Review* in 1779 was not taken in—'Philo is the hero of the piece.' Indeed, though Hume had himself remarked that 'nothing can be more cautiously and more artfully written', it seems astonishing that any careful reader should have been taken in at all. If the edifying Cleanthes were really the triumphant hero of the piece, what need for such anxieties and pre-cautions? Why handle a package of soft soap as gingerly as if it were dynamite? One may question the value of so much evasive ambigu-ity; but I suppose Hume might have answered that, like Pindar, he wrote only for men of understanding.

Sainte-Beuve, discussing the *Apologie de Raimond Sebond*, has pictured Montaigne as a demon who leads us deep into the dark labyrinth of opinions; points out that in their tangled and perplexing maze there is no lamp but faith; then suddenly snuffs out the lamp—'et l'on n'entend plus qu'un petit rire'.

Some might think that picture appropriate to Hume, as to Mon-

---

[1] They did. Compare the familiar story of d'Holbach's reply to a doubt expressed by Hume as to the existence of real atheists—'My dear David! . . . Here are fifteen round the table.'

taigne. But I do not feel that it genuinely describes either. As so often, the criticism most reveals the critic himself. Sainte-Beuve, great man as he was, had a certain bitterness foreign to these other two sceptics; the author of *Mes Poisons* might have been capable, at moments, of that demonic 'petit rire'. But I doubt if there was anything 'demonic' about Montaigne or Hume. Both of them are good-natured beings who follow with a circumspect passion the elusive trail of Truth, because they love her and believe her better than Falsehood. Most men, they might plead, do not think in any case; the heads of the few who do think, will rest better by resigning themselves to doubt, than by fuddling themselves with dogmas and fanaticisms.

Such was Hume's philosophy—a profound, but good-natured and courageous scepticism. And by it he seems to me to have lived in practice, with a good deal of consistency and success. Whether philosophers do or do not live by their own philosophic principles, can indeed prove little. Schopenhauer's 'Vanity of Vanities', for example, contrasts comically at moments with his own somewhat childish vanity about academic medals. But failure to practise what one preaches need not disprove the truth of what one says, or one's sincerity in saying it. All the same, it is more satisfying when a man does succeed in living up to his principles. And Hume, I think, did.

Few men have been, in the everyday sense, more truly 'philosophic'. One cannot say whether his temperament more moulded his philosophy, or his philosophy his temperament. 'People of this character,' he says, of the sensitive and emotional, 'have, no doubt, more lively enjoyment, as well as more pungent sorrows, than men of cool and sedate tempers: But, I believe, when everything is balanced, there is no one, who would not rather be of the latter character, were he entirely master of his own disposition.' This seems to me one of Hume's less intelligent remarks; for there are surely many passionate persons, like Blake or Byron, who would reject with loathing the idea of becoming 'cool and sedate'.[1] Hume was ex-

[1] Contrast La Rochefoucauld: 'Ceux qui ont eu de grandes passions se trouvent toute leur vie heureux,' (this seems highly questionable) 'et malheureux d'en être guéris.' Vauvenargues rings truer: 'Nous ne connaissons pas l'attrait des violentes agitations. Ceux que nous plaignons de leurs embarras méprisent notre repos.' Similarly Byron, in one of his finest and most self-discerning passages:

> Their breath is agitation, and their life
> A storm whereon they ride to sink at last,

tremely eighteenth-century, and had little conception of Romantics. Yet even he was to write, as we have seen, to Mme de Boufflers: 'You have saved me from a total indifference towards every thing in human life.' This is almost identical with Benjamin Constant's confession to Mme Récamier: 'Aimer c'est souffrir, mais aussi c'est vivre. Et depuis si longtemps je ne vivais plus.'

Still, on the whole, Hume seems to me to have kept a very happy balance—far happier than, for example, Musset, Flaubert, or Baudelaire—between too much passion (which means suffering) and too little (which means ennui).

Equally typical is his wise remark to Gibbon, that, in revising his books, he 'always laboured to reduce the superlatives and soften the positives'.

But though 'calm passions' may make more for happiness than violent ones, a cool head becomes egoistically unattractive if combined with a cold heart. That Hume escaped. 'Le bon David' had both humanity and humour, warmth and gaiety. 'Give me my choice,' he wrote at the end of his *Enquiry concerning Morals*, 'and I would rather, for my own happiness and self-enjoyment, have a friendly humane heart, than possess all the other virtues of Demosthenes and Philip united.' Hence his many, enduring friendships; hence his disarming charm, even for enemies. Robert Adam, despite his mother's ban on bringing 'Hume the atheist' to the house, once introduced him incognito. 'Thon big jolly mon,' she remarked afterwards, 'wha sat neist me 's the maist agreeable o' them a".' 'That, mother, is the very atheist you was so feart of.' 'Nay, then, Robbie, ye may bring him here as aften as ye please, for I'se warrant he's the maist innocent, agreeable, facetious mon I ever met wi'.' Similarly Rogers told that Hume once asked Cadell the bookseller to make up a party of as many as possible of those that had written against him; and, when they came, delighted them all.

It was hard to hate a man who hated so little; hard to laugh at one

> And yet so nursed and bigoted to strife,
> That should their days, surviving perils past,
> Melt to calm twilight, they feel overcast
> With sorrow and supineness, and so die;
> Even as a flame unfed that runs to waste
> With its own flickering, or a sword laid by
> Which eats into itself, and rusts ingloriously.

who laughed so freely at himself, in health or even in sickness. Hume jests, for example, at what his own plumpness would have cost him, were some 'Harpy of the Treasury' to revive the law of some Gallic cities recorded by Strabo, where 'the Senate kept a measure, beyond which, if any Belly presum'd to increase, the Proprietor of that Belly was oblig'd to pay a fine to the Public, proportionable to its rotundity'. 'I weighed myself t'other day,' he writes, in contrast, to Adam Smith, when wasted by illness six months before his death, 'and find I have fallen five compleat Stones. If you delay much longer, I shall probably disappear altogether.'

True, one could wish this wise and good man less peevish, at times, towards the English—'that pernicious People'—'the most stupid and factious Barbarians in the World'. But such splenetic outbursts were not unprovoked; they were written in private letters; and they date largely from the demagogic tumults of John Wilkes.

Towards individuals Hume could be disarmingly generous. He encouraged Andrew Millar to publish Philip Skelton's[1] *Ophiomaches*, which was an attack on himself. When Hume's protégé, the blind poet Blacklock, was published by Dodsley (1756), with an introduction by Spence, Oxford Professor of Modern History, Spence insisted on the alteration of a stanza praising Hume.[2] Blacklock would have dropped the whole scheme sooner than omit this tribute to his benefactor; but Hume himself wrote direct to Spence telling him to cut the offending passage. He lacked even that last infirmity of literary minds—literary jealousy. When Millar hesitated to publish Robertson's *History of Scotland* lest it compete with Hume's, Hume brushed the objection aside. And after the publica-

---

[1] Philip Skelton (1707–87) an Ulster-born cleric, of extraordinary generosity, but some eccentricity; as rector of Templecarn, near Lough Derg, he assembled his flock so many times to see him die, that one of them protested—'Make a day, Sir, and keep it, and don't be always disappointing us thus.'

[2] The wise in every age conclude
  What Pyrrho taught and Hume renewed,
    That dogmatists are fools.

Joseph Spence (1699–1768), friend of Pope, Professor of Poetry at Oxford (1728), now remembered for his *Anecdotes*. Johnson would only allow him to be 'a pretty scholar', not a good one; Horace Walpole described him as 'a good-natured, harmless little soul, but more like a silver penny than a genius'.

For Blacklock, see note on p. 13.

tion he lightheartedly wrote to Robertson himself: 'A plague take you! Here I sat near the historical summit of Parnassus, immediately under Dr Smollett; and you have the impudence to squeeze yourself by me and place yourself directly under his feet! Do you imagine that this can be agreeable to me?'

Here indeed is a tone that contrasts curiously with the growl of Johnson on Hume—'I know not indeed whether he has first been a blockhead and that has made him a rogue, or first been a rogue and that has made him a blockhead'; or with the shriller denunciation of Gray—'I have always thought David Hume a pernicious writer. . . . Is not that *naiveté* and good humour, which his admirers celebrate in him, owing to this, that he has continued all his days an infant, but one that unhappily has been taught to read and write?'

To this peevish squeak I prefer the brevity of Gibbon—'A letter from Mr Hume[1] overpaid the labour of ten years.'

More surprising to me is Mossner's modern comment, in his excellent biography—'To call Hume *good* would be misleading, for he was certainly no saint.'[2] Mossner will only grant him 'good in many ways'.

Adam Smith talked very differently. Now Adam Smith himself appears to me a man both wise and good; he had known Hume long and intimately; and he had 'always', he says, considered his friend 'as approaching as nearly to the idea of a perfectly wise and virtuous man, as perhaps the nature of human frailty will admit.' Of course one must form one's own judgement from the evidence as a whole. Adam Smith may have been partial. All the same it seems to me a little bold, after such a tribute, to refuse even 'to call Hume good'; a little rash, at the dim distance of two hundred years, to suppose one can know Hume so much better, and pronounce him so much worse, than did this honest and intelligent contemporary.

Charles Lamb was, in the ordinary sense of the word, 'no saint' either. And yet, for Wordsworth, 'Oh he was good, if ever good man was.' 'Good', indeed, is a terribly vague word, about the meaning of which men have never agreed. Such precise ethical gradings are beyond me. I can only say that I like and admire Hume; and believe that many of the troubles of mankind would long have

[1] On *The Decline and Fall*.
[2] *Hume*, pp. 3–4.

vanished, were half of them half as kindly and as wise as he.

As a historic type, Hume remains, above all, the great sceptic. To many it is a type far from sympathetic. But there are really two different questions. First, is Hume's general view of life a true one? Secondly, is it a good and salutary one?

On the truth of his beliefs our verdict is likely to be decided more by temperament than by reason. Indeed, it may be in general that the reflections of philosophers are often only reflections of their own temperaments or projections of their own characters and wishes on the cyclorama of infinity; that they are often like pigeons cooing at their own images in mirrors, and mistaking themselves for the universe.[1] Still, to the sceptical arguments of Hume's reason I can myself see no answer but those of intuition; which seem dubious.

It *may* be that there is a mystical approach to reality, though mystics have reached very odd and discrepant conclusions; it *may* be that knowledge can be attained through direct intuition, though intuitions prove often conflicting or absurd. When, for instance, Cardinal Wiseman's Master of the Ceremonies suddenly halted a procession on the ground that he had so been instructed, that very moment, by special revelation, the Cardinal, it is said, coped with this awkward impasse by the smiling reply—'You may let the procession go on. I have just obtained permission, by special revelation, to proceed.' But such things may breed some distrust of intuitions;[2] except when they may reveal some useful or important mental process working in one's own Unconscious. And even then it may be

---

[1] In Nietzsche's philosophy, for example, one may see the thwarted ambitions of an invalid. And when Spinoza states that God loves no one, only Himself with infinite intellectual love, it may perhaps be inferred that Spinoza was on no bad terms with Spinoza.

[2] Cf. Tennyson, *In Memoriam*:

> He fought his doubts and gather'd strength,
> He would not make his judgment blind.

The second line seems to me to contradict the first. Darwin, pondering Evolution, did not fight his doubts; he carefully collected them.

> A warmth within the breast would melt
> The freezing reason's colder part,
> And like a man in wrath the heart
> Stood up and answer'd 'I have felt'.

That, unhappily, is what Hitler's heart was constantly doing. He followed his intuitions 'like a somnambulist'. We are still paying for them.

Tennyson's thought seems to me often as shaky as his artistry was sound and sure.

wise to distrust. For the Unconscious is a tricky, wayward, incalculable creature.

But, secondly, an opponent might still reply: 'Even if Hume's scepticism were rationally unanswerable, it would still remain dangerous and soul-destroying. Even if logically right, it would still for mankind at large, be psychologically wrong. Mental and spiritual health is to be preferred even to truth itself, where that truth would cripple and paralyse. Such demoralizing doubt must be met by faith, by the will to believe. Even were that faith no more than the rum needed to carry an army to victory, it would still be folly to refuse. As de Bonald wrote, hating doubt like poison:"Les esprits supérieurs sont naturellement portés vers l'absolu et tendent toujours à simplifier leurs idées. . . . Le doute où les esprits médiocres se reposent est pour les esprits forts ce que l'indécision est pour les forts caractères, un état d'inquiétude et de malaise, dans lequel ils ne sauraient se fixer." '

Yet I doubt de Bonald. He seems erecting his personal preferences into a universal law. On the other hand it may be granted that, for many, religious faith does remain a real psychological need. It can be argued that Hume, not at his best as a psychologist, underestimated that need; and that his scepticism became too militant. Possibly. Yet it is also fair to recognize that the religions of his day in Europe were often intolerant, oppressive, and cruel; that they made some men's days a burden to them with fears of the next world, and restrictions in this; and outraged the liberties, even the lives ,of others. Even in the later half of the eighteenth century Huguenots were still being judicially murdered in France; women burnt for witchcraft in Switzerland and Poland; wretches sent to the stake by the Inquisition in Spain. Voltaire was not without a good deal of justification for his war-cry of *Écrasez l'infâme*.

To-day, when some of the more civilized religions have ceased to exploit the infernal furnaces to generate cheap power for themselves, and look forward, in the next world also, to a kind of celestial Welfare State for everyone, there seems less justification for the deadly points and slashing edges of Voltaire or Hume. Still, intelligent men cannot possibly be debarred from discussing such problems; and their discussions are unlikely to affect the unintelligent very much, either way. Again, men with religious temperaments are always likely to find themselves a religion; but the religion they find is more likely to be free from dogmatism or tyranny, if it is freely criticized.

Even in 1955 a free-thinking broadcast could cause a queer outburst of indignation. True, responsible churchmen took it with praiseworthy calm; but many less level-headed persons were outraged. Their vehemence, indeed, suggested that they were really exasperated at being reminded of what they wished to forget—the existence of doubts in other minds, perhaps even the existence of doubts in their own; just as the exasperation of Johnson, and the consternation of Boswell, at Hume's philosophic tranquillity in the face of death suggest that, on this topic, their own minds were far from tranquil. Had they possessed more faith and hope, they would have shown more charity. The only conclusion seems the eternal importance of tolerance. The religious should not assume a tone of dogmatic superiority. And the unreligious should avoid offence, except in self-defence. The less fanaticism on either side, the better.

But, quite apart from religion, there remains the wider question, highly relevant to our violent and illiberal century, whether the strong beliefs preferred by de Bonald are really preferable to a 'mitigated scepticism' like Hume's. Obviously Hamlets and Ivanovs are of not much use to the world, nor the world to them. 'Why should I waste my time,' wrote Lord Fisher, 'looking at all sides when I know that mine is the right one? The cleverest man we ever had at the Admiralty was Goschen and he was the worst failure of all. He was always looking at all sides and we never got anything done.' Often faith *has* moved mountains; often the history of the world *has* been shaped by men of vehement conviction like St Paul or Mohammed, Luther or Calvin, Marx or Lenin, Stalin or Hitler (on whose lips the words 'fanatical', 'fanaticism' recurred like a *Leitmotiv*, as terms of the highest praise).

But to this it can be answered, first, that though fervent beliefs have brought spectacular results, too often it would have been better for mankind if they had not. If faith has enabled men to move mountains, too often it has been only to drop them on the heads of hapless millions. One may suspect that we owe far less good than evil to those drastic characters who have slammed the doors of history till the world shook.

Secondly, de Bonald seems rash in assuming that strong characters must cherish strong convictions, and that those are weak who doubt. The Hamlets and Ivanovs are neurotics, whose impotence is due to causes deeper than mere intellectual scepticism. And though Hamlet might have been better had he doubted less, he might also have been better had he doubted still more—had he questioned the highly questionable value of vengeance itself. Few would call feeble the doubting Socrates. The ever moderate Aristotle yet accomplished the labours of a dozen ordinary men. The sceptic Montaigne set his calm example of tolerance and courage amid the barbarities of civil and religious wars. The sceptic Gibbon shouldered for twenty years the fall of an Empire. Frederick the Great and Napoleon were only too efficient despite a lack of principles that often became wholly cynical. And few writers have led more active and satisfactory lives than Hume himself.

Vigour of action seems often a matter of strong vitality rather than of strong beliefs. To men of strong beliefs one may prefer men of strong feelings (for human fish are poor fish), combined with strong self-control. People talk of having the courage of one's convictions: it might sometimes be better to have less conviction and more courage. That Negative Capability praised by Keats, which dispenses with dogmatic conclusions, appears by no means a form of incapacity.

It is, indeed, far from obvious why it should be thought a virtue to believe things on inadequate rational evidence. If a man loses his fortune by persistently trusting a bogus security, he is not generally regarded as admirable. The best type of soldier does not try to persuade himself that the chances of victory are one whit better than they in fact are: it is part of his duty to see them precisely as they are, and act, if necessary, in defiance of them.

I believe that, for persons of intelligence and vitality, life can be lived with far fewer certainties than is commonly supposed. Not only are our beliefs often extravagant: the quantity of them is often extravagant also. To many of the problems of this odd universe the best answer may be 'Wait and see'; likely though it may remain that we shall wait and never see. To-day there is much prate of 'Angst'; whatever the bleakness of his philosophy, few men can have suffered less from such feeble hysteria than Hume.

It may well be, of course, that men like Hume can never have a wide appeal to mankind at large. Yet for mankind at large it may be highly important that there should be men like Hume. It may or may not be desirable to think as he did: but it is at least highly desirable to think as honestly and good-humouredly as he.

Had men taken him to heart, there would have been no French Terror, no Paris Commune, no Marxism and no Nazism, no World Wars. Our own century, more fanatical than any of its predecessors since the seventeenth, has certainly no less need to learn from his 'mitigated' scepticism; unlikely as it may be that it ever will. The family motto of the Humes was 'True to the end'; as that of the Boswells was 'Vraie Foye'. Such high-sounding mottoes, as poor Boswell found, are not easy to live up to. But Hume, I think, succeeded. His philosophy may or may not have been true: *he* was.

HORACE WALPOLE

I do not like to think an author is trying to write a book. I like to imagine he is talking to me.... Our writers of to-day have bodies of iron, not in their health, but in their style.

MADAME DU DEFFAND

Horace Walpole was born on September 24, 1717, the sixth and youngest child of Robert Walpole and Catherine Shorter (grand-daughter of a rich timber-merchant, Lord Mayor of London in 1688). Though his parents took their marriage-tie lightly, and though Horace was strangely different from his father and brothers, there seems no adequate reason to believe the gossip that Horace was really the son of Carr, Lord Hervey, half-brother to Pope's 'Sporus'. Indeed he appears to have closely resembled his half-sister, Sir Robert Walpole's natural daughter, Lady Mary Churchill.

At nine the future historian of Georgian society collected his first material—just in time. He plagued his mother to see George I. 'As the infinite good nature of my father never thwarted any of his children, he ... permitted her to gratify the first vehement inclination that ever I expressed.' So at 10 p.m. on June 1, 1727, his mother took the little boy to St James's and handed him over to Melusina, Lady Walsingham (the future Lady Chesterfield), who led him to kiss the hand of a pale elderly gentleman in snuff-coloured clothes. Ten days later, on his way to Hanover, George I was struck down by apoplexy at Osnabrück.

Though not yet ten, Walpole was already at Eton; and, when George II was proclaimed there, he wept to think how, only a few days before, he had kissed the late king's hand. At Eton he remained till 1734.

'I can't say I am sorry,' he recorded at nineteen, 'that I was never quite a schoolboy.' Indeed, brutal though eighteenth-century education often was, he seems to have had an easy time at Eton; instead of batting at cricket, or battling with bargees, he enjoyed himself in a dream-world of Virgilian pastoral and French romance, happy with his school-friend Thomas Gray. Despite its aristocracy, the eighteenth century could be curiously unsnobbish. Walpole, the Prime Minister's son, and Gray, whose mother supported him by keeping a shop, formed a 'Quadruple Alliance' with West, the grandson of Bishop Burnet, and Ashton, whose father was only a Lancaster schoolmaster. And yet, in the words of Gray twenty years later—

81

> Alas, regardless of their doom
> The little victims play!
> No sense have they of ills to come,
> Nor care beyond to-day.

Soon Walpole and Gray were to be estranged by a four years' quarrel; both were to drop Ashton as a quite impossible person; and West was to meet an early death—embittered, it is said, by finding the tragedy of *Hamlet* reenacted in his own home, when his mother formed a *liaison* with her late husband's secretary and gave rise to more horrid suspicions still.[1]

In 1735, as a fellow-commoner of his father's college, King's, Walpole came up to Cambridge, whither Gray and Ashton had preceded him the year before. He tried mathematics; but found he had no aptitude:[2] he tried religion and prayed with the prisoners in Cambridge prison; but, here too, found he had no aptitude. In 1737 he lost his adored mother—perhaps the greatest grief of his whole life. Indeed, when one surveys his somewhat feminine career, with no deep attachments to women, except for Mme du Deffand, who was far older, and the Miss Berrys, who were far younger, it does not seem fantastic to suspect some degree of mother-fixation.[3]

Materially, his future was soon provided for. In 1737 the Prime Minister's son received a sinecure in the Customs, replaced in 1738 by three other sinecures. Thus at twenty-one he was assured of £1200 a year (which soon after his father's death became over £3000) from the public funds. He was also assured, when the time should come, of a Cornish borough to elect him M.P. Horace Walpole was an expensively spoilt child of his country; it has been estimated that he cost it, first and last, a quarter of a million. And yet, in the long run, England has often spent her money with considerably less return.

In 1738 he took leave of Cambridge, without the superfluity of a

---

[1] That her husband had been poisoned.

[2] The blind Professor Sanderson sent him away after a fortnight, as hopeless; and the young Walpole wept with mortification.

[3] Cf. Walpole's curious drama *The Mysterious Mother*. And his remark to Conway (6/8/1754)—'There is a beautiful tiger at my neighbour Mr. Crammond's here, of which I am so fond, that my Lady Townshend says it is the only thing I ever wanted to kiss.'

degree; at Easter 1739 he left England, with Gray, for his Grand
Tour. Paris—Rheims—Lyons—the romantic precipices of the
Grande Chartreuse—Geneva—Lyons again—the romantic horrors
of the Mont Cenis (where Walpole's fat spaniel was gobbled by a
wolf)—Turin—Genoa—Florence—Rome—Naples—Rome—
Radicofani[1]—Florence again—it was all, no doubt, much more
comfortable than Goldsmith's way of seeing Europe; though less
thrilling than Boswell's. At Florence, where Walpole became *cicis-
beo* to the fair Signora Grifoni, and made friends with Sir Horace
Mann (to whom his tireless pen was still writing when Mann died
forty-six years later,[2] although they never met again), Walpole and
Gray lingered, in all, some fifteen months. But Gray grew restive.
Travel is always liable to strain tempers. Little wonder, then, if after
a couple of years in close company a quarrel broke out between two
young men, both proud, but one studious and one sociable; one
melancholy and one gay; one socially inferior and financially obliged
to the other. The only wonder is that they did not quarrel sooner.
Writing of it thirty years later, Walpole very generously took the
blame.[3] But one may doubt if there was really much blame to take.
The open clash came at Reggio in Emilia. From Venice they returned separately to England in the late summer of 1741. Walpole
had already been duly elected M.P. for Cornish Callington.

But Horace Walpole's place in politics was to be, not on their
central stage, but in the front row of the auditorium or behind the
scenes. Early in 1742, after twenty years as first lord of the treasury,
Sir Robert fell; early in 1745 his doctors killed him.

In 1747 Horace Walpole bought beside the Thames, just south of

---

[1] Whence (5/7/1740) he wrote his cousin Conway a typically burlesque account of
the relics preserved 'in a small hovel of Capucins on the side of the hill'—'Among
other things of great sanctity there is a set of gnashing of teeth, the grinders very entire; a bit of the worm that never dies, preserved in spirits.'

[2] There still exist 848 letters from Walpole to Mann; 887 from Mann to Walpole. A
letter every 20 days, on a rough average, for half a century! (And what letters!) There
can be few parallels to such fidelity.

[3] This was all the more generous since it was a question of making the facts public.
Walpole is writing to Gray's biographer, Mason (2/3/1773): 'The fault was mine . . . .
I treated him insolently: he loved me, and I did not think he did . . . . Forgive me, if
I say that his temper was not conciliating; at the same time that I will confess to you
that he acted a more friendly part, had I had the sense to take advantage of it—he
freely told me of my faults.' (Always a perilous act of friendship. Walpole's feeling for
Gray, it may be added, was so warm that he had made a will bequeathing all to him.)

Pope's Twickenham, a little box of a house, originally built by a nobleman's retired coachman, and later the home of Mrs Chenevix the toy-woman. For fifty years it was to be his toy, his Gothic pleasure-dome—though less kindly described by the megalomaniac Beckford of Fonthill as 'a Gothic mousetrap'.[1] Here he soon began to amuse himself by adding, first (1750–3), Gothic battlements, a Gothic staircase, Gothic wallpaper, a Gothic library with bookcases modelled on the choir-doors of old St Paul's, and fireplaces modelled on medieval tombs; then, in 1760–7, a Gothic cloister and gallery, a Round Tower of three stories, and a 'chapel' with roof vaulted in imitation of the Chapter-house at York.[2]

In 1757 there budded also the Strawberry Hill press, whose first fruit was a quarto edition of Gray's *Bard* and *Progress of Poesy*; followed by Walpole's own *Catalogue of Royal and Noble Authors* and *Fugitive Pieces* (both 1758), and his *Anecdotes of Painting*, vols I–III (1762–4),[3] a work of serious and valuable labour, compiled from some forty notebooks of the engraver and antiquary George Vertue (1684–1756). In 1764 Walpole also turned, with equal success, from Gothic building to Gothic fiction—*The Castle of Otranto*.

All this was combined with a flow of letters, a buzz of social life, and intervals of what his critics called 'political frenzy'. In 1757 he generously, though vainly, tried to save Admiral Byng from being shot 'pour encourager les autres'; in 1763–4 he persuaded his cousin Conway to oppose the legality of general warrants (by which Wilkes had been arrested); and when Conway was deprived of his regiment for it, he worked passionately in support of his brave, but somewhat chilly kinsman.

In 1765, as part of the Rockingham ministry, Conway became Leader of the House of Commons; but Walpole, now wounded by what he considered Conway's neglect, set out for Paris. There at

---

[1] William Beckford (1760-1844), the author of *Vathek*, having inherited, it is said, a million in hand and a hundred thousand a year, could well afford to outbuild the author of *The Castle of Otranto*; and did. Fonthill with its 300-foot tower (which twice collapsed) cost over a quarter of a million. Hazlitt called it a cathedral turned into a toy-shop; all the same, in its absurd way, it was perhaps more impressive than Strawberry Hill. (See G. Chapman, *Beckford*.)

[2] Strawberry Hill is still well worth a visit; though it is necessary to write for permission.

[3] Vol. IV appeared in 1780.

least, like Hume two years before, he became a vast success; and, at forty-eight, found it pleasant, as he pleasantly puts it, 'to totter into vogue'. Above all, he fascinated the blind, yet penetrating Mme du Deffand, aged sixty-eight. So began a friendship of fifteen years, and one of the most famous correspondences in European literature—some eight hundred letters on either side.

At this time he also mischievously composed a letter purporting to be written by Frederick the Great to Rousseau, and offering the exiled philosopher an asylum, together with all the persecution that his perversity might desire. This squib was only too successful, both in France and in England. It considerably upset the neurotic Rousseau, and provided one of his main pretexts for quarrelling with poor Hume.[1]

In 1768 Walpole published his *Historic Doubts on the Life and Reign of Richard III*, an attempt to vindicate Crookback's character, which involved him in irritating controversy, and has been repeated in recent years. In 1766–8 he also wrote a five-act verse drama, *The Mysterious Mother*, on the curious theme of a mother, the Countess of Narbonne, who, without his knowledge, has a daughter by her own son; when the daughter grows up, the son marries her, the mother reveals the horrid secret, and stabs herself. The play has been praised, by Byron and others; Scott thought it, though 'disgusting', 'horribly impressive'. But the action seems to me neither likely to have happened, nor very interesting even if it had happened; nor do I see anything in the treatment to redeem so unpractical a plot. It falls far short of becoming an English *Oedipus*.[2]

In this same year 1768 Walpole retired, after twenty-seven years, from Parliament. His public activity, never violently active, was over;[3] but for nearly thirty years more, he continued extremely alive, and far happier, I imagine, than Johnson or Gray. He had

[1] See pp. 20–5.

[2] Incest seems to me an unpromising theme—it tends to produce either shrieks or yawns. Fanny Burney shrieked—'Dreadful was the whole! truly dreadful! . . . Mrs. Smelt and myself heartily regretted that it had come our way.' However Mme du Deffand found the subject 'très intéressante'; and Lady Diana Beauclerk made seven drawings to illustrate the play, which were hung at Strawberry Hill. (See A. S. Brandenburg in *Mod. Lang. Quart.* X (1949), 464-74.)

[3] Though in 1770 the Duc de Choiseul would have liked him for Ambassador in Paris. Walpole, however, gave warning that, much as he loved France, and peace, he would make a far from compliant ambassador.

learnt pretty well to be constantly busy, without being overwhelmed with business; to enjoy affection, without being lacerated by it; to relish the comedy, though without forgetting the tragedy, of life. He knew how to make the past enliven the present, and to escape from the present into the past.

He added to the buildings of Strawberry Hill, to the endless museum of curiosities it contained; he printed;[1] he collected, annotated, and bound plays or pamphlets; and, day after day, that nimble pen slid over the paper like a wise serpent renewing its youth by constantly changing its skin.

In 1769 his tranquillity was disturbed, his reputation lastingly and unjustly injured, by Chatterton. That not very pleasant youth, now sixteen, who had been planting antique plays on Dodsley, now turned his attention to planting antique prose and verse on Walpole. At first Walpole was duped and delighted; but Gray and Mason pronounced Chatterton's documents to be forgeries; and in a second letter Walpole very reasonably advised the young poet to stick to his job in the law, and so earn enough solid security to follow his own bent later on. Chatterton, angry at being, as he felt, merely patronized where he had sought patronage, grew insolent; came up to London; and scathingly lampooned Walpole's antiquarianism in the *Town and Country Magazine*. Then, not yet eighteen, he poisoned himself. He was hard up, but not apparently starving; he may have been suffering painfully from venereal disease; and he was mentally ill-balanced. But as queues of sentimentalists gathered round the memory of the 'marvellous boy', there gradually grew up the persistent legend that he had been 'cruelly rebuffed'—in effect, murdered—by the callousness of Walpole.[2] The eighteenth century did not at all understand neurotics; but that, as Hume found with Rousseau, could prove a very costly ignorance—as, indeed, it often does to this day.

But apart from such worries and annoyances as were caused by Chatterton, or by the marriage of Walpole's illegitimate niece with the King's brother, the Duke of Gloucester, or by the extrava-

---

[1] E.g. annotated *Mémoires du Comte de Grammont* (1772); *Anecdotes of Painting*, vol. IV (1780); *Hieroglyphic Tales* (1785).

[2] For a very thorough discussion of the matter see E. H. W. Meyerstein, *A Life of Chatterton* (1930).

gances of Walpole's lunatic nephew, Lord Orford, or by the growing crowds that pressed to see his too successful toy of Strawberry Hill,[1] the years slipped smoothly by him, gaily tranquil as an old Chinese sage.

And yet, as the Greeks knew, disdaining such wishful complacencies as those of *Rabbi ben Ezra*, old age has always its bitterness. Friends died—Lady Suffolk (1767), Lady Hervey (1768), Gray (1771), Mme du Deffand (1780), Cole the antiquary (1782), Kitty Clive the actress (1785), Horace Mann (1786). Finally, in 1791 the death of his mad nephew brought to the old man of seventy-four the title of his father, dead forty-six years earlier. He became, ironically, fourth Earl of Orford.

Yet the lively letters still flowed on. Like the wise Bonstetten, if he could not replace old friends, at least Walpole recruited new. He had long grown distrustful of deep feeling; he had grown reticent; but he felt far more than he confessed. And in 1788, at seventy, just as Mme du Deffand had once loved him at sixty-eight, as the old Goethe was to love Ulrike von Levetzow at seventy-four, Horace Walpole was swept off his feet by two young ladies, 'my twin wives', 'mes très chères Fraises', Mary and Agnes Berry—above all by Mary (1763–1852), now twenty-four. Gossip said that he even wished to marry her, or her sister. But, as usual, gossip may well have lied.[2] Enough that this relationship, repaid on their side by lasting devotion, sweetened the last nine years of that long life; though it also cost him agonies of anxiety while the two girls and their father faced the dangers of travel through that revolutionary France which Walpole abhorred, even more passionately than he had sympathized with revolutionary America.

In the March of 1797 the liveliest chronicler of that now expiring century, whose boyhood had seen George I, passed quietly away,

[1] In the end he had to draw up printed rules, limiting visitors to parties of four (children being excluded), and to one party a day. 'I shudder when the bell rings at the gate. It is as bad as keeping an inn.'

[2] The two sisters, each of whom got engaged, yet never married, were to form an almost inseparable pair for the prodigious period of eighty-eight years.

Walpole's niece, the Duchess of Gloucester, is said to have asked him, in jealousy, 'Do you mean to marry Miss Berry, or do you not?'; to which he answered, 'That is as Miss Berry herself pleases.' So Mary Berry told Charles Greville; adding that Walpole never thought of marrying Agnes. But this suggests that he had at least *thought* of marrying Mary.

while Bonaparte and Masséna pushed back the shattered armies of Austria through the passes of Carinthia and Tyrol.

Horace Walpole did not find much favour with nineteenth-century critics. Yet Lord Orford seems to me in many ways to have made a success of life where Lord Chesterfield failed. Both set a high value on the graces of life; it is largely as examples of eighteenth-century grace that they are valuable still. But Walpole did not sin like Chesterfield against what is perhaps the first commandment of the Graces—'Thou shalt not be a bore'. He did not nag, nor reiterate, nor share Chesterfield's tendency to turn worldly wisdom into tyranny, politeness into pedantry.

Again, a large part of human grace lies in gaiety. Chesterfield could be witty, pungent, sardonic. But he remains a man who never laughed. His wit has often the glitter of an icicle—or of a crystal chandelier in an elaborate salon. Walpole too could be bitter. He could hate passionately—especially anyone who had lifted a finger against his beloved father, or his beloved cousin, Conway. He enjoyed scandal in a way that some precisians might call malicious. But I own that I enjoy scandal, provided it is gay, not priggish. If one is interested in human nature, one is interested in its oddities. And it is sometimes the smallest details that are the most revealing. I doubt if Walpole's gossip did anyone much harm, even then; the world is certainly a little gayer for it now. Even if his stories were not always true, even if he was sometimes naughty to pass them on, they remain interesting as pictures of what his age thought credible, discreditable, or comical. Walpole was not, I think, either cold or cruel—on the contrary, he could be unusually humane, and quixotically generous. In fact, whatever his faults or frivolities, he had that vital quality which I feel conspicuously lacking in Chesterfield —warmth. Where Chesterfield remains a rather glacial acquaintance, for Walpole one can feel friendship—not as warm as for characters like Montaigne, Ronsard, Dorothy Osborne, Edward Fitz-Gerald, or Thomas Hardy—but still friendship.

This difference between Chesterfield and Walpole comes out vividly in their style.[1] And it is, above all, his style that has kept Walpole alive.

[1] Saintsbury's verdict that Chesterfield was 'a much greater master of English' seems to me very strange.

There is perhaps no form of literature, except lyric poetry, where success depends so much on style as it does in letters. Ordinary letters are of little interest to anyone but the recipients (if even to them). Some correspondences, no doubt, have become interesting as antiquarian or historical documents. The *Paston Letters*, for example, do not often come to life; they need to be animated by the touch of a poetess like Virginia Woolf; but they are precious to the medieval historian. Again, the student of Browning, often so admirable in his lyrics, must also read his letters, though, to me, their prosaic dullness is such that often they seem written in tar with a pen of lead. But the common reader looks in letters for things he can value either for their matter, or for their manner, or for both.

Sometimes the matter may be important because it is religious, as in St Paul's Epistles, or ethical, as in Seneca's Letters; or because it is critically revealing, as in Flaubert's correspondence; or again there may be the passionate interest of love-letters like those of Héloïse or the Portuguese Nun, Dorothy Osborne or Mlle de Lespinasse. But even in such letters, as in any kind of literature, the manner, the style, remains also vitally important. And for the everyday letter-writer, who deals, not with the fate of hearts, or souls, or nations, but with the little trivialities of ordinary life, almost everything depends on style, and on the personality that style reveals. At times, no doubt, there is the thrill of historic interest, when Mme de Sévigné writes of the trial of Fouquet, Walpole of the trial of the Jacobite rebels after the '45; but, apart from such setpieces, both of them gain their readers simply by their power of making even small beer intoxicating, their gift of extracting grace, or gaiety, even from straws. That too is the essential gift of Lady Mary Wortley Montagu, Gray, Cowper, Lamb, Byron, FitzGerald, or Mrs Carlyle.

Perhaps the most essential quality with letter-writers like these is liveliness; whether it takes the form of vitality, or fantasy, or gaiety. But without grace the vitality can become clumsy; the fantasy, bizarre; the gaiety, crude. Perhaps that is one reason why so many of the best letters have been written by women ('pennis non homini datis', as Walpole put it, 'with quills denied to man')—by Dorothy Osborne, Mme de Sévigné, Lady Mary Montagu, Julie de Lespinasse, Jane Welsh Carlyle; or, sometimes, by rather feminine men, like Cowper or Walpole himself.

On Lady Mary's letters (much though he disliked her) Walpole comments: 'It is very remarkable, how much better women write than men'; and again—'It is the fair part of creation which excells in that province . . . orators write affectedly, ministers obscurely, poets floridly, learned men pedantically, and soldiers tolerably, when they can spell.'

Walpole's own imagination is uncommonly vivid, and often uncommonly gay. He does not seem to suffer, like most of us, from days when the brain feels stale as a week-old loaf, and a sheet of notepaper looks forbidding as the Sahara. Just as Pope could make one of the most charming poems in English out of a few snipped hairs,[1] so Walpole can put new colour even into that threadbare theme of every English bore, the English weather. The theme may be eternal: the phrases are new—'being the first of July and consequently the middle of winter'—'somebody said lately that the winter was come over to pass the spring in England'—'yet one must have seen such a thing as spring or one could not have invented the idea'—'my poor hay has not a dry thread to its back. . . . The best sun we have is made of Newcastle coal, and I am determined never to reckon upon any other'—'the month of June, according to custom immemorial, is as cold as Christmas. I had a fire last night, and all my rose-buds, I believe, would have been very glad to sit by it'. This last was in June 1784. Again, in June 1755, as usual, it rained. But what a rainbow his sunny gaiety makes of it!—

'About four arrived such a flood, that we could not see out of the windows: the whole lawn was a lake, though situated on so high an Ararat. . . . I had but just time to collect two dogs, a couple of sheep, a pair of bantams, and a brace of gold-fish; for, in the haste of my zeal to imitate my ancestor Noah, I forgot that fish would not easily be drowned. In short, if you chance to spy a little ark with pinnacles sailing towards Jersey, open the skylight, and you will find some of your acquaintance.'[2]

The formula may be simple—fantasy and humorous exaggeration.

[1] Whereas, says Walpole, he 'laboured his letters as much as the *Essay on Man*, and as they were written to everybody, they do not look as if they had been written to anybody.'

[2] To Richard Bentley, 11/6/1755.

But this form of art, like most, remains far easier in theory than in practice. For example:

(On a social upstart) 'I thought he had not had a grandfather since the Creation, that was not born within these twenty years.'

(On his father's Norfolk squires) 'I here every day see men, who are mountains of roast beef, and only seem just roughly hewn out into the outlines of the human form, like the giant-rock at Pratolino.'[1]

(On the daughter-in-law of the Spanish ambassador) She 'they say is not ugly, and has as good a set of teeth as one can have, when one has but two and those black.'

(On French *philosophes*) 'They think me quite profane for having any belief left.' 'There was no soul in Paris but philosophers, whom I wished in heaven though they do not wish themselves so. They are so overbearing and so underbred.' 'I think they are ten times more foolish since they took to thinking.'

(On French landscape) 'Trees cut into fire-shovels, and stuck into pedestals of chalk, compose their country.'

(On the Wilkes agitations of 1769) 'Mr. Hume is writing the Revolutions of Middlesex, and a troop of barnacle geese are levied to defend the Capitol.'

(On Lord Rockingham's romantic grounds) 'There are temples in cornfields; and in the little wood, a window-frame mounted on a bunch of laurel, and intended for an hermitage.'

(On modern morals) 'This sublime age reduces everything to its quintessence; all periphrases and expletives are so much in disuse, that I suppose soon the only way of making love will be to say "Lie down".'

(On himself) 'Nobody cares less than I about what they don't care for.'

---

[1] Presumably the *colosso del Apennino* (60 feet high) of Giovanni Bologna (1524-1608) in the gardens of the Medici villa at Pratolino, north of Florence.

Here the art lies in using hyperbole so as to be, not 'enormous and disgusting', but (because so light-hearted) enormously delightful—to create apparent nonsense in which the hearer is pleased to find, all the same, real sense.

Then again, as so often when one analyses the charm of a style, a great deal of Walpole's effect, as of Johnson's, comes from his brilliant gift for imagery—for simple simile and metaphor.

(Of his own letters) 'My letters depend on events, and I am like the man in the weather-house who only comes forth on a storm.' And again—'Every drop of ink in my pen ran cold.'

(Of his boredom in society) 'When I get by myself, I undress myself and seem to have had people in my pockets, in my plaits, and on my shoulders! . . . I literally seem to have murdered a man whose name was Ennui, for his ghost is ever before me.'

(On his gout) 'Cherubims that have no legs, and do nothing but stick their chins in a cloud and sing, are never out of order.'

(On his improvements of Strawberry) 'I am all plantation, and sprout away like any chaste nymph in the *Metamorphosis*.'[1]

(On the east wind, while he lingers out the spring of 1766 in Paris) 'I should not be quite sorry if a little of it tapped my lilacs on their green noses and bade them wait for their master.'

(On a disastrous period in 1757) 'It is time for England to slip her own cables, and float away into some unknown ocean.'

(How often one has felt that, since aviation shrank the English Channel to a ditch!)

(On Frederick's military exploits in 1758) 'Well! the King of Prussia is found again—where do you think? only in Poland, up to the chin in Russians! Was ever such a man! He was riding home from Olmütz; they ran and told him of an army of Muscovites, as you would of a covey of partridges; he galloped thither and shot them.'

(On the Opposition) 'The cruellest thing that has been said of the

---

[1] Should, of course, be *Metamorphoses* (of Ovid).

Americans by the court, is, that they were encouraged by the Opposition. You might as soon light a fire with a wet dish-clout.'

(On the opening of the American Revolution). 'I have seen my country's barometer up at Minden and down at Derby. . . . One has griefs enough of one's own, without fretting because Cousin America has eloped with a Presbyterian parson.'

This bachelor has indeed a fondness for such matrimonial imagery.

'An epic poem is a mixture of history without truth, and of romance without imagination. We are well off when from that *mésalliance* there spring some bastards called episodes, that are lucky enough to resemble their romantic mother, more than their solemn father.'[1]

And again—'Our passions and our understandings agree so ill, that they resemble a Frenchman of quality and his wife . . . the passions, like the lady, affect to have great deference for the husband, the understanding.'

With so fertile an imagination, Walpole might have made, in the age of Campion or Herrick, a charming minor poet.[2] And these lively little fantasies are never livelier than when they are compressed into a single vivid word; as when Bubb Dodington entertains the Spanish ambassadress—'indeed the ambassadress could see nothing; for Dodington stood before her the whole time, *sweating* Spanish at her'; or again when Pitt appears, histrionically swathed and bandaged, in the House of Commons (1757)—'In short, no

---

[1] Conceivably Walpole might have heard of the sixteenth-century decision of the Accademia della Crusca, 'che eroico e romanzo è tutt' uno, e s'intende romanzo per un eroico allegro, ed eroico per uno romanzo noioso e spiacevole'.

[2] At rare moments, he *is* one; in parts, for example, of *The Portrait of Mme du Deffand* (see p.117), or of *The Entail*; where a poor butterfly, blind to time and fate, wishes to entail its favourite residence, a rose, (like another Strawberry Hill) on its posterity.

> A CATERPILLAR grovel'd near,
> A subtle slow conveyancer . . .
> Each leaf he binds, each bud he ties
> To eggs of eggs of BUTTERFLIES.

The next instant, a mischievous boy crushes the butterfly, and ruins the rose.

aspiring Cardinal ever *coughed* for the Tiara with more specious debility.'[1]

Largely, I imagine, because of this gay liveliness of temper, Walpole kept to the end of his long life, despite his delicacy and his gout, a curious youthfulness. 'I am Methusalem on most things, and a boy on others.' And because he had no love of philosophical abstractions, aimed at the conversational style of good society, and was in close contact with the French mind, his style is not only light, but youthful in another sense also—it seems strangely modern, and far less old-fashioned than much of Johnson, Gibbon, or Burke. This does not make Walpole necessarily better, but it brings him closer. Much of the time he talks just as we might talk to-day—if we had the wit.

Indeed so much is his success due to charm of style, that it is his lightest touches, often, that have left the deepest mark, and his gaiety that has done most to make him a serious figure in the literature of his age. Like eighteenth-century poetry, he seems to me best when laughing or biting. His serious letters tend often to be formal, heavy, and laboured in compliment. Had he written to Mann or Lady Ossory as he wrote to Pinkerton or Robertson, he might himself long since have become mere food for antiquarians.

But though a good letter-writer, like a good cook, can concoct wonders out of almost nothing, both, if they are wise, will prefer good materials. From his own private journal Boswell contrived to make in the end the biography of a great contemporary; from his own private correspondence Walpole contrived, with similar insight and assiduity, to make a historical picture of his contemporary world. Letter-writers like Cicero or Mme de Sévigné had, of course, done something of the kind before him; but no one, to my knowledge, either before or since Walpole has so deliberately chosen to do in history what Richardson did in fiction—tell the course of events in letters. As early as 1746 Gray was inquiring about Walpole's historical 'Memoires'. These eventually covered the long stretch from 1741 to 1791; and he arranged for their publication

---

[1] *Memoires of the Last Ten Years of George II*, III, 8. The point is that a Cardinal might have more chance of being elected Pope if he seemed unlikely to live too long. Thus Sixtus V is reported to have hobbled feebly on a staff till elected—and then to have flung it triumphantly away.

after his death. But, though often trenchant, vivid, and interesting, for the ordinary reader these Memoirs have been completely overshadowed by the letters. As early as 1748 Walpole took steps to recover those he had written to Horace Mann. For he was not in general one of those inconceivably industrious persons who keep copies of their letters—as if writing them even once were not grind enough. Even so, it must have needed no little energy to write some four thousand letters, then to become one's own archivist, and keep them from falling into the chaos which quickly threatens all who preserve old correspondence. Sometimes he even annotated them.

Further, as Dr W. S. Lewis has pointed out, there seems to have been some careful planning—a sort of general scheme, by which Walpole contrived, like a newspaper-editor, to have different correspondents for different subjects; though, in this case, it was the correspondents' job not so much to write as to be written to.

Thus for politics there was the diplomatic Mann far off in Florence; for social gossip, George Montagu, then Lady Ossory; for literary matters, Gray, then Mason, then Hannah More; for antiquarianism, Cole, then Lort and Pinkerton. Naturally, such divisions could not be hard and fast; and they could only be developed by degrees.

Nor, I think, should one stress *too* much the deliberate calculation with which Walpole thus covered the history of his age in his private letters. It could have become a very cold-blooded and artificial affair. And it would need most skilful dissimulation. For surely any addressee who suspected that he was being used as a mere stalking-horse for posterity, might well have liked it as little as Queen Victoria when she complained that Mr Gladstone addressed her as if she were a public meeting. Besides, many of Walpole's correspondents fall under no specialized heading; and his multitudinous letters to Mme du Deffand, for example, were recalled by him only to be burnt; so that only a few survive.

My guess would be that Walpole wrote with, perhaps, half of one eye on posterity. His letters may have belonged, for him, in part to the art of literature; but they were meant, I imagine, first and foremost, to be part of the art of life.

In any case the upshot is that we possess a contemporary picture of eighteenth-century England comparable only with the picture left us, from a very different angle, by Boswell. It does not make one wish one had lived then—far from it; but it brings before us a number of persons—particularly, Walpole himself—with whom, for a while, it is very charming and amusing to live. Through most periods, the general mass of human doings and sufferings grows depressing to contemplate. History is largely crimes and follies. It is the individuals, that redeem it; the individuals, that attract; the individuals, that really matter.

In his own way, Walpole has painted the decline and fall of Whig aristocracy. Born when the party was supreme under his father, he lived to see it splintered into ineffectual fragments, while the government of Pitt grappled with the French Revolution. If Walpole seems superficial beside Gibbon, still let us not underestimate the labour of all these letters that fill far more volumes than *The Decline and Fall of the Roman Empire*; remembering, too, that Gibbon, on his part, found his own colossal toil 'amusing'—'this work amused and exercised nearly twenty years of my life'—'some fame, some profit, and the assurance of daily amusement encourage me to persist'. For Gibbon was not like that type of erudite historian who spouts and flounders like a surfeiting whale in the throes of chronic mental indigestion.

But perhaps Walpole is really closer to Saint-Simon. Both were clever aristocrats, concerned, not with philosophic principles or historic trends, but with portraying the decay of a brilliant régime of extraordinary individuals. Both watched from the wings a drama of real life in which they themselves figured only dimly; yet with a passionate, indefatigable curiosity, and an unerring eye for those slight touches, those dramatic details which alone can bring to immortal life persons or scenes long dead. True, Saint-Simon is something of a maniac, of a demoniac snob, far less balanced and rational than Walpole. He is less gay. In any case, the monologue of memoirs tends to be less gay than dialogue—which letters, in effect, are. Yet Saint-Simon too remains similarly unforgettable in his best sketches of idle aristocracy, with all its arrogance, frivolity, and futility—such as that Duc de Guise who was never allowed to seat himself at table with his lordly Duchess, niece of Louis XIII, till she had first given him permission; or the stupid M. de Navailles who, when M. le Prince in Flanders failed to find some brook upon the map, obligingly ran and fetched a globe; or M. le Prince letting loose, like another Samson, three or four hundred foxes in the garden at Chantilly of a M. Rose who had refused to sell the Prince his house; or that other intolerable noble, Charnacé, who coveted the site of a peasant-tailor's cottage, which marred his avenue in Anjou, and, having lured the man away to make him a livery, spirited the whole building, saucepans and all, to a distance of four musket-shots in a single day—so that in the evening the poor tailor, returning, thought himself victim of some strange sorcery; or that incredible M. de Vivonne, who having stared some time, leaning against a table, at his dying son, the Duc de Mortemart, calmly remarked, to the scandalized horror of the weeping family, 'Ce pauvre homme-là n'en reviendra pas; j'ai vu mourir tout comme ça son pauvre père'. (For he suspected that his son's real father was one of his own equerries.)

Walpole, however, if less astounding than Saint-Simon, is more humane, and more humorous; the observer of a world as dissipated perhaps, but less artificial and inbred. Walpole disliked the Duke of Newcastle as Saint-Simon disliked the Duc de Noailles. But one cannot conceive Walpole exclaiming, of his bête noire, as Saint-Simon does: 'Je ne cache pas que le plus beau et le plus délicieux jour de ma vie ne fût celui où il me serait donné par la justice divine de l'écraser en marmelade et de lui marcher à deux pieds sur le ventre.' Walpole prefers to present *his* enemy as a figure of comedy, a more grotesque Polonius. The Duke, he will observe, 'though approaching to seventy, still appeared in the full vigour of his nonsense'. Or he inserts his victim as comic relief in that famous set-piece describing the funeral of George II—amid the muffled drums, tolling bells, booming cannon, in the torchlit Abbey, while the Duke of Cumberland, his face distorted by a recent stroke, gazes down into the vault where he must soon follow his dead father, enter Newcastle:

'He fell into a fit of crying the moment he came into the chapel, and flung himself back in a stall, the Archbishop hovering[1] over him with a smelling-bottle—but in two minutes his curiosity got the better of his hypocrisy, and he ran about the chapel with his glass to spy who

[1] It would surely be hard to find a more vivid verb—one instantly visualizes the Archbishop as a large, bedraped, eighteenth-century angel, winged with lawn sleeves.

was or was not there, spying with one hand, and mopping his eyes with t'other. Then returned the fear of catching cold, and the Duke of Cumberland, who was sinking with heat, felt himself weighed down, and turning round, found it was the Duke of Newcastle standing upon his train to avoid the chill of the marble.'

Then there is the proud Duke of Somerset[1] who expected his daughter always to watch his after-dinner nap; and when, one day, he woke on the floor and found she had left her post, forbade any person in his household to speak to her for a year.

There is the Whig Lord Peterborough who, when asked by the monk that was showing him the Sainte Ampoule at Rheims, 'Monsieur, est-ce que vous sacrez vos rois?', replied with ferocious humour, 'Non, Monsieur, nous les massacrons' (a lesson the French were only too soon to learn).

The Duke of Montagu makes a malicious dinner-party at Bath of all the people he can collect that stutter. Lord Derby's cook gives notice, worn out with preparing suppers at 3 a.m. The English scene darkens; but not England's social frivolities. In May 1778 France is joining America against us; but—'Lady Melbourne was standing before the fire, and adjusting her feathers in the glass, says she, "Lord! they say the stocks will blow up: that will be very comical".' Three years later, a month after Cornwallis surrendered at York-town, 'in the height of four raging wars, I saw in the papers an account of the Opera and of the dresses of the company; and thence, the town, and thence of course the whole nation, were informed that Mr Fitzpatrick had very little powder in his hair'.

Or there are the diversions of the hopeful young.

'The gaming at Almack's, which has taken the *pas* of White's is worthy the decline of our Empire, or Commonwealth, which you please. The young men of the age lose five, ten, fifteen thousand pounds in an evening there. Lord Stavordale, not one-and-twenty, lost eleven thousand there last Tuesday, but recovered it by one great hand at hazard: he swore a great oath,—"Now, if I had been playing *deep*, I might have won millions." His cousin, Charles Fox, shines equally there and in the House of Commons. He was twenty-one yesterday se'nnight; and is already one of our best speakers.

[1] Cf. Cooper, *Annals of Cambridge*, IV, 3.

Yesterday he was made a Lord of the Admiralty. We are not a great age, but surely we are tending to some great revolution.' (2/2/1770)

They were. And yet, in contrasting Walpole and Saint-Simon, one can partly see, even in little things, why the really terrible revolution was to burst, not here, but beyond the Channel. Walpole's English aristocracy, with all its riot and folly, is still in contact with Parliament, with trade, with the robust, open-air life of the English countryside; while Saint-Simon's French nobility were crowding an insanitary Versailles in order to hold the king's candlestick, or watch him take off his shirt, with no serious occupation in life but war— 'elle n'est bonne,' in Saint-Simon's phrase, 'qu'à se faire tuer'. Walpole himself may seem frivolous; yet he worked hard enough at subjects not contemptible, like early English painting. He did not, like Saint-Simon, spend twenty-four years of his life in the futile masquerade of Versailles; nor break his heart because the presidents o the Paris *parlement* dared to keep their bonnets on—'l'usurpation énorme du bonnet'—when addressing dukes and peers.

Hence it was that, while Walpole sleeps sound in Houghton Church, in 1794 a shrieking mob tore up the coffin of Saint-Simon, which he had ordered to be fastened with iron bands to that of his Duchess, outraged their bodies, and flung them into the 'fosse commune'.

The same interesting contrast emerges for a moment in Walpole's pictures of the kings of France and England. Neither dynasty makes one nostalgic for the eighteenth century. Yet the difference remains significant. On the one hand there are Louis XV and the du Barry— 'Catin diverts herself and King Solomon the wise with tossing oranges into the air after supper, and crying "Saute, Choiseul! saute, Praslin!" and then Solomon laughs heartily.' (Poor Mme du Barry had no vision, happily, of the day when, after she had vainly screamed to the executioner to spare her one moment longer, her own head was to leap as lightly into the basket of the guillotine.)

In England the royal tragi-comedy is of a different kind, hardly less fatal, but far more respectable. Poor George III at least tried to do his job—though he overdid it. And how vivid the glimpse of him, in Walpole's *Last Journals* (supposing it true)—running into the Queen's room at the news of Burgoyne's taking Ticonderoga, with the cry: 'I have beat them!—beat all the Americans!'

Next there is the Church which, seen through the windows of Strawberry Hill, is not much more edifying. True, the second half of the century could hardly parallel Archbishop Blackburne of York[1] (d. 1743), of whom Walpole records: 'I often dined with him, —his mistress (Mrs. Cruwys) sat at the head of the table, and Hayter, his natural son by another woman, and very like him, at the bottom, as chaplain.'

After this, it is a bagatelle to hear of the Bishop of Worcester's wife in 1778 needing three hours each night to be undressed by her maid, so that the wretched Abigail never got to bed till 3 or 4 a.m.— 'do not mention this, for I did not take the girl, and she still assists at the daily and nightly revolutions of Babel'.

Or there is the aviary established in Gloucester Cathedral, where the Chapter allowed accommodation near the high altar, complete with troughs for water and bird-seed, to a benefactress who believed the soul of her favourite daughter transmigrated into a robin-red-breast.

True, there were religious revivals; though not for Walpole, who was himself a vague sort of deist, disliking irreligion much more than he liked religion. The Lisbon earthquake of 1755[2] badly jolted the complacency of eighteenth-century Europe. 'Between the French and the earthquakes,' writes Walpole, 'you have no notion how good we are grown; nobody makes a suit of clothes now but of sackcloth turned up with ashes.' Far more lasting in effect was that human earthquake, John Wesley; yet Wesley was hardly for Walpole's class[3]—

'My health advances faster than my amusement. However, I have been at one opera, Mr. Wesley's. They have boys and girls with

[1] Lancelot Blackburne (1658-1743) was said by scandal to have been a chaplain of buccaneers. He is also reported to have congratulated Queen Caroline on her good sense in putting up with her husband's new mistress. On the other hand it seems that Walpole maligns him in supposing his chaplain (Thomas Hayter, 1702-62, later Bishop of Norwich, then of London) to have been his natural son.

[2] Cf. the effects of the London earthquakes of 1750 (p. 11).

[3] So Wesley himself was apt to find; for example, at Holyhead in 1750: 'In the evening I was surprised to see, instead of some poor plain people, a room full of men daubed with gold and silver . . . several of them (I afterwards learned) being eminently wicked men. I delivered my soul, but they could in no wise bear it.'

charming voices, that sing hymns, in parts, to Scotch ballad tunes;
but indeed so long, that one would think they were already in
eternity, and knew how much time they had before them. The
chapel is very neat, with true Gothic windows (yet I am not converted). . . . Wesley is a lean elderly man, fresh-coloured, his hair
smoothly combed, but with a *soupçon* of curl at the ends. Wondrous
clean, but as evidently an actor as Garrick . . . towards the end he
exalted his voice, and acted very ugly enthusiasm.'

One is reminded of Chesterfield with his Methodist lady-friends;[1] or
of the Maréchale de Luxembourg's shocked comment on the Bible
—'Quel ton! Quel effroyable ton!'

Then, again, there are the military. War in those years still kept at
least a certain chivalry (everyone remembers 'Will you fire first?' at
Fontenoy)[2] that it has now long lost; except at times in the air. Thus
in 1758, when we took Cherbourg, to the poor of the town Prince
Edward gave a hundred guineas; the general and the admiral in command, twenty-five each. 'I love charity,' comments Walpole, 'but
sure this is excess of it, to lay out thousands, and venture so many
lives, for the opportunity of giving a Christmas-box to your
enemies!'

The prince also gave the ladies of Cherbourg a ball, 'and told
them he was too young to know what was good breeding in
France, and therefore he would behave as he should if meaning to
please in England—and kissed them all'.

A little later when the Duc d'Aiguillon took English prisoners
near St Malo, to spare their feelings he politely forbad bell-ringing
or rejoicings in the places they were marched through; a little earlier
he had sent back to the Duke of Marlborough, under flag of truce,
some silver tea-spoons the English commander left behind in a
hurry. And in 1759, when in Germany Prince Ferdinand of Brunswick was invested with the Garter, the French general, M. de Con-
tades, fired a salute of twenty-one guns in his honour from the
enemy camp.

Even the rank and file could be quixotic. In 1779 Walpole records

[1] See *The Search for Good Sense*, p. 136.
[2] The truth of that tradition has, however, been questioned (Fortescue, *History of
the British Army*, II, 115). In fact, the French seem to have fired first; in the story, they
politely refused to.

that, at the storm of San Fernando de Omoa, a sailor with two sabres, meeting a disarmed Spaniard, tossed his enemy one of them —'Now we are on equal terms.'

Not, it goes without saying, that all the military of the age were Bayards 'sans peur et sans reproche'. There is, for example, Clive loaded with the loot of India—'General Clive is arrived all over estates and diamonds. If a beggar asks charity, he says "Friend, I have no small brilliants about me." ' Or there is that General Braddock destined to fall at Fort Duquesne[1]—'a very Iroquois in disposition', who, when his sister had hanged herself after gambling away her fortune at Bath (1731), merely remarked: 'Poor Fanny! I always thought she would play till she would be forced to *tuck herself up!*'

Last, but not least, in Walpole's eighteenth-century gallery are the women's portraits; such as that spirited Miss Fanny Murray[2] who, being given a twenty-pound note by Sir Richard Atkins, replied, 'Damn your twenty pound, what does that signify!'— clapped it between two pieces of bread and butter, and eat it; or the lovely Gunnings, two Irish girls without fortune, one of whom became Duchess of Hamilton, then Duchess of Argyll; and the other, Lady Coventry.[3] The first was so beautiful that seven hundred people sat up all night at a Yorkshire inn to see her get into her chaise; the second, Lady Coventry, was lovelier still, but something

---

[1] See p. 225.

[2] Fanny Murray (1729-78), daughter of a Bath musician called Rudman, began as a Bath flower-girl; was linked with Marlborough's grandson Jack Spencer, Beau Nash, Lord Sandwich, James Maclean 'the gentleman highwayman', and others; and was the heroine of Wilkes's *Essay on Woman*. There were rumours that Sir R. Atkins might marry her; but he died in 1756. Arrested for debt, she was given £200 a year by Jack Spencer's son, and married off to the Scottish actor, David Ross; to whom she remained a faithful wife till her death over twenty years later.

[2] The Gunnings, Maria (1733-60) and Elizabeth (1734-90), were daughters of a needy Irish gentleman of County Roscommon, and so poor that they are said to have thought of going on the stage. In 1749 they came to England; by 1751 they were the rage of London; in 1752 Elizabeth married the Duke of Hamilton, Maria the Earl of Coventry. In 1759 Maria, having been mobbed by an admiring rabble in Hyde Park, was provided by the old King, to the amusement of the time, with an escort of two sergeants and twelve privates of the Guards. Next year she died of consumption, whether or not aided by the white lead of her cosmetics. Elizabeth (who seems the finer character of the two) was widowed in 1758, and married in 1759 the future Duke of Argyll. Johnsonians will recall how she was gracious to Johnson, snubbing to Boswell, at Inverary. (See H. Bleackley, *The Beautiful Duchess*.)

being sepulchrally solemn themselves, yet lack the least gift of grace; and so they are inclined to take harshness or laboriousness, being 'serious' things, for strength; while grace and gaiety are dismissed as superficial trifling. Caliban they can appreciate; not Ariel. Chaucer lacks 'high seriousness'.

In such eyes a man like Horace Walpole who, at forty-five, could stick sweet-peas in his hair and sing to a party of quadrille-playing dowagers at Lady Blandford's, must clearly have been a quite impossible and contemptible person.

With Walpole, as with Johnson and Boswell, the loudest lion in the path is, of course, Macaulay. For him, Johnson was damned as a Tory; Boswell and Walpole, as mere fribbles. The great historic scenes in Macaulay are full of life and colour; but his portraits are usually painted too exclusively in Indian ink and Chinese white. The result, though lively, is not life. But at least it is unambiguous; and so can provide a good starting-point.

With Walpole, Macaulay happily begins by comparing his works to *pâté-de-foie-gras*, a delicacy derived only from disease in the wretched goose that provides it.

'Whatever was little seemed to him great, and whatever was great seemed to him little. Serious business was a trifle to him, and trifles were his serious business. . . . After the labours of the print-shop and the auction-room, he unbent his mind in the House of Commons. And, having indulged in the recreation of making laws and voting millions, he returned to more important pursuits, to researches after Queen Mary's comb, Wolsey's red hat, the pipe which Van Tromp smoked during his last sea-fight, and the spur which King William struck into the flank of Sorrel. . . . While he was fetching and carrying the gossip of Kensington Palace and Carlton House, he fancied that he was engaged in politics, and when he recorded that gossip, he fancied that he was writing history. . . . About politics, in the high sense of the word, he knew nothing, and cared nothing.'

'No writer surely,' continues Macaulay, with one of the most sweeping generalizations of his Goliath-scythe, 'was ever guilty of so much false and absurd criticism. . . . There is indeed scarcely any writer in whose works it would be possible to find so many contradictory judgments, so many sentences of extravagant nonsense. . . . He sneered at everybody. . . . He never convinces reason, or fills the imagination, or touches the heart.'

of a goose; and, when the old George II asked if she were not sorry that Masquerades had been abolished for 1756, because of the Lisbon earthquake, she tactfully replied that there was only one sight left that she really wished to see—a coronation. But by twenty-seven the fair Lady Coventry was dead; poisoned, so whispered rumour, by the white lead she persisted in daubing on her complexion. This world, as Walpole so wisely repeated, is a comedy to those that think, a tragedy to those that feel.[1] He has left us, like Balzac, a *Comédie Humaine*; it is, in tone, a gayer comedy than Balzac's; but, in the background, tragedy is there.

But of course the main figure in this endless gallery remains Walpole himself. In so personal a form as the letter it is almost inevitable that the writer's personality should become more vital than in any other branch of literature except perhaps the lyric, the journal, and some types of essay.

His own countrymen have not, I think, been very kind, or very grateful, to Walpole. Perhaps Mérimée was right in thinking him more French than English. 'It is the fashion,' wrote Byron (who, when not romantically mad, could be remarkably sane) 'to underrate Horace Walpole; firstly, because he was a nobleman, and secondly because he was a gentleman.' But I am a little doubtful of Byron's explanation; if this belittlement of Walpole has long persisted, it is due, I think, rather to a certain owlishness commoner in English criticism than in French, a kind of hypocrisy of seriousness which condemns gaiety as frivolity, and finds it easier to be charitable to the sort of vicious maniac that Swift could sometimes become, because he was at least in deadly earnest. After all, this is perhaps not unnatural; many critics find not the least difficulty in

---

[1] 'His entirely meaningless epigram,' writes a recent critic, 'about the world's being a comedy to those that think, a tragedy to those that feel, would suggest that he had no idea what any of those terms meant'. I do not see why it should be 'meaningless', or why Walpole should be supposed ignorant of the meaning of 'tragedy' or 'comedy', 'think' or 'feel'. It is very much Hardy's view—'Laughter always means blindness.'

> Yea. Tragedy is true guise,
> Comedy lies.

The theatre laughs at Falstaff's methods of recruiting—'food for powder, food for powder; they'll fill a pit as well as better; tush, man, mortal men, mortal men'. Retold from the viewpoint of the poor devils who fattened the crows on Shrewsbury field, the episode would become less amusing. 'Comedy lies.'

being sepulchrally solemn themselves, yet lack the least gift of grace; and so they are inclined to take harshness or laboriousness, being 'serious' things, for strength; while grace and gaiety are dismissed as superficial trifling. Caliban they can appreciate; not Ariel. Chaucer lacks 'high seriousness'.

In such eyes a man like Horace Walpole who, at forty-five, could stick sweet-peas in his hair and sing to a party of quadrille-playing dowagers at Lady Blandford's, must clearly have been a quite impossible and contemptible person.

With Walpole, as with Johnson and Boswell, the loudest lion in the path is, of course, Macaulay. For him, Johnson was damned as a Tory; Boswell and Walpole, as mere fribbles. The great historic scenes in Macaulay are full of life and colour; but his portraits are usually painted too exclusively in Indian ink and Chinese white. The result, though lively, is not life. But at least it is unambiguous; and so can provide a good starting-point.

With Walpole, Macaulay happily begins by comparing his works to *pâté-de-foie-gras*, a delicacy derived only from disease in the wretched goose that provides it.

> 'Whatever was little seemed to him great, and whatever was great seemed to him little. Serious business was a trifle to him, and trifles were his serious business. . . . After the labours of the print-shop and the auction-room, he unbent his mind in the House of Commons. And, having indulged in the recreation of making laws and voting millions, he returned to more important pursuits, to researches after Queen Mary's comb, Wolsey's red hat, the pipe which Van Tromp smoked during his last sea-fight, and the spur which King William struck into the flank of Sorrel. . . . While he was fetching and carrying the gossip of Kensington Palace and Carlton House, he fancied that he was engaged in politics, and when he recorded that gossip, he fancied that he was writing history. . . . About politics, in the high sense of the word, he knew nothing, and cared nothing.'
>
> 'No writer surely,' continues Macaulay, with one of the most sweeping generalizations of his Goliath-scythe, 'was ever guilty of so much false and absurd criticism. . . . There is indeed scarcely any writer in whose works it would be possible to find so many contradictory judgments, so many sentences of extravagant nonsense. . . . He sneered at everybody. . . . He never convinces the reason, or fills the imagination, or touches the heart.'

of a goose; and, when the old George II asked if she were not sorry that Masquerades had been abolished for 1756, because of the Lisbon earthquake, she tactfully replied that there was only one sight left that she really wished to see—a coronation. But by twenty-seven the fair Lady Coventry was dead; poisoned, so whispered rumour, by the white lead she persisted in daubing on her complexion. This world, as Walpole so wisely repeated, is a comedy to those that think, a tragedy to those that feel.[1] He has left us, like Balzac, a *Comédie Humaine*; it is, in tone, a gayer comedy than Balzac's; but, in the background, tragedy is there.

But of course the main figure in this endless gallery remains Walpole himself. In so personal a form as the letter it is almost inevitable that the writer's personality should become more vital than in any other branch of literature except perhaps the lyric, the journal, and some types of essay.

His own countrymen have not, I think, been very kind, or very grateful, to Walpole. Perhaps Mérimée was right in thinking him more French than English. 'It is the fashion,' wrote Byron (who, when not romantically mad, could be remarkably sane) 'to underrate Horace Walpole; firstly, because he was a nobleman, and secondly because he was a gentleman.' But I am a little doubtful of Byron's explanation; if this belittlement of Walpole has long persisted, it is due, I think, rather to a certain owlishness commoner in English criticism than in French, a kind of hypocrisy of seriousness which condemns gaiety as frivolity, and finds it easier to be charitable to the sort of vicious maniac that Swift could sometimes become, because he was at least in deadly earnest. After all, this is perhaps not unnatural; many critics find not the least difficulty in

---

[1] 'His entirely meaningless epigram,' writes a recent critic, 'about the world's being a comedy to those that think, a tragedy to those that feel, would suggest that he had no idea what any of those terms meant'. I do not see why it should be 'meaningless', or why Walpole should be supposed ignorant of the meaning of 'tragedy' or 'comedy', 'think' or 'feel'. It is very much Hardy's view—'Laughter always means blindness.'

> Yea. Tragedy is true guise,
> Comedy lies.

The theatre laughs at Falstaff's methods of recruiting—'food for powder, food for powder; they'll fill a pit as well as better; tush, man, mortal men, mortal men'. Retold from the viewpoint of the poor devils who fattened the crows on Shrewsbury field, the episode would become less amusing. 'Comedy lies.'

And then follows a most curious comparison of Walpole's wit, as 'in its essential properties, of the same kind', with the metaphysical wit of Cowley or Donne. Metaphysical wit has hardly more resemblance, for me, to Walpole's than an octopus to a humming-bird.

Finally, after all this objurgation one next reads, with some astonishment, Macaulay's equally sweeping eulogy—'No man who has written so much is so seldom tiresome.'

Some of Macaulay's accusations seem worth considering in more detail. 'No writer, surely,' he has said, 'was ever guilty of so much false and absurd criticism.' That many of Walpole's literary judgements now seem bizarre, like Hume's and even Johnson's, is doubtless true (though one should always remember how many of our own judgements will seem equally bizarre a century hence). He was, no doubt, blind to many writers whom the world agrees to be excellent (although, less frank than Walpole, the world does not always in practice show vast avidity to read them). For him, Lucan was better than Virgil—'To speak fairly, I prefer great sense, to poetry with little sense'. Dante is 'a Methodist parson in Bedlam'. Chaucer's work he belittled, despite his passion for the 'Gothic', as 'a lump of mineral from which Dryden extracted all the gold, and converted (it) into beautiful medals'. Spenser is 'John Bunyan, in rhyme'. Thomas Warton is 'an old fool' for thinking Prior spoilt *The Nutbrown Maid* in *Henry and Emma*. As for Montaigne, 'what signifies what a man thought who never thought of anything but himself; and what signifies what a man did, who never did anything?' Foolish; but at least neatly put. Swift, again, was 'a wild beast who baited and worried all mankind almost, because his intolerable arrogance, vanity, pride, and ambition were disappointed' (not wholly untrue, I think; but far from the whole truth). Richardson's *Clarissa* and *Grandison* are 'deplorably tedious lamentations ... pictures of high life as conceived by a bookseller, and romances as they would be spiritualized by a Methodist teacher'. Goldsmith 'is a fool, the more wearing for having some sense'—'an idiot, with once or twice a fit of parts'. As for Sterne, 'the second and third volumes of *Tristram Shandy*, the dregs of nonsense, have universally met the contempt they deserve'. (But, as might be expected, Walpole had far more liking for the *Sentimental Journey*—'infinitely preferable to his tiresome *Tristram Shandy.*'[1]) Johnson, above all, doubly odious as a Tory and a denigrator of Gray, makes Walpole lose both temper and judgement—'mountebank'—'babbling old woman'—'saucy Caliban'—'the gigantic littleness of a country schoolmaster'.

One can see, I think, in these judgements, or misjudgements, a common factor—like Chesterfield, Walpole was one of those over-civilized minds that cannot endure any departure from the polished and the polite. Rousseau and the Romantics were soon to change all that, often plunging into the opposite extremes of the irrational and the barbarous. For the human mind is, unfortunately, like an ill-ballasted ship that rolls excessively from right to left, and back from left to right. No wonder humanity is often sea-sick.

Accordingly the writers that Walpole does appreciate are of the more sophisticated kind. There is, for example, Congreve—'we are so charmed with what everybody says, that we have no leisure to be interested in what anybody does'. There is Montesquieu, whose *Esprit des Lois* Walpole once pronounced, in Macaulayesque fashion, 'the best book ever written'. There is Voltaire.[2] 'Gray could not hear Voltaire's name with patience, though nobody admired his genius more; but he thought him so vile, that for the last years of his life he would read nothing he wrote. Well! but one must read him! Is there another author left in Europe who one wishes would write?' (9/9/1773.)

To Gibbon's *Decline and Fall* Walpole gave an instant welcome; though he annoyed the historian by finding (as he well might) the second and third volumes less entertaining than the first.[3]

Again he is shrewd on Fanny Burney and the falling off in her later work (*Camilla*)—'this author knew the world and penetrated characters before she had stepped over the threshold; and, now she

[1] Coleridge took precisely the opposite view: 'I think highly of Sterne—that is of the first part of *Tristram Shandy* . . . the *Sentimental Journey* is poor sickly stuff.'

[2] 'He could not deny,' says Macaulay, 'that Voltaire and Rousseau were clever men; but *he took every opportunity of depreciating them*.' As regards Voltaire, this seems an error so wild that Macaulay's schoolboy could have corrected it. (Cf. p. 108.) Walpole particularly admired Voltaire's *Universal History*—'a marvellous mass both of genius and sagacity'. (To Lady Ossory, 8/11/1789.)

[3] 'He coloured; all his round features squeezed themselves into sharp angles; he screwed up his button-mouth, and rapping his snuff-box, said, "It had never been put together before"—*so well* he meant to add—but gulped it.'

has seen so much of it, she has little or no insight at all.'

About Gray, of course, Walpole was enthusiastic. This might be thought merely the blind generosity of friendship. But Walpole's affection was by no means blind. He criticized a certain tendency in his friend to affect melancholy, when 'humour was his natural and original turn'. Nor could he (very characteristically) swallow Gray's Scandinavian themes[1]—'who can care through what horrors a Runic savage arrived at all the joys and glories they could conceive, the supreme felicity of boozing ale out of the skull of an enemy in Odin's hall?' Once more the castellan of Strawberry Hill shrinks back from too Gothic realities.

But this should not be exaggerated. Over-civilized, perhaps, Walpole was. But he was less narrow than Chesterfield; whose artificialities justly irritated him. He was himself a precursor of Romanticism (little as he might have liked some of its later productions). There is substance in his preface to the *Castle of Otranto* (which, after all, looks forward to Scott):

> 'It was an attempt to blend the two kinds of romance, the ancient and the modern. In the former all was imagination and improbability: in the latter, nature is always intended to be, and sometimes has been, copied with success. Invention has not been wanting; but the great resources of fancy have been dammed up, by a strict adherence to common life.'

In fine, Romanticism and Realism need each other—as in Shakespeare, they are stronger together than alone.[2] It was something to see that as early as 1764. To be as imaginative as Malory or *Sir Gawain and the Green Knight*, yet as natural as Defoe or Fielding—the idea was daring, even if the execution was miserable.[3]

[1] There *is* perhaps at times a touch of factitious over-compensation in the violent bloodiness of some valetudinarian writers—such as Stevenson, Henley, or D. H. Lawrence.

[2] In the Yale *Walpole* (vol. 29, Appendix 3) there is a passage by Walpole on the gravediggers' scene in *Hamlet*, and Garrick's blindness in cutting it, that seems to me admirable sense.

[3] Like *The Mysterious Mother*, *The Castle of Otranto* itself seems to me mainly remarkable as an instance of how badly, sometimes, clever minds can write when they attempt to create. Even Walpole's style, so admirable in his letters, here becomes at moments almost illiterate; and the story, with its casques big as courtyards, swords

Like his friend Gray, Walpole sensed the need for some revolution in literature. 'Je ne l'ai point écrit pour ce siècle-ci, qui ne veut que de la raison froide'; but though he felt the need, he had little hope of the Romantic harvest he was helping to sow. For about English literature he became extremely pessimistic. He expected little from contemporaries; from posterity, still less. 'For my part,' he wrote in 1774, 'I take Europe to be worn out. When Voltaire dies, we may say, "Good-night!" I don't believe this age will be more read than the Byzantine historians.'[1] A singularly bad guess. Still it was not really for Macaulay to cavil. For in 1850 Macaulay himself wrote:

> 'It is odd that the last twenty-five years, which have witnessed the greatest progress ever made in physical science—the greatest victories ever achieved by man over matter—should have produced hardly a volume that will be remembered in 1900.'

He was under no obligation to like contemporary literature himself; but it was surely rash to predict that in fifty years no one would like it.

If we recall that even the *two* years 1849–50 saw the publication of Arnold's first volume of poems, *Shirley*, *David Copperfield*, Macaulay's own *History*, Ruskin's *Seven Lamps*, *Sonnets from the Portuguese*, *The Scarlet Letter*, *Alton Locke*, *In Memoriam*, and *The Prelude*, it must be admitted that this type of doleful criticism is rash. It was hardly for Macaulay, who thus cried 'Famine!' in the midst of plenty, who compared Milton's fondness for Euripides to Titania's passion for Bottom, and who, if I remember, once des-

---

that take a hundred men to carry, cowled skeletons, sighing pictures, and bleeding statues, set in a scene that compounds Strawberry Hill with Trinity Great Court, recalls the chilling somnambulations of surrealism. The dreaming author remains (like the reader) half asleep; but only half asleep. Indeed it seems, rather, a daydream by a too sophisticated antiquarian, uneasily conscious, from the corner of his eye, of irreverent wags like George Selwyn. There is more, I feel, of the magic of real dreaming even in Macpherson; to say nothing of Chatterton or Blake, Coleridge, Scott, or Beddoes. That *The Castle of Otranto* should have passed through sixty editions appears to me a strange instance of public suggestibility.

[1] It does not much mend matters that in 1791-2 Walpole developed a fantastic admiration for Erasmus Darwin. Twelve lines of Darwin's describing creation 'are in my opinion the most sublime passage in any author'.

cribed Wordsworth as 'a humbug, a bore, and a rat', to condemn Walpole for 'false and absurd criticism'.[1]

To counterbalance Macaulay's extravagant unfairness to Walpole, it is worth contrasting the no less exaggerated eulogy written on him by Byron (1821)—

> 'to say nothing of the composition of his incomparable letters, and of *The Castle of Otranto*, he is the "Ultimus Romanorum", the author of *The Mysterious Mother*, a tragedy of the highest order, and not a puling love-play. He is the father of the first romance and of the last tragedy in our language, and surely worthy of a higher place than any living writer, be he who he may.' (Preface to *Marino Faliero*.)

One may not unjustly, I think, suspect Byron here of a desire not only to praise Walpole, but also to snub the living writers—particularly that 'puddle of water-worms', the Lake Poets—whom he disliked and despised.

But in any case it is only fair to Walpole to remember that he never set up for a professional critic. He had as much right to his tastes as we to ours. And it seems to me a little impertinent to damn any man for literary judgements expressed in private letters.

Secondly, there is Macaulay's tirade against Walpole's rather jackdaw antiquarianism. Now if a man likes to collect such oddities as Edward IV's hair, Wolsey's red hat, Anne Boleyn's clock, Mrs Hampden's wedding-gloves, the Duke of Monmouth's white teapot, or Van Tromp's pipecase, it all seems harmless enough. One may smile at the concourse of over 50,000 persons drawn, largely by such curiosities, to the Strawberry Hill sale of 1842; or at the gibes of *The Times* on that occasion about 'a pip and part of the stalk of the apple which Eve plucked from the tree of Knowledge'. One may be reminded of Steele's Don Saltero proudly exhibiting a straw-bonnet from Bedford as 'Pontius Pilate's wife's chambermaid's sister's hat'. But plenty of purchasers would rush to buy

---

[1] In justice to Macaulay, it should be recalled that he later became quite excessively modest about his own criticism (for his remarks on literature seem to me often interesting). 'I have never written,' he said in a letter to Napier, 'a page of criticism on poetry, or the fine arts, which I would not burn if I had the power.'

Walpole's curios to-morrow; plenty of antiquarians busy themselves with things far duller.

Nor was Walpole merely an accumulator of kickshaws. His collection of engraved English heads was the largest any individual had yet made, and in 1842 took ten days to sell. Nor was it exactly dilettante indolence that could persistently take notes of eighty country-houses visited between 1751 and 1784. Again, his reputation has now risen as a historian of painting.

> 'Of the earlier English portraiture,' says Dr W. S. Lewis, 'he was and still is the chief historian. He had the immense advantage of owning Vertue's MSS and modern scholars have only admiration for his use of them. He was an expert editor and he had an "eye" and a memory which, even if he had not been able to buy Vertue's MSS, would have made him a remarkable critic. . . . Walpole's claim to be the English Vasari is as sure, I believe, as his claim to the primacy of English letter-writers.'[1]

This is impressive evidence. *Anecdotes of Painting* does not, I own, strike me as a very impressive work; yet it must have proved a very toilsome one to extract from thirty-nine MSS of Vertue's jumbled and illegible jottings. And far into old age Walpole's gnarled and gouty fingers went on painfully writing their own tireless annotations on endless other matters.

However, it is as a letter-writer that Walpole matters to most of us. And the charm of his letters can be seriously impaired by imperfect sympathy with his character. I cannot fully enjoy him if I am to picture him as a sort of toad with butterfly's wings. Hence the far graver importance of Macaulay's other, more personal indictments—that Walpole knew nothing and cared nothing about politics; that he trifled with everything serious and was serious only about trifles; that he 'sneered at everybody' and never 'touches the heart'.

Indifference to public affairs and world issues seems to me a

[1] For details, see L. Cust and A. M. Hind in vol. III (1913-14) of the Walpole Society; also W. S. Lewis, *Horace Walpole, Antiquary*, in *Essays presented to Sir Lewis Namier* (1956), and *Horace Walpole's Library* (1958). Anyone who imagines Walpole a mere butterfly should look at Vertue's MSS as published (with some facsimiles) by the Walpole Society; the drudgery of making them into a book would reduce anyone lacking in true antiquarian zeal to howl aloud for sheer boredom.

strange charge to bring against one who devotes more space to such matters than any other great letter-writer in English. Far from being indifferent, Walpole was passionately loyal to his father's policy and memory. He may have been as a rule, like Gibbon, a dumb member of parliament. But he could become an ardent pamphleteer and intriguer behind the scenes. Indeed he was so much the reverse of inert or nonchalant, that he could be accused at times by contemporaries of 'political frenzy' and 'ardour for factious intrigues'. His general creed was strongly Whiggish (as was natural enough in his father's son). And he well described himself as 'a quiet republican, who does not dislike to see the shadow of monarchy, like Banquo's ghost, fill the empty chair of state, that the ambitious, the murderer, the tyrant, may not aspire to it; in short, who approves the name of a King, when it excludes the essence.' If that is folly, it is precisely the folly which the British constitution has since pursued; and if only other nations had shared it, the world might have been a far happier place for the last two centuries.

In 1757, after the loss of Minorca, Admiral Byng was sentenced to death for negligence. Walpole did not know Byng, and disliked him at sight; but he bestirred himself with considerable energy to obtain a fortnight's delay; and was deeply distressed to find that he had gained for the victim only a fortnight more of suspense.

In 1763–4 came the Wilkes agitation and the question of the legality of general warrants, as used by Grenville's government against him. Walpole persuaded his cousin Conway to oppose them; was furious when the King and Grenville retaliated by depriving Conway of his regiment; and did not rest from violent political activity till the Rockingham ministry came into power, with Conway as a Secretary of State and Leader of the Commons. Then indeed, though he would have refused office, Walpole hoped some important post would at least be offered him; but Conway failed to stir a finger; and deeply hurt, though silent, Walpole betook himself to Paris (1765). On his return in 1766 he was again for a time Conway's adviser, and a kind of power behind the scenes; but in 1768 with Conway's resignation and his own withdrawal, after twenty-seven years, from Parliament, Walpole's active politics were over.

But not his political interest. When, later, he felt that Lord Hertford was inert about securing Conway's seat, 'on the stairs I trembled so with passion that I had like to have fallen from the top to the bottom'—curious behaviour for a man who, according to Macaulay, took nothing seriously except frivolity, and neither knew nor cared about real politics or real people.

Nor was Walpole one of those 'patriots' who have thought liberty was not for export, but began and ended at home; quite indifferent, provided Britons were not slaves, how much they might enslave others. For the Slave Trade he shared Johnson's passionate detestation.

> 'We have been sitting this fortnight,' he writes to Mann in 1750, 'on the African Company: *we*, the British Senate, that temple of liberty, and bulwark of Protestant Christianity, have this fortnight been pondering methods to make more effectual that horrid traffic of selling negroes. It has appeared to us that six-and-forty thousand of these wretches are sold every year to our plantations alone!—it chills one's blood. I would not have voted in it for the continent of America! . . . We reproach Spain, and yet do not even pretend the nonsense of butchering these poor creatures for the good of their souls!'

Again, in 1773 the House has been discussing an expedition sent to subdue, or deport, the Caribs of St Vincent.

> 'Caribs, black Caribs, have no representatives in Parliament; they have no agent but God, and he is seldom called to the bar of the House to defend their cause; 206 to 88 gave them up to the mercy of their persecutors. . . . Alas! dare I complain of gout and rheumatism, when so much a bitterer cup is brewed for men as good as myself in every quarter of the globe!'

Where Caribs were concerned, Richard, and even Edmund, Burke seem to have taken things much more calmly.[1]

When the American Revolution came, it found Walpole as clear and vehement in his view of it as Burke himself—'I most heartily wish success to the Americans. . . . If England prevails, English and American liberty is at an end.'

[1]See p. 136.

After revolution in America, revolution in France; but, again like Burke, Walpole felt towards this second upheaval a horror as violent as his sympathy for the first. And understandably. Whatever the follies and cruelties that attended it, as they must attend any war, the American rising was typically eighteenth-century in its rationalism and its belief in common sense; and so was the United States constitution that emerged. But Franklin, Jefferson, or Washington were very different types from Danton, Robespierre, or Marat. As Gouverneur Morris pointed out at the time, the French wanted the liberties of the American state without possessing the solidity of the American character. And so the French Revolution plunged into rhapsodies, frenzies, and fanaticisms of a far more Romantic type. And extreme Romanticism seems to me to work a great deal better in literature than in life.

'Two thirds of France,' writes Walpole in 1790, 'who are not so humble as I, seem to think they can entirely new-model the world with metaphysical compasses; and hold that no injustice, no barbarity, need to be counted in making the experiment.' We, too, have come to know those 'metaphysical compasses'; and our century will bear the scars of them to its end. Another comment of Walpole's from the close of that same year remains no less true to-day, of 'democracy' east of the Elbe—'Imprisonment is the characteristic of liberty, and when all men are equal, accidents are punished as only crimes used to be.' The Paris massacres of August 10, 1792, wrung from him a cry that is, again, only too recognizable for our own generation—'I did not apprehend that you could educate and polish men, till you made them ten times worse than the rudest ignorance could produce. I have been shocked at scalping Indians— but I never despised savages, because they are only cruel to *enemies*, and have had no instruction.' Walpole, according to his lights, valued liberty; but he was not, like poor Mme Roland, one of those who do not realize till they are themselves on the scaffold, what crimes and follies can be committed in its name.[1]

Macaulay's further charge that Walpole was emotionally callous seems to me no better grounded than the charge that he was in-

[1] In 1793 she is said to have cried to the giant statue of Liberty in the Place de la Révolution, as she faced the guillotine: 'O Liberté! que de crimes on commet en ton nom!' or, in another version, 'Liberté! comme on t'a jouée!'

tellectually frivolous and indifferent. Indeed one could make as good a case for calling him over-emotional and sentimental. William Cole did think him over-sensitive. And of himself Walpole wrote: 'Indiscreet and abandoned to his passions, it seemed as if he despised or could bear no constraint; yet this want of government of himself was the more blameable, as nobody had greater command of resolution whenever he made a point of it.' He could never forgive the opponents of his father or of his cousin. He could not bring himself to dismiss, after twenty-five years of incompetence, a gardener of his —though 'incredibly ignorant, and a mule', and belonging to 'that odious nation', the Scots.

> 'I have offered him fifteen pounds a year to leave me, and when he pleads that he is old, and that nobody else will take him, I plead that I am old too, and that it is rather hard that I am not to have a few flowers, or a little fruit as long as I live. . . . I will take the liberty of letting you know, if I can persuade the serpent that has reduced my little Eden to be as nasty and barren as the Highlands, to take a pension and a yellow ribbon.'

Or again, when he is fifty-eight, his dog falls ill—'My poor Rosette is dying . . . I have been out of bed twenty times every night, have had no sleep, and sat up with her till three this morning; but I am only making you laugh at me; I cannot help it—I think of nothing else.' When Mme du Deffand died, he took over her yapping and snapping Tonton, because he doubted if anyone else would be kind to the little beast; and after its death, nine years later, in the fullness of its obesity—'I shall miss him greatly,' writes Walpole, 'and must not have another dog; I am too old, and should only breed it up to be unhappy when I am gone.' Not all dog-lovers think of *that*.

Of an edition of Walton's *Angler* he wrote to Dalrymple (28/6/1760):

> 'It is published by Mr Hawkins,[1] a very worthy gentleman in my neighbourhood—but who I could wish did not think angling so very *innocent* an amusement. We cannot live without destroying animals —but shall we torture them for our sport, sport in their destruction?

[1] Dr Johnson's unclubbable Sir John.

I met a rough officer at his house t'other day, who said he knew such
a person was turning Methodist, for in the middle of a conversation
he rose, and opened the window to let out a moth—I told him I did
not know that the Methodists had any principle so good, and that I,
who am certainly not on the point of becoming one, always did so
too.'

When he read in the newspaper of condemned criminals, he was
(some may think) so sentimental as to put his finger over the date
fixed for their execution, so as not to be oppressed by the thought
of it. He was, as we have seen, sufficiently ahead of his time to feel
(like Johnson, though less intemperately) that negro slavery remained an ugly blot on the American cause—'I should think the
souls of the Africans would sit heavy on the swords of the Americans.' He was even more ahead of his time in his detestation for the
futility of most wars.

'If all this did but starve us,' he comments in 1761 on Pitt's advocacy
of hostilities with Spain, 'I should not much mind it: I should look as
well as other people in haughty rags, and while one's dunghill is the
first dunghill in Europe, one is content. But the lives! the lives it will
cost! to wade through blood to dignity! I had rather be a worm than
a vulture.'

And again in the following year, 1762—

'You may imagine I am anxious to have the Peace . . . in one word, I
have no public spirit, and don't care a farthing for the interests of the
merchants. Soldiers and sailors who are knocked on the head, and
peasants plundered or butchered, are to my eyes as valuable as a lazy
luxurious set of men, who hire others to acquire riches for them; who
would embroil all the earth, that they may heap or squander.'

In 1770 he grows prophetic: 'By the next century, I suppose, we
shall fight for the Dog-star and the Great Bear.' 'They talk,' he
comments on the petitions to Parliament in 1780, 'of the waste of
money; are silent on the thousands of lives that have been sacrificed
—but when are human lives counted by any side?'
I must own that I do not find such things very easy to reconcile
with Macaulay; or with Wordsworth's animus against 'that cold
and false-hearted, Frenchified coxcomb, Horace Walpole'; or with

Leslie Stephen's 'we cannot regard him with much respect, and still less with much affection'.

And of course there have been judges still more severe. Lord Liverpool wrote to J. W. Croker (23/8/1824): 'I believe Horace Walpole to have been as bad a man as ever lived.' Croker replied to Lord Liverpool (13/10/1824): 'I entirely agree with your lordship's opinion of Horace Walpole—there never lived a more selfish man; a more factious politician; a more calumnious writer.' It seems a little harsh that Lord Liverpool should deny even Nero and Judas Iscariot their usual pre-eminence in iniquity. As for Croker (by poetic justice, though not altogether justly) he is now remembered only for his scourgings of Keats and Tennyson.

Those who knew Walpole better were apt to take strangely different views from these. 'Ce n'est point flatterie,' writes the critical Mme du Deffand, whose brain, at all events, was far from blind, 'c'est que l'esprit, les talents, et l'extrême bonté ne se sont pas jamais trouvés réunis qu'en vous.' And again—'vous êtes sincère et bon, vous êtes variable, mais constant, vous êtes dur, mais sensible, oui, sensible, et très sensible, quoi que vous puissiez dire; vous êtes noble, fier, généreux, humain; eh bien! n'est-ce pas assez pour que vous puissiez être impunément fantasque, bizarre, et quelquefois un peu fol?' That, I should have thought a very shrewd portrait. No man, they say, is a hero to his valet. Yet Walpole's valet in Paris appears to have found him more attractive than many heroes. 'Le laquais qui vous suivait ici,' writes Mme du Deffand, 'qu'on appelait La Jeunesse, vient sans cesse demander à mes gens si l'on n'a pas de nouvelles de votre retour; il quittera tout, dit-il, pour entrer à vous.' Or there is Conway's letter to his brother—'Horace Walpole has on this occasion shown that warmth of friendship, that you know him capable of, so strongly that I want words to express my sense of it.' Conway seems to have been an upright, but somewhat icy person. He is all the better witness.

The 'occasion' was this. In April 1764 Conway had been deprived of his regiment, and his office as Groom of the Bedchamber, for opposing general warrants; Walpole at once wrote to him: 'I have six thousand pounds in the funds; accept all, or what part you want. Do not imagine I will be put off with a refusal.'[1] Nor was it

---

[1] Conway did in fact refuse.

the first time. Twenty years before, in 1744, Conway, then a needy young officer, had been in love with Lady Caroline Fitzroy. Walpole deplored the match, for Lady Caroline had a loose reputation; none the less, to make the marriage possible, he offered to share his own income with his cousin. In the end, however, Conway married Lady Ailesbury, and lived happily ever after. Now I must admit certain doubts whether Walpole's high-minded censors ever did, or would have done, anything so generous.

Then there is the whole strange story of Walpole's relations with Mme du Deffand. Here again I cannot breathe at the moral altitudes attained by some of the saints of criticism.

Mme du Deffand was one of the most intelligent women of an intelligent age, and one of the most disillusioned daughters of that century of sense. (Sainte-Beuve[1] called her 'avec Voltaire, dans la prose, le classique le plus pur de cette époque, sans même en excepter aucun des grands écrivains'.) Born in 1697, married at twenty-one to a husband who bored her to extinction, she passed through one love-affair after another (though there seems to have been little love about them)—including a liaison of a fortnight with the Regent Orleans, and one lasting many years with the Président Hénault. At her first meeting with Walpole in 1765, he was forty-eight and she twenty years older with already twelve years of blindness behind her. Yet her vitality, her courage, were still inexhaustible; returning from supper in the country at one in the morning, she would set off to drive round Paris, because it was too early to go to bed.[2] But her nightmare, her evil spirit, her bottomless pit was—ennui. In her hard sense, and in her senses, she had always been cold—to use her own words, 'ni tempérament ni roman'; like Mme de Charrière (Boswell's Zélide), she had long vivisected every human feeling, every happiness, till it died. But now, with Walpole, the

---

[1] To see her importance it is enough to glance at the index to his *Causeries de Lundi*; where she is linked with Voltaire, Montesquieu, Necker, Mlle de Staal, and many more.

[2] In 1766 Walpole wrote a verse portrait of her which seems to me not only sincere in its admiration, but in parts really moving; particularly in the lines—

> Where does Patience, tell who know,
> Bear irremediable woe;
> And, though of life's best joy bereft,
> Smile on the little portion left?

repressed affection, the stifled passion, of three-score years suddenly burst out. He was like nothing she had ever known. And she showed how strongly a dry log at last can blaze.

Walpole was moved, but acutely embarrassed. He dreaded ridicule almost as desperately as she dreaded boredom. And to be gossiped of as the Corydon of a blind beldame nearly seventy would have been very ludicrous indeed. In particular, he feared that the *cabinet noir* of Louis XV might open their correspondence—and this was no mere alarmism, for in fact copies of fourteen of his letters to Mme du Deffand, or of parts of them, have been found in the French archives.

Accordingly, whenever Mme du Deffand became too effusive, he would check and scold her without mercy. For instance—'Suis-je fait pour être l'héros d'un roman épistolaire? Parlez-moi en femme raisonnable, ou je copierai les réponses aux *Lettres Portugaises*.' For this, critics in their turn have scolded him. But here, too, they seem to me a little impertinent. Mme du Deffand might complain bitterly; she might reproach him bitterly; but she was not alienated—death alone could dissolve this strange devotion. It is sometimes wiser, as well as more charitable, to consider what people do rather than what they say. To this old woman in Paris Walpole wrote weekly for fifteen years. When in 1770 she was threatened with the loss of 3,000 livres of pension, he begged to be allowed to pay her yearly that amount from his own purse—'laissez-moi goûter la joie la plus pure, de vous avoir mise à votre aise, et que cette joie soit un secret profond entre nous deux'. For her sake he revisited Paris in 1767, 1769,[1] 1771, and 1775; in 1780 she died, and he never went abroad again. He was ageing, delicate, tormented with gout;[2] and a journey to Paris then was much more laborious and fatiguing than a trip to Australia to-day. If this sort of conduct indicates a character selfish and callous, it seems a pity that there are not more of them. And one is again driven to wonder whether the high-souled censors who carp at Walpole have ever themselves taken half as much devoted trouble

---

[1] 'It costs me many a pang, when I reflect that I shall probably never have resolution enough to take another journey to see this best and sincerest of friends, who loves me as much as my mother did! but it is idle to look forward—what is next year?—a bubble that may burst for her or me . . . .' (To George Montagu, 7/9/1769.)

[2] In 1792, despite his abstemiousness, he looks back on 'almost half a century of gout'.

for anybody.[1] Indeed, it is not very noticeable that critics in general make it their object in life to render other writers happy.

Further, in Walpole's recurrent anxiety and distress over a relationship where he also showed such kindness and devotion, there may have been, besides the rational dislike of ridicule, an irrational, neurotic element. I have already suggested that this somewhat feminine author, who was somehow driven to dramatize a theme so unattractive to normal minds as *The Mysterious Mother*, shows what may be signs of mother-fixation. Now Mme du Deffand was just old enough to be his mother; her attachment was both maternal and passionate; one can imagine the neurotic turmoil and conflict such a situation might possibly arouse in one with Walpole's temperament, without his being able to understand himself. Even his habit of calling this old Marquise 'ma petite' could be seen as an unconscious attempt to reverse, and so neutralize, this disquieting relationship. One can only guess at this distance of time. But I suspect some irrational factor of the kind. One of the great values of modern psychology, whatever its errors in detail, should surely be to help towards more understanding, more sympathy, more tolerance, than were possible for our forefathers. A pity that so few literary biographers, even now, seem to learn that lesson.

Moreover, one need not have read Stefan Zweig's *Beware of Pity* to realize how dangerous it can prove in life to encourage, out of compassion, feelings that one cannot lastingly satisfy. Kindness to-day may have consequences that, to-morrow, turn out all too cruel. Indeed Walpole gives at times the impression of having come, from bitter experience, to dread strong feelings in general.

> 'Consider,' he wrote (6/3/1766) to John Craufurd, 'how little time you have known me, and what small opportunities you have had of knowing my faults. I know them thoroughly; but to keep your friendship within bounds, consider my heart is not like yours, young, good, warm, sincere, and impatient to bestow itself. Mine is

[1] In view of this I find unfair Virginia Woolf's sentence (*Death of the Moth*, p. 51) 'He seemed sometimes as heartless as a monkey; drove Chatterton, so people said, to suicide, and allowed Madame du Deffand to die alone in despair.' Tattle so absurd as this 'so people said' surely deserved clearer contradiction. Like Macaulay, Virginia Woolf was a vivid portraitist; but in both writers the love of violent contrasts and incongruities led at times to over-colouring. Their work, at times, can be the cream of literature; but often they whip it too much. (For Chatterton, see p. 86.)

worn with the baseness, treachery, and mercenariness I have met with. It is suspicious, doubtful, and cooled. I consider everything round me but in the light of amusement, because if I looked at it seriously, I should detest it. I laugh that I may not weep. . . . I converse with Mesdames de Mirepoix, Boufflers, and Luxembourg, that I may not love Madame du Deffand too much—and yet they do but make me love her the more. But don't love me, pray don't love me. Old folks are but old women, who love their last lover as much as they did their first. I should still be liable to believe you, and I am not at all of Madame du Deffand's opinion, that one might as well be dead as not love somebody. I think one had better be dead than love anybody.'

I find this sort of utterance hard to reconcile with Macaulay's portrait of a man whose 'works are destitute of every charm which is derived from elevation, or from tenderness of sentiment'. On the contrary, the passage seems to me movingly sincere. True, it is wildly inconsistent. But that makes it seem only the more sincere. It is our reason that bothers over consistency; much our real feelings care about it!

One supreme inconsistency, however, was to overtake Walpole in his own old age. Then he in his turn was to dote on the young Miss Berrys, especially on Mary Berry, just as Mme du Deffand had doted upon him. It brought pain and anxiety to his last years; but it brought also a great deal of happiness. And Mary Berry not only responded to the old man's affection; she cherished his memory till she died, an old lady in her turn, in 1852. To her, it appears, Macaulay actually admitted, later on, that he had been unjust to Walpole; but he never retracted in print.

In reality Walpole was, I think, a far less shallow and more complex character than has been commonly supposed—and a far more interesting character than most of his critics. Men can display frivolity either because their heads are merely empty, or because their eyes are too keen, and their hearts too full. They may laugh because they are gay; or because, underneath, they are far from gay—and realize that if they waited for gaiety before indulging in laughter, they might wait for ever without laughing at all—just as Nietzsche wrote, 'Laugh, my young friends, if you are at all determined to remain pessimists' (meaning, I take it, that without that indomitable gaiety one may let oneself lapse into comforting delusions).

Now, beneath all his gaiety, Walpole's view of life was very far from gay. Mme du Deffand can be gloomy enough—'Ah! je le répète sans cesse, il n'y a qu'un malheur, celui d'être né. Quelle cruauté de se marier, de tirer des individus du néant! Tout ce qui existe est malheureux, un ange, une huître, peut-être un grain de sable; le néant, le néant, voilà ce qui vaut le mieux.' And yet Walpole more than once rebukes this pessimistic old lady for foolish optimism.

> 'Vous renoncez, dites-vous, au projet d'être heureuse. Ma petite! ma petite! comment un tel projet a-t-il pu rester si longtemps? ... Toute expérience mondaine prouve qu'on ne peut arriver qu'à la tranquillité, à moins d'être fol. La félicité est une chimère, et qui, existant, se détruirait elle-même, parce qu'on serait au désespoir de la certitude qu'elle finît.'

In 1761, he had to go down to his paternal home at Houghton, now falling into ruin by the neglect of his mad nephew. His letter on that occasion is a curious utterance for a man supposed incapable of taking anything seriously.

> 'Here I am, probably for the last time of my life, though not for the last time[1]—every clock that strikes tells me I am an hour nearer to yonder church—that church, into which I have not yet had courage to enter, where lies that mother on whom I doted, and who doted on me! There are the two rival mistresses of Houghton,[2] neither of whom ever wished to enjoy it! There too lies he who founded its greatness, to contribute to whose fall Europe was embroiled—there he sleeps in quiet and dignity, while his friend and his foe, rather his false ally and real enemy, Newcastle and Bath, are exhausting the dregs of their pitiful lives in squabbles and pamphlets! ... For what has he built Houghton? for his grandson to annihilate, or for his son to mourn over!'

This is Walpole's prose counterpart of his friend Gray's *Elegy in a Country Churchyard*; and, for me, it contains an intenser and more

---

[1] He would be buried there.

[2] The first Lady Walpole, Horace's mother; and the second Lady Walpole, Sir Robert's mistress, Maria Skerrett, who died in childbirth three months after her marriage.

tragic poetry than most eighteenth-century verse. Is this what Thackeray called 'Horace's dandified treble'? Is this the man who seemed to Macaulay incapable of seriousness? So Chaucer seemed to Arnold; who would, indeed, have hated to be compared to Macaulay—but here he deserves it. How dangerous it can sometimes be to laugh among the English (and the Scots)!—they are liable to nail one's cap-and-bells to one's head.

And yet one of Macaulay's own most sombre poems is so close an echo of another passage in Walpole's prose that one half suspects direct influence, conscious or unconscious.[1] 'My dear Sir,' writes Walpole at sixty-seven, 'life is like a chessboard,—the white spaces and the black are close together; it does not signify of which hue the last square is; the border closes all!' And here is Macaulay's echo, from his *Sermon in a Churchyard* (1825):

> The plots and feats of those that press
>   To seize on titles, wealth, or power,
> Shall seem to thee a game of chess
>   Devised to pass a tedious hour.
> What matters it to him who fights
>   For shows of unsubstantial good,
> Whether his Kings, and Queens, and Knights
>   Be things of flesh, or things of wood?
>
> We check and take; exult and fret;
>   Our plans extend, our passions rise,
> Till in our ardour we forget
>   How worthless is the victor's prize.
> Soon fades the spell, soon comes the night:
>   Say, will it not be then the same,
> Whether we played the black or white,
>   Whether we won or lost the game?

I by no means share the scorn of some for the verse of Macaulay. This, to me, rings sincerely. But if life is so, what remedy? Men may seek it in worldly ambition; or in hopes beyond this world.

[1] Similarly it looks as if Macaulay's famous New Zealander sketching the ruins of St Paul's from a broken arch of London Bridge might have been suggested by Walpole's words to Mann: 'At last, some curious traveller from Lima will visit England and give a description of the ruins of St Paul's, like the editions of Balbec and Palmyra.' (24/11/1774.)

Some for the Glories of This World; and some
Sigh for the Prophet's Paradise to come.[1]

But Walpole had seen the hollowness of ambition; and he shared
the fine resolve of many eighteenth-century minds not to believe
simply what one wishes to believe. For they felt (rightly, I think)
that factitious consolations are often like alcohol in a snowstorm—
fortifying at first with a new sense of warmth, because it brings the
blood to the surface; but liable to bring only a worse chill in the end.
Indeed one of Walpole's most memorable rebukes to Mme du Deffand is for allowing herself, for a moment, to sacrifice honest commonsense to wishful dreaming—

'Rendez-vous à la raison, prends le monde comme il est, n'attendez-
pas à le refaire à votre gré, et ne ressemblez pas à ce prince dans les
Contes persans qui courait le monde pour trouver une princesse qui
ressemblât à un certain portrait qu'il avait vu au trésor de son père, et
qui se trouva avoir été la maîtresse de Salomon.'

One should study, in fact, what Hardy called 'the sad science of
renunciation'.

Walpole himself had few illusions. He was, no doubt, a deist.
'Tyrants are proof of an hereafter. Millions of men cannot be formed
for the sport of a cruel child.' And he detested the French *philosophes*
for playing, as he judged, with mental and moral dynamite. But I
see no sign that religious comforts ever really comforted him at all.[2]

About this world he was still more disillusioned. He shared none
of the facile and premature faith in human progress and perfectibility that were to land France in the Terror, and Europe in the
Revolutionary Wars. In 1783 the world was on tiptoe at the Mont-
golfiers' invention of balloons. 'Ah,' cried an old French lady, 'next
they will find how to live for ever—and *we* shall be dead.' But Walpole's comment (like that of Johnson in *Rasselas*) was sounder and
more sombre.

---

[1] Why is that strange, oriental, un-English *Ruba'iyat* of FitzGerald's one of the
most popular poems in England? Because, I suspect, though so alien to English
thought and belief, in their hearts, without admitting it, even the English feel much
of it fundamentally true.

[2] Pinkerton quotes him as saying: 'Fontenelle's Dialogues on the Plurality of
Worlds first rendered me an infidel' (*i.e.* deist).

'Now that the dream is so near to an end, I have no occasion for lesser pageants—much less for divining with what airy vehicles the atmosphere will be peopled hereafter, or how much more expeditiously the east, west, or south will be ravaged and butchered, than they have been by the old-fashioned clumsy method of navigation. ... I observe that no improvements of science or knowledge make the world a jot wiser.'[1]

After two more centuries of science it is only too easy for us to agree; but it was far less obvious then. Humanity's worst enemy is, is fact—humanity. That lesson Walpole had early heard from the lips of his father; more than thirty years after Sir Robert's death, his son recalls his saying that 'very few men ought to be Prime Ministers: for it is not fit many should know how bad men are'.

More fatal even than human badness is perhaps human blindness. 'It is idle to cure the world of any folly, unless one could cure it of being foolish.' That seems to me a desolating, but vital truth. At the end of his long career Clemenceau's verdict was, in essence, the same:

'Il ne faut pas taper sur la République et la démocratie parce que vous voyez qu'elles sont incarnées par quelques fumistes.[2] . . . La chose ennuyeuse dans tout cela, et irrémédiable, ce n'est pas qu'on soit en République ou en Monarchie, qu'il y ait à la tête de l'Etat Doumergue, Deschanel ou Charles IX, c'est que tout ça ce soient des hommes, rien que des hommes.'

But that, of course, the planners of New Jerusalems, golden or iron, always refuse to see. One may hope for things to grow better. But it seems naïve to dream of their growing anything like perfect.

And so with life's lesser dreams. What is fame? 'If one means to make a lasting bustle, one should contrive to be the hero of a village; I have known a country rake talked of for a riot, whole years after the battle of Blenheim has grown obsolete.' 'One likes to see men

[1] Contrast Victor Hugo on the balloon:
> Où va-t-il, ce navire? Il va, de jour vêtu,
> A l'avenir divin et pur, à la vertu,
> A la science qu'on voit luire,
> A la mort des fléaux, à l'oubli généreux,
> A l'abondance, au calme, au rire, à l'homme heureux.

Great writers can be singularly naïve.
[2] Humbugs.

that posterity will wish to have seen: bate that curiosity and they are commonly not just the men one would wish to see much of.'[1]

What, again, is fashion? 'Is not it a persuasion that nothing was ever right till the present moment, and that the present moment will immediately be as wrong as all its predecessors?' So much for fools who pique themselves on being 'in the movement'.

What is erudition? Often it is no more than the superstition of the learned, the folly of the wise. 'I have often thought that young men ought not to be made scholars, lest they should grow to reverence learned blockheads, and think there is any merit in having read more foolish books than other folks.' And again—'Gray says (very justly) that learning never should be encouraged, it only draws out fools from their obscurity.'

What, then, remains in so bleak a world that is worth doing or pursuing? First of all, Walpole answers, good humour and gaiety; not the rage of Swift, dying, in his own words, like a poisoned rat in a hole. 'I find all men are like all men; and how can one be angry with everybody?' 'I have never yet seen or heard anything serious that was not ridiculous. . . . Rabelais brightens up to me as I see more of the world; he treated it as it deserved, laughed at it all, and (as I judge from myself) ceased to hate it.' 'My greatest ambition is not to grow cross.' In short, *vive la bagatelle!*

Secondly, since life is intolerable without some form of intoxication, let it be of a mild kind that does not besot or degrade. Illusions are degraded, ridiculous, dangerous; better than illusions are distractions. They need not dupe one. There are friendship and affection—Walpole might doubt them, suspect them, fear them; but he never became a misanthrope; and at eighty he was perhaps even fonder of Mary Berry than of anyone in his earlier life.

Then again there is the spectacle of the present world and the fascination of the past.

> 'Visions, you know, have always been my pasture; and so far from
> growing old enough to quarrel with their emptiness, I almost think
> there is no wisdom comparable to that of exchanging what is called
> the realities of life for dreams. Old castles, old pictures, old histories,

---

[1] Cf. T. E. Lawrence (in a letter): 'Too much glory or none? Why, I think the nones, who eat and drink and chase their appetites, are wholesomer. And I like camels and cats, therefore.'

and the babble of old people, make one live back into centuries, that cannot disappoint one. One holds fast and surely what is past. The dead have exhausted their power of deceiving—one can trust Catherine of Medicis now.'

That sad irony might almost have come from the pen of Hardy, or of Proust.

And so one catalogues noble authors, one whitewashes Richard III, one collects anecdotes of painting, one revives the Gothic age at Strawberry; well knowing that these things are also vanity. Yet they emancipate one a moment from the tyranny of Time.

Strawberry Hill, with its 'pie-crust' battlements, might be a bauble, a plaything. But there were moments when he well knew that himself.

Where then, for Walpole, lay the secret of such success as he did achieve? Above all, I think, in being what almost everyone finds it so hard to be—himself. Writers, indeed, often find it particularly difficult; so do public speakers on platforms. All publicity brings its temptation to poses, to pretensions, to pretence. And for eighteenth-century writers that temptation was specially strong; for it was the most social of centuries. One may recall Stendhal's description of social converse in France—'le commerce armé de deux vanités'. The more conscious one is of one's self, the harder it becomes to be it.

Here Chesterfield often suffers—he is too obsessed with cutting a figure. Here Burke often suffers—he is too constantly on the platform. But Johnson, often too pompous in his formal writing, remains himself in his talk; because he was too fearless to pretend. Boswell, so often irritating in public, acquires a fascinating if ridiculous self when tête-à-tête with his journals. Goldsmith, fooled in society by his rage to shine, regains his spontaneous Irish self when alone at his desk.

But a closer parallel to Walpole here is, I think, Walpole's friend Gray. Even more than the prose-writers, the poets of the eighteenth-century were tempted to artificiality by being embedded in an artificial society. They were acutely conscious of snuff-taking critics; they sang to be heard rather than overheard. And so even Gray tends to jar and chill many readers by fits of stilted formality—'tall by walking on tiptoe'; especially in the two famous odes of 1757, where a poet already, by nature, as shy as an owl forced upon daylight, seems further embarrassed by the burden of a reputation now to be kept up. But the true Gray, for many, is the melancholy Gray, forgetting the garish world in his moods of loneliness and bereavement; or the playful Gray, forgetting himself in light verse about drowned cats, or ladies' visits, and in easy letters to his real intimates.

So with Walpole. What he printed for the public seems often hardly worth publication; it is among the things he did *not* publish that one finds what lastingly deserves it. I am always disappointed when I return to his controversial or antiquarian works, to his tragedy, his Gothic romance, his *Hieroglyphic Tales*. Even his verses, though sometimes charming trifles, remain trivial. Even his letters to persons outside his inmost circle are apt to be heavy. And so (though parts of the *Memoirs* are vivid and biting) one may ask oneself if one has not overestimated him, and underestimated the incisive judgement of Macaulay.

Really to know Walpole, you must go back to the letters he wrote to the men and women he really knew. It is not only his playfulness—that delightful, airy sparkle of a Puck or Ariel; not only his moments of amused and amusing malice. Often, no doubt, it is this playfulness which wins him a serious place among English writers; often the things he threw off light as thistledown that have taken most lasting root. But there is also a graver sincerity in him, too often forgotten. Life 'is a tragedy to those that feel'. There are times when the real Walpole unmasks his heart—a heart that seems to me neither black nor hollow—that one can remember, whatever its faults, with liking and respect. 'Werde was du bist'—'become what you really are'.

There are people who go through life all sweetness, like walking wedding-cakes, covered with sugar Cupids and iced so thick that one sickens. They make one value dry wine, dry light, dry humour, as never before. Mentally, as physically, men need both light and warmth. Light without warmth can become as melancholy and sterile as moonlight on a cemetery; warmth without light can become very like Hell. The eighteenth-century mind tended at times to light without warmth; the Romantics, and fanatics in general, to warmth without light. A large part of the art of life consists in balancing both. Like Hume and Franklin, Walpole does not seem to me to have succeeded so badly.

He remains, no doubt, a smaller figure in literature than Johnson, Goldsmith, Gray, Hume, or Burke. But at least, I think, he got more out of life—thanks partly to good fortune, but partly also to good sense—than any of them, except Hume. No doubt, one could admire Walpole more if, like Benjamin Franklin, with his gaiety and grace he could have combined also a greater usefulness to mankind. But, after all, how many men have left as much to teach men, if they would but learn; and to amuse them, if they had more taste for understanding life and the past? He would have smiled to know that the enthusiasm of an American collector has constructed a 'diurnal' recording all that is known of every single day of that long life, from its twentieth year to its eightieth.[1] He would, no doubt, also have been flattered. It shows how seriously he can be taken. But his head was too level to have been turned by it. He would have felt that this too was, in the end, vanity; as when, ten months before he died, the old man wrote to Lady Ossory, deprecating her handing round his letters, as if they were still remarkable.

> 'Oh, my good Madam, . . . pray send me no more such laurels, which I desire no more than their leaves when decked with a scrap of tinsel and stuck on twelfth-cakes that lie on the shop-boards of pastry-cooks at Christmas. I shall be quite content with a sprig of rosemary thrown after me, when the parson of the parish commits my dust to dust. Till then, pray, Madam, accept the resignation of your
>
> > Ancient servant,
> > Orford.'

'There's rosemary, that's for remembrance.' Horace Walpole has had far more remembrance than he could ever have dreamed of. But I still think that some of it might with justice have been kinder.[2]

---

[1] See W. S. Lewis, *Collector's Progress*—a fascinating book, even for the non-collecting type of mind which can feel some sympathy with Rossetti's growl that, even if presented with the authentic daisy of Burns, he would sooner swallow the thing than carry it twenty yards (though *that* seems a little extreme).

[2] Some readers will think I have been too kind to Walpole (and too harsh, in the previous volume, to Chesterfield). Sympathies of temperament are incalculable, and may bias one more than one knows. But I have tried to hold the balance even, and to give fair space to Walpole's accusers. My readers will judge for themselves. Still, I am fortified in my impression of Walpole by what seem to me the very similar views of Mr Ketton-Cremer, in his excellent biography, and of Dr W. S. Lewis, the completest of all Walpolians.

EDMUND BURKE

With grave
Aspect he rose, and in his rising seem'd
A Pillar of State; deep on his Front engraven
Deliberation sat and publick care;
And Princely counsel in his face yet shon,
Majestick though in ruin: sage he stood
With Atlantean shoulders fit to bear
The weight of mightiest Monarchies; his look
Drew audience and attention still as Night
Or Summers Noon-tide air, while thus he spake.

MILTON

I N most eyes, Burke is a far finer figure than Horace Walpole. He laboured terribly. Fate, indeed, foiled him again and again, till he seems at times the Cassandra of the eighteenth century. But many would claim that his wisdom, often unheeded in his own day, has yet outlived him, as a lasting political influence. On the other hand, just because his field *was* political, his memory remains still subject to the contentiousness of politics. I have heard a clever and sincere modern historian treat him as a pretentious pretender, who has duped posterity too long. What is the answer?

Before he was twenty, Burke had written his famous treatise on the Sublime and Beautiful; he was himself at times to attain the sublime; but I do not find in his work much of beauty, or of grace. He had the passionateness of the Irish, and their passion for the past,[1] and their power of hatred; but of Irish wit and humour, unlike Goldsmith or Sheridan, he had little. His wit has found defenders; but it seems to me usually poor, sometimes appalling. 'I never heard him,' said Johnson to Boswell, 'make a good joke in my life. . . . No, Sir, he is not the hawk there. He is the beetle in the mire.' But other great men have shared that defect—for example, Milton.[2] More serious, I feel, was the lack of humour. With more humour Burke might have been more winning, more persuasive, more balanced, less liable to become a noble bore. It might have saved him from a tendency, at times, to arrogant pontification and false profundity that exasperates those who cannot take themselves, or anyone else, with quite such solemnity. Johnson, too, could pontificate; but with Johnson, or at him, one can laugh.

[1] In the nineteen-thirties I found the telegraph-poles in a small village near Sligo pasted with green-printed I.R.A. posters headed 'Remember 1167'. (Imagine English villagers being adjured to remember 1066!) Elsewhere slogans about Cromwell, whitewashed on walls in two-foot letters, showed his memory to be still as burning as that of William of Orange beyond the Ulster border. It seems to me not improbable to see something of this trait in Burke, with his fervour for the traditions of the past. (Compare the remark of an Irish peasant-woman on Bertrand Russell's daughter, aged five—'She's a bonny girl, *in spite of Cromwell*'.)

[2] For Wit, and for Humour, Mrs Thrale gave Burke 0 out of 20. (Religion, 16; Morality, 10; Scholarship, 14; General Knowledge, 19; Person and Voice, 12.) More surprisingly she gave him 0 also for Good Humour; whereas for *that* she awarded Mrs Burke 18.

Still, had Burke been as humorous as Hume, he might have weakened in himself that indomitable conviction, that indefatigable energy, which made him, at the end, a power in Europe.[1] He wrote with effort; and to read him takes effort. But I do not think he would have complained of this judgement. He chose the hard way. He was, in politics, a deeply serious person; and his strength lay elsewhere than in humour. He was content to be used up and worn out in causes that he felt to be more important than any happiness of his own.

Burke, indeed, exemplifies one of the grimmer paradoxes of life —that it is often very hard both to *do* good and to *be* good. Hephaestus, the god of smiths, sweats at his forge; he may fashion masterpieces; yet he himself remains lame and sooty, and the Immortals smile at the Halt-foot as he limps through the halls of Heaven. It is his wife Charis—Grace—whose effortless fascination enchants both gods and men. It is the laughter-loving Aphrodite who inspires Praxiteles or Botticelli. It is Apollo, that fickle ravisher of nymphs, that ruthless archer, that wayward truant who, even when condemned to keep the sheep of Admetus, thinks more of his lyre than his shepherd's crook—it is Apollo whose laurels men adore, and to whose wise oracles men bow.

How unfair! Yet, often life *is* so. Suppose you spend fifty years on slumming, or on missions—how noble; yet, often, how narrowing! Think of Wesley rising at four, for over fifty years, and travelling more than a quarter of a million miles to preach; yet never allowing himself to laugh, nor children at school to play—'he who plays as a child will play as a man'; and think, on the other hand, of Goethe, that sublime egotist, his life and personality polished, year after year, like a jewel. 'Thought widens, but cripples,' he said, 'action animates, but narrows'. And remember his praise of Schiller —'Each time I saw him, he was a different, a completer, person.' Wesley, no doubt, was a happier man than Goethe—in his long life he knew hardly a quarter of an hour's depression; whereas Goethe complained at seventy-five that he had never enjoyed a single month

[1] I say this because one is anxious not to be unfair. Yet I own that a sense of humour does not seem to have weakened one whit the tenacity of men like Wellington, or Churchill. And without that humour they would have been far inferior as human beings.

of comfort.[1] And yet . . . I would far rather listen to Goethe's talk than Wesley's.

I suppose that, as so often, the wise solution lies in a happier mean —in balance between thought and action, between cultivating one's own garden and cultivating the common field. For all slavery—even slavery to high causes—remains to some extent an evil.

Burke is a less extreme case than Wesley, of the man who makes himself a human sacrifice to great causes. He found time, no doubt, for talking at The Club with Johnson and the rest; time to become a country gentleman with a large estate that he might, I suspect, have done very much better not to buy. But over his life there hangs, all the same, a somewhat dusty cloud of overstrain and overwork[2]—or, in Goldsmith's phrase about him, of 'cutting blocks with a razor';

> Tho' fraught with all learning, yet straining his throat,
> To persuade Tommy Townsend to lend him a vote.

To-day few English classics—certainly few English classics so famous—can be less thumbed than Burke. There are even histories of English Literature that go the strange length of wholly ignoring his existence—which no history of England could possibly do. This is one of the penalties of political oratory.

Hazlitt has said that no woman could read Burke through. A little rash. Hazlitt meant, I suppose, that about general ideas on politics women are sceptical, or indifferent, or both. This seems to ignore women like Mrs Macaulay in the eighteenth century, George Eliot in the nineteenth, Beatrice Webb in the twentieth. If women tend to be sceptical about general ideas, it is not I that shall blame them. Yet to be too indifferent about general ideas is to miss one of the great interests of life. I think one *should* read Burke—I will not say, read him *through*.

Edmund Burke was born in Dublin on New Year's Day, 1729. His name, though it sounds now so Irish, seems in origin Norman.

---

[1] One is not, however, compelled to believe him.

[2] An early poem of Burke's to his future father-in-law, Dr Nugent (1751), describes himself as, two years before, 'a Youth of body broke, infirm of mind'; and a pencil note adds 'Then nineteen his studies had nearly destroyed him'. There seems to have been another crisis in 1766—'Then, in the vigor of my manhood, my constitution sank under my labor . . . I seemed to myself very near death'.

His father was a Protestant attorney—but, we are told, 'by giving way to splenetic humours, he did in a manner voluntarily contract his practice'. 'In a manner' the same might be said of the last phase of his famous son.

The great-aunt of Burke's mother had married the son of Edmund Spenser, the poet. Like this famous kinsman and namesake, Edmund Burke himself was to become a figure noble, unfortunate, long remembered, but not much read—indeed both writers might be read much more, had they written much less.

In the years 1744-9, spent at Trinity, Dublin, Burke was already flinging himself, with typical passion, into one subject after another. First he was seized by a 'Furor Mathematicus'; then in succession by other 'furores'—'Logicus', 'Historicus', 'Poeticus'. There was also, already, a phase of political fury; which made him publish seven anonymous pamphlets before he was even twenty. All this contrasts strikingly with the indolence of Goldsmith, or the calm concentration of Hume. But much of Burke's life was to be hectic with the same touch of mental fever.[1]

As with some other Celtic politicians of our own century, this passionate temperament kept aflame in him a heat of oratorical vehemence which can fill the creeping Saxon with admiration, or at least astonishment. And yet the English, not in the eighteenth century alone, have felt also (and I trust always will feel) a certain distrust, in the long run, for all emotionalism that grows *too* purple and impetuous—

> Or some fierce thing replete with too much rage,
> Whose strength's abundance weakens his own heart.

In 1750 Burke's father packed him off to London, to study law in the Middle Temple. But, like Hume, and Boswell, the young man preferred literature; till finally his father cut off his allowance. The year 1757 saw his marriage to Jane Nugent, daughter of a Catholic physician at Bath—a union that seems to have been happier than most in the eighteenth, or indeed in any, century.[2]

---

[1] H. V. F. Somerset, *A Notebook of Edmund Burke* (1957), p. 38.
[2] In his notebook Burke wrote a character of her, rather honeysuckle in style. (H. V. F. Somerset, *A Notebook of E. Burke*, 52-4.)

In the same spring of 1757 appeared his *Essay on the Sublime and Beautiful*. Its main merit seems to me that it prefers to approach aesthetics through psychology; asking what it is in ourselves—in human nature, rather than what it is in objects, that makes them seem beautiful or terrible. I doubt if the book has much to say to the modern reader. But it brought the young Burke a reputation. A more solid support was the editorship of Dodsley's new *Annual Register* (1758), at £100 a year. No gold mine; but it may have helped Burke to gain that encyclopedic knowledge which so awed his contemporaries.[1]

In 1759 he became also secretary to 'Single-Speech' Hamilton, who was shortly after made Chief Secretary to the Viceroy of Ireland (1761–4). But after six years as Hamilton's 'genius', in 1765 Burke quarrelled with this too exacting patron, whom he then typically denounced as 'an infamous scoundrel', 'the most consummate villain that ever lived';[2] and became, instead, secretary to Lord Rockingham, the new Prime Minister. Conveniently provided with a seat at Wendover, in 1766 he quickly made a parliamentary reputation by speeches in favour of the American Colonies, and against the Stamp Act.[3]

However in July 1766, after only a year in office, Rockingham was dismissed, in favour of Grafton; and for sixteen years Burke was condemned to be the rallying-point and energizer of an indolent and dispirited opposition, led by Whig nobles often inclined to throw up the whole weary business, and withdraw themselves to spacious country-seats far more temptingly comfortable than the tent of Achilles can have been.

Indeed, in 1768, Burke himself blossomed, somewhat mysteri-

[1] It was long believed that Burke continued to be 'principal conductor' of the *Annual Register* for twenty-five years or more. See D. C. Bryant, *Burke and his Literary Friends*, (*Washington University Studies*, No. 9) 1939, ch. XV; T. W. Copeland, *Burke* (1950), ch. III. But B. D. Sarason (*PMLA.* LXVIII (1953), 496-508) brings what seems to me strong evidence that Burke gave up the editorship in 1765.

[2] In Burke's place, Hamilton seems to have employed Johnson; who liked and esteemed him to the last. Behind Burke's hysterics about Hamilton's 'villainy', and being treated as 'one of Mr H.'s cattle', one suspects some queer psychological tangle. (See T. W. Copeland in *History To-day*, June 1952, 394-9.)

[3] The exact date of Burke's maiden speech (apparently on the Stamp Act) was January 17, 1766 (see Dixon Wecter, 'Garrick and the Burkes' in *Philological Quarterly*, XVIII (1939), 367-80).

ously, from a needy young Irishman into an English country-gentleman. He became master of the estate of Gregories, at Beaconsfield in Buckinghamshire, once possessed by the poet Waller. It now contained a Palladian mansion, resembling Buckingham Palace, with no less than six hundred acres of land. All this cost Burke £20,000 down, and a considerable annual upkeep—perhaps £2,500. This he called 'casting a little root' in the country. The root was hardly 'little'. Indeed it was to prove the root of considerable evil.

It would perhaps have been better had Burke never seen the place. No doubt country retirement helped his health; but health hardly requires six hundred acres. All his life Gregories hung round his neck, with its debts and mortgages, as Abbotsford came to hang round Scott's.[1]

This, indeed, is the side of Burke most depressing for his admirers. He had to draw deeply on the purses of Whig lords. Rockingham in his will forgave him, it is said, debts of thirty thousand pounds. Burke denied gambling in East India stock; but his 'kinsman' William Burke and his brother Richard gambled in it heavily. And Edmund's financial affairs were long and lamentably involved with this shady couple, who shared with him a common purse and home; so that even his friend, the Bishop of Chester, could later describe his house as a 'hole of adders'.[2] It seems, at the least, unfortunate that, while Edmund Burke denounced corruption in England and extortion in India, Richard Burke should have been busy swindling poor Caribs of their lands in the West Indies, and William Burke no less busy with embezzlement and financial jugglery in India itself.

Possibly the best that can be said is that Burke was so preoccupied

---

[1] On June 30, 1795, for example, when threatened with foreclosure of a mortgage, he wrote, 'Had I foreseen this, I might perhaps in America, Portugal, or elsewhere, have found a refuge; and the sale of what I have might have gone some way toward doing justice to my creditors . . . . I cannot quite reconcile my mind to prison with great fortitude.' (See T. W. Copeland, *Burke*, 51-6.)

Cf. too the story of a creditor's clerk who failed to recognize Burke ploughing his own land at Beaconsfield; asked him if Mr Burke were at home; and was told, 'Mr Burke is out'. (Another link with Montesquieu, who would sometimes be mistaken for a peasant as he worked on his lands of La Brède.)

[2] Similarly a letter from Samuel Rogers of September 11, 1783, refers to the Burkes as 'Such monsters'. (See H. V. F. Somerset, 'New Light on Edmund Burke', in *Discovery*, December 1932, 396-7.)

with the public finances that he gave little heed to what was happening to his own; which he came to leave in the hands of his wife and son, to an extent for which he later reproached himself bitterly.[1] And perhaps Irish clannishness blinded him to the dubious characters of William and Richard Burke, whom he would eulogize as the noblest of men. For, personally, he could show a fine disinterestedness. He was a most generous giver. And he well knew, as he once said publicly, that his way of opposition was 'not the road to preferment'. During his last twenty-five years in Parliament he held a government position for less than twelve months; and as Paymaster in 1782 he reduced the proceeds of his own office from £27,000 a year to £4,000; whereas Lord Holland, the father of Burke's friend Fox, had held the balances of that office from his retirement, in 1765, till 1778, thus pocketing nearly £250,000 in interest. Such was eighteenth-century political finance.

And so even the shifty William Burke may have spoken truth when he remarked, 'Ned is full of real business, intent upon doing solid good to his country, as much as if he was to receive twenty per cent from the commerce of the whole empire, which he labours to extend and improve.'

None the less one could wish that this champion of freedom had not bartered away his own financial liberty; that he had kept his hands as scrupulously clean as Pitt (though even Pitt died £40,000 in debt); that he had preferred the sage economy of Hume, or the proud poverty of Johnson; that he had more remembered the lines of George Herbert—

> Yet in thy thriving still misdoubt some evil
> Lest gaining gain on thee, and make thee dim
> To all things else. Wealth is the conjurer's devil
> Whom when he thinks he hath, the devil hath him.
> Gold thou mayst safely touch; but if it stick
> Unto thy hands, it woundeth to the quick.

In 1771 Burke became agent (at £500 a year) for the New York

---

[1] 'They both kept from me, personally, everything that was fretful, teasing and disquieting.' For details of the shabby story of the Burkes' finances see Sir Philip Magnus, *Burke*, ch. III; Dixon Wecter, *Burke and his Kinsmen* (*Univ. of Colorado Studies*, Series B, vol. I, 1939-41).

Assembly—a post which he kept till the clash of 1775. In 1773 he visited Paris. Mme du Deffand liked him[1] (though she could not like his frightful French). He was himself captivated by that sight of Marie Antoinette, 'glittering like the morning star', which twenty years later was to inspire one of his most purple, though not, I think, of his happiest passages. But he did *not* like French rationalism. He could never feel happily at home with it, like Hume or Franklin; he could not even smile ironically at it, like Walpole. It already appalled that conservative, religious, Romantic side of his nature which was to inspire, and sometimes unbalance, his final phase.

But meanwhile, for the quarter-century from 1765 to 1790, the scene is finely filled by Burke the liberal. His denunciations of the Stamp Act in 1766 are followed by a whole series of great political speeches and writings—in 1769, *Observations on a late Publication*, attacking a tract of Grenville's; in 1770, *Thoughts on the Causes of the Present Discontents;* in 1774-5, perhaps the wisest of all his utterances, those *On American Taxation* and *On Conciliation with America*.

In 1774 he was elected for Bristol; and in the same year the Rockingham Whigs were joined by Burke's fellow-champion, Fox, who could so happily reinforce his friend by following up the heavy cannonades of Burke in the lighter skirmish of debate, with a grace and magic that Burke himself never approached.

In 1776 Burke supported two more motions for conciliation with America; in 1778 he denounced our use of Red Indians against the colonies; in 1780, amid the ruinous expense of the American War, he brought in an elaborate bill for economical reform (which was rejected by the Lords); and in the same year he attacked in the House the legal barbarity which sentenced homosexuals to the pillory, where two wretches had lately been pelted to death. But, also in this same year 1780, his liberalism towards Irish trade and Roman Catholics cost him his seat at Bristol; and indeed his tolerance towards the Catholic faith in which his mother and his father-in-law had lived could have cost him his life in the anti-Papist Gordon Riots.

---

[1] In 1780, however, she judged less favourably his speech on economies—'Je le trouve verbeux, diffus, obscur, plein d'affectation.' A most terrible old lady; her eyes might be sightless, but her ears and wits were as sharp as her tongue. For anything precious or pretentious she developed a ruthless horror; compare Mercier's story of her coming into a company where Rivarol was holding forth—'What bad book is this,' said she, 'that you are reading here?'

He had to take refuge in the house of General Burgoyne, now home on parole after his surrender at Saratoga; and pleaded afterwards for leniency towards the arrested rioters.

At last, in 1782, George III and Lord North had to accept the inevitable—the victory of America; and after sixteen years a Rockingham ministry once more came into power, with Burke as Paymaster-General. But within three months Rockingham had died; and was succeeded for a moment by Shelburne, a gifted yet distrusted person, odious both to Fox and to Burke; who, with that hysteria now growing upon him, described Shelburne as having the principles of Machiavelli, the morals of Catiline and Caesar Borgia. Picturesque; but a trifle simplified.

Within eight months Shelburne was duly forced out of office by that infamous coalition of Fox with the very North whom he had for years been denouncing as a wretch devoid alike of honour and of honesty.[1] Burke's participation does not seem much to his credit. But once more he found himself Paymaster (February 1783).

Yet this brief return to office proved far from happy. Two officials of the Pay Office, Powell and Bembridge, had been suspended on suspicion of embezzlement. Burke tactlessly reinstated them, and repeatedly defended his action in the House more tactlessly still. On one occasion he had to be pulled down by Sheridan into his seat. On another, he embellished his arguments with a stupid anecdote of raving indecency. Powell and Bembridge, he claimed, were 'men of business and religious integrity'; but at the end of the month (May 1783) Powell cut his throat; Bembridge was tried, fined, and imprisoned. After his release in 1784 he appealed to Burke for help. But Burke, at last out of patience, had come to regard him as 'a wild, precipitate and now desperate wretch'. The whole affair seems one more example of the passionate blindness of that brilliant mind (as with William and Richard Burke) to the shady characters of those with whom he felt himself leagued in loyalty.

However the unholy alliance of Fox and North, too cynical even for eighteenth-century politics, failed to outlast the year. In Decem-

[1] North doubtless bore no malice for this. He had none. He was a delightful, though disastrous, person. Cf. the story of the blunderer who asked him in the theatre, 'Who is that plain-looking woman?' 'That, sir, is my wife.' 'Oh no, I mean the one next her.' 'That, sir, is my daughter. And let me tell you, sir, we are considered to be three of the ugliest people in London.'

ber 1783 George III turned successfully to the young Pitt, aged twenty-four. Never again was Burke to hold office; and yet his days of greatest influence were still in store. The rest of his career was absorbed by India and France. In 1786, he moved the impeachment of Warren Hastings, whose trial dragged on for seven whole years till his acquittal in 1795. Well might Gibbon remark that he had heard of eternal punishment, but never till now of an eternal trial.

But long before his old enemy finally eluded him, Burke's passions had been roused still more fiercely by the Revolution in France; which wrung from him in succession some thirteen philippics, including his *Reflections on the Revolution* (1790), his *Appeal from the New to the Old Whigs* and *Thoughts on French Affairs* (1791), and his *Letters on a Regicide Peace* (1796). From his break with Fox in May 1791 till his retirement from the Commons in 1794, except when compelled by his part in the Hastings trial, Burke hardly spoke in the House. He had turned from Parliament to his pen and the English people.

Now for the first time he found himself at one with king and country. His name filled Europe. Though he missed the peerage for which he had hoped (and even chose the title of Lord Beaconsfield), his financial difficulties were lightened by pensions totalling £3,700—more than twelve times as much as Johnson's.[1] Yet this

[1] A curious and rather pathetic memorandum from Burke to Pitt about this has been published by Mr H. V. F. Somerset (*Eng. Hist. Review*, XLV (1930), 110-4). 'Mr Burke,' it begins,' has never asked for anything, nor suggested any reward. It never did become him, nor does it now become him, to suppose that he has any merit to entitle him to the particular favour of the Crown or of the publick. He is sensible that he has done nothing beyond his strict Duty.' Then follow sixty lines of argument that his 'merit' *does* so 'entitle him'. Barré has had a pension of £3000; Dunning, £4000 and a peerage. 'Mr. Burke certainly does not mean to compare his Abilities with those of the two Gentlemen he alludes to. It is allowed to a man to speak of his Industry. As for real Labour of Mind and body, he had even then, that is as long ago as 1782, worked more in any three months than they had done in their whole Lives.' (This seems a little ungracious.) 'In the twelve years since, notwithstanding his very advanced Age, his Industry has not been relaxed in any Course in which such small abilities as his could possibly employ it'. But his circumstances are straitened. 'A total neglect of a man's private affairs is likewise the inevitable consequence of occupations that engross the whole man.' (A principle that would have odd results if generally adopted.) Then follows a similar contrast with the rewards bestowed on Lord Auckland.

Burke had, I suspect, like most of us, more selves than one; but this seems to me a document that Johnson, Hume, or Franklin would have been, not proud, but much *too* proud, to write.

last phase too was not happy. In 1791 he lost his friendship with Fox;[1] three years before his own death in 1797, he lost also the son whom he adored (though others apparently did *not*). Nor is it a very happy period for many of Burke's admirers either. Too often his visions of the future grow unmeasured in their gloom. Too often the old prophet's voice breaks into a scream. The Age of Reason is fast yielding to Romanticism. Poetry gains: but thought, it seems to me, does not.

How much further Burke was moving along the road towards the Romantics than more typical figures of his century such as Chesterfield, Johnson, or Goldsmith, Hume, Crabbe, or Jane Austen, can already be seen from a passage in an early notebook, where 'Enthusiasm' already becomes a term of praise—very different from what Byron mocked at as 'entusy-musy'.

'I know the Clergy, shamed and frightened at the Imputation of Enthusiasm, endeavour to cover Religion under the Shield of Reason, which will have some Force with their Adversaries. But God has been pleased to give Mankind an Enthusiasm to supply the want of Reason; and truely, Enthusiasm comes nearer the great and comprehensive Reason in its effects, though not in the Manner of Operation, that the Common Reason does; which works on confined, narrow, common, and therefore plausible, Topics. The former is the lot of very few. The latter is common; and fit enough for common affairs—to buy and sell, to teach Grammar and the like; but is utterly unfit to meddle with Politics, Divinity and Philosophy. But Enthusiasm is a sort of Instinct, in those who possess it, that operates, like all Instincts, better than a mean Species of Reason.

'It is true indeed that enthusiasm often misleads us. So does reason too. Such is the Condition of our Nature; and we can't help it. But I believe that we act most when we act with all the Powers of our Soul; when we use our Enthusiasm to elevate and expand our Reasoning; and our Reasoning to check the Roving of our Enthusiasm.'[2]

This seems to me very typical, but very dubious doctrine. In the

---

[1] After the famous renunciation of friendship in the Commons, when Fox burst into tears (May 6, 1791), Burke is said to have paced his room till nearly 4 a.m., in such a paroxysm of passion that his friend Therry dared not leave him alone.

[2] H. V. F. Somerset, *A Notebook of E. Burke*, 68-9.

hands of a sadist or a fanatic, a Tamburlaine or a Hitler, it could lead to hideous conclusions. 'Instinct' and enthusiasm—spontaneous impulse and passion—may, indeed, provide a vital source of energy; but they give a poor kind of guidance. They may resemble the charge in a gun, essential to drive the projectile; their satisfaction may serve for target; but they are likely to prove useless or disastrous without sights and range-finder. Impulse and passion can also inspire new ideas, called up from less conscious levels of the mind. But the ideas may be false, foolish, or frenzied. And how hard it is for 'our Reasoning to check the Roving of our Enthusiasm' was to be tragically shown by Burke's own later years.

It may now be simplest to consider some typical utterances of Burke; then to try to estimate him as political thinker, as artist, and as man.

First, from the speech on American taxation (1774)—that fatal token-payment of 3d. on the pound of tea which cost us the First British Empire. Never indeed was there an instance more appalling of mere penny-wisdom.

'No man ever doubted that the commodity of tea could bear an imposition of three-pence. But no commodity will bear three-pence, or will bear a penny, when the general feelings of men are irritated, and two millions of people are resolved not to pay. The feelings of the colonies were formerly the feelings of Great Britain. Theirs were formerly the feelings of Mr Hampden when called upon for the payment of twenty shillings. Would twenty shillings have ruined Mr Hampden's fortune? No! but the payment of half twenty shillings, on the principle it was demanded, would have made him a slave.'

'Again, and again, revert to your old principles—seek peace and ensue it—leave America, if she has taxable matter in her, to tax herself. I am not here going into the distinctions of rights, nor attempting to mark their boundaries. I do not enter into these metaphysical distinctions; I hate the very sound of them. Leave the Americans as they antiently stood, and these distinctions, born of our unhappy contest, will die along with it. . . . Be content to bind America by laws of trade; you have always done it. Let this be your reason for binding their trade. Do not burthen them by taxes; you were not used to do so from the beginning. Let this be your reason for not taxing. These are the arguments of states and kingdoms. Leave the rest to the schools; for there only they may be discussed with safety.'[1]

'Sir William Temple says, that Holland has loaded itself with ten times the impositions which it revolted from Spain, rather than submit to. He says true. Tyranny is a poor provider. It knows neither how to accumulate, nor how to extract.'

Next, there is Burke's speech to his Bristol constituents, after his election there in 1774. He is urging that important point, important (but not always recognized) still, that a Member of Parliament should *not* be a mere delegate, pledged to his constituents to vote for this, and against that.

'Certainly, gentlemen, it ought to be the happiness and glory of a representative, to live in the strictest union, the closest correspondence, and the most unreserved communication with his constituents. Their wishes ought to have great weight with him; their opinion high respect; their business unremitted attention. It is his duty to sacrifice his repose, his pleasures, his satisfactions, to theirs; and, above all, ever, and in all cases, to prefer their interest to his own. But, his unbiassed opinion, his mature judgement, his enlightened conscience, he ought not to sacrifice to you; to any man, or to any set of men living. These he does not derive from your pleasure; no, nor from the law and the constitution. They are a trust from Providence, for the abuse of which he is deeply answerable. Your representative owes you, not his industry only, but his judgement; and he betrays, instead of serving you, if he sacrifices it to your opinion. . . . Parliament is not a *congress* of ambassadors from different and hostile interests; which interests each must maintain, as an agent and advocate, against other agents and advocates; but parliament is a *deliberative* assembly of *one* nation, with *one* interest, that of the whole; where, not local purposes, not local prejudices ought to guide but the general good, resulting from the general reason of the whole. You chuse a member indeed; but when you have chosen him, he is not member of Bristol, but he is a member of *parliament*.'

[1] Actually Burke believed that Parliament *had* a constitutional right to tax the colonies. And it appears from the *Annual Register* for 1765 that he was opposed to American representation at Westminster because, even had the remoteness of America allowed it, slave-owners were not fit to sit in a parliament of free men.

It was, indeed, Burke's proud claim that he was 'the first man who on the hustings, at a popular election, rejected the authority of instructions from constituents'.[1]

This too seems sound enough. And it leads to a very living question—whether it is well that party discipline should to-day have become so strict that, even if a member shows some freedom from control by his constituents, he has very little freedom from the control of his party whip. This is still a free country; we still have free votes; but, paradoxically, those who govern us do not—except on very rare occasions.[2] It may have become inevitable; it may still be regrettable.

Again, Burke would to-day, I think, have scented a considerable danger in a certain tendency of the Trades Union Congress to try at times to dictate to the House of Commons. One cannot have two kings of Brentford. And so public opinion showed itself convinced in the general strike of 1926.

And now for that masterpiece of true liberalism, *On Conciliation with America*.

After making the important point that English export trade to North America alone in 1772 was worth almost as much as the export trade of England to the whole world had been in 1704, Burke passes to that famous, though at times perhaps too florid character-sketch of the rugged vitality of these colonists whom it had become our infatuated policy to provoke. His insight has already singled out that eager energy which, whatever their national defects, remains still one of the most striking and formidable qualities of the United States.

> 'Pass by the other parts, and look at the manner in which the people of New England have of late carried on the whale fishery. Whilst we follow them among the tumbling mountains of ice, and behold them penetrating into the deepest frozen recesses of Hudson's Bay, and Davis's Streights, whilst we are looking for them beneath

[1] Cf. Macaulay at Leeds: 'It is not necessary to my happiness that I should sit in Parliament, but it is necessary to my happiness that I should possess, in Parliament or out of it, the consciousness of having done what is right.'

[2] Still less, of course, do M.P.s possess the secrecy of voting enjoyed by their constituents. But no doubt ballot-boxes in Parliament would increase irresponsibility and instability of government.

the arctic circle, we hear that they have pierced into the opposite region of polar cold, that they are at the antipodes, and engaged under the frozen serpent of the south. Falkland Island, which seemed too remote and romantic an object for the grasp of national ambition, is but a stage and a resting-place in the progress of their victorious industry. Nor is the equinoctial heat more discouraging to them, than the accumulated winter of both the poles. We know that whilst some of them draw the line and strike the harpoon on the coast of Africa, others run the longitude, and pursue their gigantic game along the coast of Brazil. No sea but what is vexed by their fisheries. No climate that is not witness to their toils. Neither the perseverance of Holland, nor the activity of France, nor the dexterous and firm sagacity of English enterprize, ever carried this most perilous mode of hardy industry to the extent to which it has been pushed by this recent people; a people who are still, as it were, but in the gristle, and not yet hardened into the bone of manhood. When I contemplate these things; when I know that the colonies in general owe little or nothing to any care of ours, and that they are not squeezed into this happy form by the constraints of watchful and suspicious Government, but that through a wise and salutary neglect, a generous nature has been suffered to take her own way to perfection: when I reflect upon these effects, when I see how profitable they have been to us, I feel all the pride of power sink, and all presumption in the wisdom of human contrivances melt, and die away within me. My rigour relents. I pardon something to the spirit of liberty. . . .

' America, gentlemen say, is a noble object. It is an object well worth fighting for. Certainly it is, if fighting a people be the best way of gaining them. . . .

'First, Sir, permit me to observe that the use of force is but *temporary*. It may subdue for a moment; but it does not remove the necessity for subduing again: and a nation is not governed, which is perpetually to be conquered. . . .

'If you do not succeed, you are without resource; for, conciliation failing, force remains; but, force failing, no further hope of reconciliation is left. . . .

'A further objection to force is, that you *impair the object* by your very endeavours to preserve it. The thing you sought for is not the thing which you recover; but depreciated, sunk, wasted, and consumed in the contest. Nothing less will content me, than *whole America*. I do not choose to consume its strength along with our own; because in all parts it is the British strength that I consume. . . .

Let me add, that I do not choose wholly to break the American spirit, because it is the spirit that has made the country.'

Then another classic passage on the power of geography over history—

'Three thousand miles of ocean lie between you and them. No contrivance can prevent the effect of this distance, in weakening government. Seas roll, and months pass, between the order and the execution: and the want of a speedy explanation of a single point, is enough to defeat an whole system.[1] . . . Nature has said it. The Turk cannot govern Aegypt, and Arabia, and Curdistan, as he governs Thrace; nor has he the same dominion in Crimea and Algiers, which he has at Brusa and Smyrna. Despotism itself is obliged to truck and huckster. The Sultan gets such obedience as he can. He governs with a loose rein, that he may govern at all; and the whole of the force and vigour of his authority in his centre, is derived from a prudent relaxation in all his borders. Spain, in her provinces, is, perhaps, not so well obeyed, as you are in yours. She complies too; she submits; she watches times. This is the immutable condition: the eternal law, of extensive and detached empire.'

Then a return to the high traditions of English liberty—

'The temper and character, which prevail in our colonies, are, I am afraid, unalterable by any human art. We cannot, I fear, falsify the pedigree of this fierce people, and persuade them that they are not sprung from a nation, in whose being the blood of freedom circulates. The language in which they would hear you tell them this tale, would detect the imposition; your speech would betray you. An Englishman is the unfittest person on earth, to argue another Englishman into slavery.'

And so to the immortal climax, perhaps too long delayed (brevity except in some of his finest sentences, was not a virtue of Burke's):

'As long as you have the wisdom to keep the sovereign authority of this country as the sanctuary of liberty, the sacred temple consecrated to our common faith, wherever the chosen race and sons of England worship freedom, they will turn their faces towards you.

[1] As was to be seen in the campaign of Saratoga.

The more they multiply, the more friends you will have; the more ardently they love liberty, the more perfect will be their obedience. Slavery they can have any where. It is a weed that grows in every soil. They may have it from Spain, they may have it from Prussia. But until you become lost to all feeling of your true interest and your natural dignity, freedom they can have from none but you.'

Then follows the maxim that to-day stands inscribed below the statue of Burke in Washington—'Magnanimity in politics is not seldom the truest wisdom; and a great empire and little minds go ill together.'[1] (With that, I feel, he should have ended—and not half a page later.)

This, indeed, is the only cement which still holds, the only cement that has any hope of continuing to hold together the British Commonwealth of Nations. There is no precedent for it in history—an Empire permanently free to dissolve, that yet, so far, does not dissolve; precarious though the bonds may have become.

And this is also, perhaps, the only strategy that can save the free world from losing the Cold War.

And yet, so little can reason do against emotion—against greed, and self-interest, and pride, and prejudice, and sheer sheepheadedness—that we read at the end of Burke's speech the two cold lines: 'Upon this resolution, the previous question was put, and carried:— for the previous question 270,—against it 78.' It is an ironic comment on human nature that the finest eloquence of Burke never swayed men one tenth as much as the ravings of Hitler.

Yet that defeat seems to me the highest point in Burke's career. Passion in him has not yet blinded common sense. On the contrary, each strengthens the other.

Burke's eloquence had four special fields—America (the finest), India, Ireland, and France. The speech of 1783, on Fox's India Bill, brings us to the second of these. What matters here is not Burke's defence of Fox, but his attack on British misrule.

'The several irruptions of Arabs, Tartars, and Persians, into India

[1] Cf. Wordsworth (1838): 'Blest Statesman He, whose Mind's unselfish will
    Leaves him at ease among grand thoughts: whose eye
    Sees that, apart from magnanimity,
    Wisdom exists not.'

were, for the greater part, ferocious, bloody, and wasteful in the extreme. . . . But the difference in favour of the first conquerors is this; the Asiatic conquerors very soon abated of their ferocity, because they made the conquered country their own. . . . Fathers there deposited the hopes of their posterity; and children there beheld the monuments of their fathers. Here their lot was finally cast; and it is the natural wish of all, that their lot should not be cast in a bad land. Poverty, sterility, and desolation, are not a recreating prospect to the eye of man; and there are very few who can bear to grow old among the curses of a whole people. . . .

'But under the English government all this order is reversed. The Tartar invasion was mischievous; but it is our protection that destroys India. It was their enmity, but it is our friendship. Our conquest there, after twenty years, is as crude as it was the first day. The natives scarcely know what it is to see the grey head of an Englishman. Young men (boys almost) govern there, without society, and without sympathy with the natives. They have no more social habits with the people, than if they still resided in England; nor indeed any species of intercourse but that which is necessary to making a sudden fortune, with a view to a remote settlement. Animated with all the avarice of age, and all the impetuosity of youth, they roll in one after another; wave after wave; and there is nothing before the eyes of the natives but an endless, hopeless prospect of new flights of birds of prey and passage, with appetites continually renewing for a food that is continually wasting. Every rupee of profit made by an Englishman is lost for ever to India. . . .

'There is nothing in the boys we send to India worse than the boys we are whipping at school, or that we see trailing a pike, or bending over a desk at home. But as English youth in India drink the intoxicating draught of authority and dominion before their heads are able to bear it, and as they are full grown in fortune long before they are ripe in principle, neither nature nor reason have any opportunity to assert themselves for remedy of the excesses of their premature power. . . . Their prey is lodged in England; and the cries of India are given to seas and winds, to be blown about, in every breaking up of the monsoon, over a remote and unhearing ocean.'

This is rapid, clear, direct, and generous—Burke at his best; yet it was the prelude to that long vendetta against Warren Hastings as an extortionate and unscrupulous satrap—a vendetta fine, no doubt, in intention, but intemperate in execution—which burdened nearly

ten years of Burke's life, from 1786, when he moved the impeachment, to 1795, when Hastings was finally acquitted, a ruined man.

There had been nothing quite like that famous and interminable
trial since Cicero impeached Verres for the plunder of Sicily (though
Burke erred in thinking Hastings another Verres); and its opening
scene has been painted by Macaulay with a rhetoric that (quite prepared to be taxed with bad taste) I prefer even to Burke's own—as
terser, more concrete, more coloured. It has become hackneyed—so
have parts of Shakespeare, for that matter; but since few can know it
by heart, I propose to quote parts of it again. For this, after all, is the
most dramatic scene of all in Burke's at times too theatrical life.

'The place was worthy of such a trial. It was the great hall of William
Rufus, the hall which had resounded with acclamations at the in-
auguration of thirty kings, the hall which had witnessed the just
sentence of Bacon and the just absolution of Somers, the hall where
the eloquence of Strafford had for a moment awed and melted a victorious party inflamed with just resentment, the hall where Charles
had confronted the High Court of Justice with the placid courage
which has half redeemed his fame. Neither military nor civil pomp
was wanting. The avenues were lined with grenadiers. The streets
were kept clear by cavalry. The peers, robed in gold and ermine,
were marshalled by the heralds under Garter King-at-arms. . . .
There were seated round the Queen the fair-haired young daughters
of the house of Brunswick. There the Ambassadors of great Kings
and Commonwealths gazed with admiration on a spectacle which no
other country in the world could present. There Siddons, in the
prime of her majestic beauty, looked with emotion on a scene sur-
passing all the imitations of the stage. There the historian of the
Roman Empire thought of the days when Cicero pleaded the cause
of Sicily against Verres, and when, before a senate which still retained some show of freedom, Tacitus thundered against the oppres-
sor of Africa. There were seen, side by side, the greatest painter and
the greatest scholar of the age. . . . There were the members of that
brilliant society which quoted, criticized, and exchanged repartees,
under the rich peacock hangings of Mrs Montague. And there the
ladies whose lips, more persuasive than those of Fox himself, had
carried the Westminster election against palace and treasury, shone
round Georgiana Duchess of Devonshire.'

A superb commencement. Yet the trial was to peter out in an

interminable anticlimax; partly because, though Hastings was defended by lawyers, he was prosecuted by parliamentarians ill versed in legal evidence or legal procedure; partly because the House of Lords was cumbrously ill fitted to try such a case, which an ordinary court might have despatched in a few months. The whole affair remains a fearful warning against verbosity. For if only Hastings himself had not bored the Commons with a prolix defence read at the bar of the House, he might never have had to endure the prolixity of his accusers, subjecting the events of thirteen years to a trial that itself took seven; so that of the 168 peers who had graced its opening pageantry, some 60, it is said, had died before it hobbled to its lame conclusion.[1]

Who was really right? Authorities still differ. Hastings, it is now generally admitted, was not a bloodthirsty harpy. His mind was set, not on plundering India, but on maintaining there the ordered power of England.

He might more plausibly be accused of grasping at power than at money. Often he became dictatorial. Still, he might have been less dictatorial, had he been more in the position of a dictator. Clive observed that only once (before Plassey) had he called a council of war; and that, had he listened to it, the British would not have mastered Bengal. (Better perhaps if they had not: but that is a different point.) When Marlborough wished to do nothing in particular, he would call a council of war. But Hastings was permanently saddled, year after year, with an obstructive council of four, including the intractable and intolerable Philip Francis. Ibsen remarked that whenever he heard the words 'a committee has been appointed', he was moved to laughter; in my experience of committees, he was not far wrong. Often they are too verbose; often too cowardly; often their members are too busy grinding private axes to cut much ice in common. To get things done, I believe it is often better to leave them to an individual with very full powers, keeping only the power of immediate dismissal if he proves unsatisfactory. Certainly eighteenth-century India was no place for committee-government.

About money Hastings seems to have been, not greedy, but care-

---

[1] Actual sittings of the Court occupied only 142 days—an average of only three weeks a year. But, for the defendant, it remained intolerable.

less and ruthless. The East India shareholders, and the government of British India, were expensive. Yet the money for these was somehow found. The repurchase of the lands of Daylesford, and the wishes of that Baroness Imhoff who played in the life of Hastings a part not unlike that of Emma Hamilton in Nelson's, were also expensive. Yet the money for these also was somehow found. Hastings was no Fabricius. It can only be pleaded that one should not commit the moral anachronism of judging a man of one age by the standards of another; and that if Clive professed to be astonished at his own financial moderation, Hastings might have said the same with considerably more justice. For, after Plassey, Clive is said to have come home worth £1,200,000.

The real charge against Hastings seems to me that at times he became *too* violent, *too* Machiavellian. He had resolved that England should dominate in India, as Frederick had resolved that Prussia should dominate in Central Europe; and, having chosen his end, like Frederick he could be crudely unscrupulous, even for his age, about the means. The treatment meted out to Chait Singh, Faizullah Khan, and the Begums of Oudh too much recalls wolf and lamb to bring much patriotic satisfaction to any decent reader. And this, I take it, was what made Pitt, to the general stupefaction, vote finally for impeachment in the matter of Chait Singh. The best that can be urged on the other side was perhaps said by George III when, with one of those disconcerting flashes of good sense which could come from that muddled head, he wrote to Pitt approving that he had voted according to his conscience, yet adding—'As for myself I do not think it possible in that country to carry on business with the same moderation that is suitable to a European country'. But this, of course, was precisely that 'geographical morality' which Burke denounced in Hastings.

And what of the part played by Burke himself? He seems to me to have made the mistake men constantly make, of lavishing on persons that hatred which should be kept only for things; and of losing in his paroxysms all sense of proportion. To talk of Hastings as 'a heart blackened to the very blackest—a heart corrupted, vitiated and gangrened to the very core' was not merely rant; it was also self-defeating folly. Voltaire knew far better how to stab tyrants home with his pen. The roll of his own periods, the cry of his own passion, bewitched Burke's ears like the song of the Sirens; but, as Sirens do, they lured to disaster.

After he had vainly done his worst against Hastings, Burke quitted the Commons for ever; and to a friend he wrote—'Let my endeavours to save the nation from that guilt and shame be my monument: the only one I will ever have. . . . If ever Europe recovers its civilization, that work may be useful. Remember! Remember! Remember!' Whether this echo of Charles I on the scaffold was deliberate, I do not know; it would hardly seem very appropriate. But in essentials one must believe Burke sincere. The evils he denounced in the system were real; and, in the end, he helped to amend them. All the same, his career has far finer moments—far finer 'monuments'—to remember him by; both as orator and as statesman.

The ultimate point of that weary seven-years trial is not how far Hastings was innocent or guilty, how far Burke was misled by the frenzied personal hatred felt for Hastings by Sir Philip Francis, the probable author of *Junius*; the vital thing, in the long run, was the stirring of the public conscience, the condemnation of the evils of what has since come to be called 'colonialism'.[1] Almost at once the governorship of Lord Cornwallis (1786–93) brought to India at least considerable reform.

But long before Hastings was at last notified from the Woolsack that the Lords acquitted him, the storm-centre, for Burke and for England, had shifted from India to France. In this his last phase, where, more and more, his style flushes like the leaves of autumn, he was to produce a greater effect on the world, and to gain a higher reputation, than ever before; but also to show how much his wisdom, though still often impressive, was in danger of sinking to become 'passion's slave'. It is also the part of his work most relevant to our own world. America is in no danger of oppression; colonialism has passed away; but we live, more perhaps than ever before, in an age of revolutions.

Already in his speech on the Army Estimates (February 1790),

---

[1] Contrast, for example, the callousness of De Quincey—'in the course of the Hastings trial, upon the concerns of paralytic Begums and mouldering queens—hags that, if ever actually existing, were no more to us and our British sympathies, than we to Hecuba—did Mr Sheridan make his capital exhibition.'

Burke drags in France as implacably as Cato dragging into the debates of the Roman Senate the need to destroy Carthage. He cannot forgive the Revolutionaries their doctrinaire irreverence for the past, their reckless policy of the clean sweep. 'The French have made their way through the destruction of their country, to a bad constitution, when they were absolutely in possession of a good one. They were in possession of it the day the states met in separate orders. . . . They first destroyed all the balances and counter-poises which serve to fix the state, and to give it a steady direction. . . . These they rashly destroyed, and then they melted down the whole into one incongruous, ill-connected mass.'

Burke is, in his way, a Fabian. He distrusts theories; he distrusts men; he distrusts the haste of fools rushing in. He believes like Montesquieu's Usbek in the *Lettres Persanes* that 'il est quelquefois nécessaire de changer certaines lois. Mais le cas est rare; et lorsqu'il arrive, il n'y faut toucher que d'une main tremblante'. He believes, like Jefferson, that liberty is only to be gained 'by inches'.

The answer to 1789 is, for him, 1688. 'With us it was the case of a legal monarch attempting arbitrary power—-in France it is the case of an arbitrary monarch, beginning, from whatever cause, to legalize his authority. . . . With us, we got rid of the man, and preserved the constituent parts of the state. There they get rid of the constituent parts of the state, and keep the man. What we did was in truth and substance, and in a constitutional light, a revolution, not made, but prevented.' For Burke, the English constitution was like an English garden, a happy blend of art and nature, wisdom and instinct; the French constitution like a French garden of Louis XIV, artificial, geometrical, blighted.

One may agree that we ordered this matter better in England. Yet one may ask if Burke fairly considered either our own advantages or the difficulties of the French. The England of 1688 had a robust aristocracy, statesmen of political experience, constitutional traditions, the sobering memories of the English Civil War. But the France of 1789 had endured a century of absolutism and oppression; redress had been too long delayed; and the success of America provided a dangerously intoxicating precedent. Yet the France of 1789 was very unlike America. It was perhaps more like the Russia of 1917. Liberalism is a tree of slow growth, that easily dies if too suddenly transplanted. 'But that', Burke might have answered, 'is the point I ceaselessly insisted on.' It was; yet perhaps he failed to distinguish enough between the strength of a healthy tradition in England and the impotence, in France, of one too long allowed to rot.

'You will observe,' he writes in the *Reflections on the Revolution* (1790), 'that from magna charta to the declaration of right, it has been the uniform policy of our constitution to claim and assert our liberties, as an *entailed inheritance* derived to us from our forefathers, and to be transmitted to our posterity. . . . This policy appears to me to be the result of profound reflection; or rather the happy effect of following nature, which is wisdom without reflection, and above it. A spirit of innovation is generally the result of a selfish temper and confined views. People will not look forward to posterity, who never look backward to their ancestors.'

'Following nature'—'wisdom without reflection'—Burke here becomes a strange mixture of the eighteenth century, with its vague 'Nature', and of the coming Romanticism, with its belief in 'wisdom without reflection'. To those who distrust reason much, but intuition still more—to those who see 'Nature' rather as something which civilized man has struggled, century by century, to tame and dominate (though he perishes if he tries to dominate it to excess), this side of Burke may seem far from satisfactory—too credulous, too nebulous, too mystical. 'You might,' he tells his French correspondent, 'if you pleased, have profited of our example, and given to your recovered freedom a correspondent dignity. Your privileges, though discontinued, were not lost to memory. Your constitution, it is true, whilst you were out of possession, suffered waste and dilapidation; but you possessed in some parts the walls, and in all the foundations, of a noble and venerable castle. You might have repaired those walls; you might have built on those old foundations . . . but you chose to act as if you had never been moulded into civil society, and had everything to begin anew. You began ill, because you began by despising everything that belonged to you.'

But when Burke says 'you might, if you pleased, have done this and that,' he seems himself to ignore the blind passions that sway human nature, and play cat and mouse with human reason. Life is not easy for Lafayettes and Kerenskys; the worm-eaten, undermined building that collapses in a tempest is a very different affair from the ballasted vessel that heels to the storm, but keeps its own strength of equilibrium. The French of 1789 were not solid Americans; and one wonders if even Franklin and Washington could have coped with that long-sowed whirlwind.

'Were all these dreadful things necessary? were they the inevitable results of the desperate struggles of determined patriots, compelled to wade through blood and tumult, to the quiet shore of a tranquil and prosperous liberty? No! nothing like it. The fresh ruins of France, which shock our feelings wherever we can turn our eyes, are not the devastation of civil war; they are the sad but instructive monuments of rash and ignorant counsel in time of profound peace.' One is reminded of Masaryk's shrewd comment on the Bolsheviks—'They *had* to shoot. But they should not have gone on shooting'. Only we know, now, once violence has begun, how hard it is to stop.

But at this point Burke himself grows too violent. His horror of extreme radicalism drives him into extremes of conservatism—into a defence of the absurdities of the English electoral system, rotten boroughs and all, as 'perfectly adequate to all the purposes for which a representation of the people can be desired or devised'. The bringing of Louis XVI from Versailles, and the exultations over it of enthusiasts like Dr Price—who seems to have indulged in the usual silly raptures of 'fellow-travellers'—goad Burke to hysteria, no less excessive, at 'the most horrid, atrocious, and afflicting spectacle, that perhaps ever was exhibited to the pity and indignation of mankind'. Where was Burke's history?

And so we come to the most famous of Burke's purple passages, the panegyric on Marie Antoinette. Here I find it hard not to agree with the comment of the unpleasant Sir Philip Francis: 'In my opinion all that you say of the Queen is pure foppery.... Pray, Sir, how long have you felt yourself so desperately disposed to admire the ladies of Germany?'

Burke could only reply that he had wept in writing the passage; and wept in re-reading it. But surely politics is better without tears. What mattered far more than the insult that day to the sovereignty of Marie Antoinette was the insult to the sovereignty of law, on which depend the peace and the happiness of all civilized states. Therefore the real question was whether the 'ten thousand swords'

Burke wished to see 'leaping from their scabbards' would in fact have strengthened or weakened law, peace, and happiness in France. I do not know the answer. Napoleon thought he did—and his 'whiff of grapeshot' proved, for the moment, unanswerable. And yet one recalls that, from then on, the grapeshot seldom ceased till Waterloo. And one is left only with the mature conviction of the shrewd victor of Waterloo, that almost *anything* is better than civil war.

In any case it seems to me that Burke badly erred in stressing so much the interests of a single woman, however queenly, romantic, and pathetic, rather than the general welfare of France, of Europe, of the world.

The eighteenth century had, no doubt, been too rational; but with the later Burke one can watch the tide fast turning towards the opposite excess. 'Prejudice,' he now claims, 'renders man's virtue his habit; and not a series of unconnected acts.' But surely prejudice may equally render man's vices 'his habit'. It would be strange to find generalizations so rash in Hume or Montesquieu.

But, though propaganda can hardly claim an honoured place among human activities, it holds sometimes a vital one; and it must be allowed to Burke that he saw the needs of that perilous time, and met them, as few of his contemporaries could. He saw that any propaganda against the revolutionary spirit must itself have real fire. In politics, as in war, the defensive is difficult, and often demoralizing—as we can see to-day in our dealings with Communism both in Russia and in Asia. Burke's *Reflections* converted many minds against the Revolution; they even converted George III to Edmund Burke. To every visitor the King exclaimed—'Read it. It will do you good!—do you good! Every gentleman should read it.'

His brother-monarch Louis XVI even occupied himself in translating it. Not, for one placed as he was, a very tactful occupation. And he might have found more pressing and more practical things to do. But that sluggish soul seemed doomed to bungle everything—including his fatal flight to Varennes.

The *Reflections*, however, also influenced far wider and more intelligent circles than those of George III and Louis XVI. They have been called by Dumont 'the first considerable check that was given to the general enthusiasm in the cause of the Revolution'. Lecky thought them more effective than any political work of the eighteenth century except perhaps Swift's pamphlet on *The Conduct of the Allies* (which I should have thought less important than Paine's *Common Sense*). And Cobban sums up: 'Disregarded in Parliament, Burke had the nation behind him. He it was, not Pitt, who rallied England against the French menace.'

This may be true enough of the early nineties; but surely it is fair to remember that Pitt, after all, bore the burden of government, and became 'the pilot who weathered the storm'—until it broke him, and other hands brought us finally to harbour after ten years more. Indeed in that last two-minute speech of Pitt's at the Guildhall— 'England has saved herself by her exertions, and will, as I trust, save Europe by her example', there was a brevity that contrasts finely with Burke's besetting sin of wordiness.

Gibbon's comments on Burke in these years seem to me delightful, and also impressive—the judgement of typical eighteenth-century calm on the passions that were soon to dethrone it. 'I admire his eloquence,' writes Gibbon to Lord Sheffield, 'I approve his politics, I adore his chivalry, and I can forgive even his superstition.' And again—'Poor Burke is the most eloquent and rational madman that I ever knew.' But I suppose Burke would only have snorted. For he held the astonishing principle that speaking to an infidel like Hume may be socially expedient, but is morally unjustifiable. His liberalism had strange limits. Indeed it may be asked whether Burke must not bear his share of responsibility for the savage repression, the spies, the sentences of imprisonment and transportation, that mar the next quarter of a century. There are moments when he seems unpleasantly close to the grim Lord Braxfield.

In 1791 followed the *Appeal from the New to the Old Whigs*. (The new Whigs are those sympathizing, like Fox or Sheridan, with the French Revolution of 1789; the old Whigs are those wiser ancients who made, or maintained, the English Revolution of 1688).

Perhaps its most interesting and eloquent passage is Burke's appeal to Montesquieu, with his admiration for the sober liberties of the British Constitution.

'Place, for instance, before your eyes, such a man as Montesquieu. Think of a genius not born in every country, or every time; a man gifted by nature with a penetrating aquiline eye; with a judgment prepared with the most extensive erudition; with an herculean robustness of mind, and nerves not to be broken with labour; a man who could spend twenty years in one pursuit. Think of a man, like the universal patriarch in Milton (who had drawn up before him in his prophetic vision the whole series of the generations which were to issue from his loins), a man capable of placing in review, after having brought together, from the east, the west, the north, and the south, from the coarseness of the rudest barbarism to the most refined and subtle civilization, all the schemes of government which had ever prevailed amongst mankind, weighing, measuring, collating and comparing them all, joining fact with theory, and calling into council, upon all this infinite assemblage of things, all the speculations which have fatigued the understandings of profound reasoners in all times!—Let us then consider, that all these were but so many preparatory steps to qualify a man, and such a man, tinctured with no national prejudice, with no domestic affection, to admire, and to hold out to the admiration of mankind the constitution of England! And shall we Englishmen revoke to such a suit? Shall we, when so much more than he has produced, remains still to be understood and admired, instead of keeping ourselves in the schools of real science, choose for our teachers men incapable of being taught, whose only claim to know is, that they have never doubted; from whom we can learn nothing but their own indocility; who would teach us to scorn what in the silence of our hearts we ought to adore?'

This is generous praise of one great man by another. And it is true enough that Montesquieu said fine and flattering things of us— 'L'Angleterre est agitée par des vents qui ne sont pas faits pour submerger, mais pour conduire au port'— 'le plus libre pays qui soit au monde, je n'en excepte aucune république. Je l'appelle libre, parce que le prince n'a pas le pouvoir de faire aucun tort imaginable à qui que ce soit'—'cette nation aimerait prodigieusement sa liberté parce que cette liberté serait vraie; et il pourrait arriver que, pour la défendre, elle sacrifierait son bien, son aisance, ses intérêts; qu'elle se chargerait des impôts les plus durs, et tels que le prince le plus absolu n'oserait les faire supporter à ses sujets.' How true that was, Napoleon and Hitler were to find.

All the same at Burke's invitations to 'adore' the British Constitution, I suspect that Montesquieu would have quietly smiled. Politicians should not talk in the strain of priests of Baal. And, as can be seen from his private notes, Montesquieu's eyes were far less wilfully closed than Burke's now were, to our political weaknesses—at times he thought we might survive only because the English people had more virtue than its governors. Even so, 'les Anglais ne sont plus dignes de leur liberté. Ils la vendent au roi; et si le roi la leur redonnait, ils la lui vendraient encore'.

Indeed, the effect of recalling Montesquieu is not, for me, what Burke intended. For the name of Montesquieu brings back to my memory precisely the qualities that Burke himself lacks—the gaiety, the balance, the level-headedness, the simplicity of style, the free-dom from emphasis or hyperbole, rapture or rhapsody, which make my admiration for Montesquieu as natural and spontaneous as breathing; whereas in my admiration for Burke there remains a sense of reluctant strain and effort. No doubt, since Burke set him-self to stir the emotions of multitudes, where Montesquieu addresses only the good sense of tranquil aristocrats and thinkers, the orator was forced to make himself a trumpet-voice. And yet, at moments, how the glare of the sun on that trumpet's brass wearies the eye; how its blare, in the long run, exhausts the ear!

There seems no need to seek further illustrations of Burke's standpoint in the long series of pamphlets poured out against the French Revolution, with indefatigable fury, by this man who was already sixty when it began—*Thoughts on French Affairs* (1791), *Remarks on the Policy of the Allies* (1793), *Letters on Peace with the Regicide Directory* (1796). They were effective propaganda in their day; they contain fine phrases, splendid paragraphs; at times they startle still by the applicability of much that they say of French Jacobinism then, to Russian Communism now.[1] But, all the same, one's eyelids droop. The scolding, nagging, screaming grow too prolonged. I cannot compare the tone of it all with the resolute irony and sombre humour of Churchill in the face of wickedness far more brutal, and of dangers far more appalling. Burke, I feel, did not know when, or where, to stop.

What, then, of Burke in general, as thinker, as writer, and as man?

---

[1] E.g. 'Benevolence to the whole species, and want of feeling for every individual with whom the professors come in contact, form the character of the new philosophy.' 'By hating vices too much, they come to love men too little.' 'A theory concerning government may become as much a cause of fanaticism as a dogma in religion.'

His thought has been praised to the skies. If he survives a hundred other orators, it is because he was also a tireless thinker—sometimes the most liberal of conservatives, sometimes the most conservative of liberals; so that he could both seem a forerunner of Disraeli, and yet be spoken of by Disraeli's enemy, Gladstone, as an 'almost divine man'. He survives, too, as one of the first sons of our Age of Reason to realize the inadequacy of bare reasoning, the mysterious intricacies of human temperament, the need for gradual and unconscious evolution; as the unheeded Cassandra of the American Revolution, the champion of Irish Catholics and negro slaves and Indian victims of colonialism, the belatedly honoured prophet who, with Pitt, fortified England to resist the fanaticism of revolutionary France.

'Systems of scientific thought,' says Acton, 'have been built up on the fragments that fell from his table.' One may not much care for this image of 'systems' being 'built' on crumbs; but never mind. And again—'Brougham and Lowe lived by the vitality of his ideas. Mackintosh and Macaulay are only Burke trimmed of all that touched the skies.' On the other hand, Acton records telling John Morley that 'I would have hanged Mr Burke on the same gallows as Robespierre. Tableau.' I am not clear how far this was said merely to tease Morley. But not entirely, I imagine.

To this day Burke's reputation as a political thinker remains high. 'Burke's stature as a philosopher of politics,' says Mr T. E. Utley (1957), 'has grown, though not steadily, since his death, and it has never seemed more impressive than it does today.'

Yet I remain a little sceptical about all the eulogies lavished on the 'philosophy' of Burke. That he should gain applause from quarters so diverse, suggests that his thought lends itself to very diverse interpretations—that it is somewhat vague, or somewhat inconsistent, or both.

The soundest basis of his politics was really, I think, a profound distrust of all political doctrines and dogmas—of what he called 'metaphysics'. Yet he had too, at times, a fondness of his own for generalizations—often generalizations of a highly dubious kind.

'Man,' he will say, 'acts from adequate motives relative to his interests; and not on metaphysical speculations.' But is this true? Surely men only too often act on motives that are rationally quite inadequate, and contrary to their true interests; and only too often they do act on 'metaphysical speculations'—think of the Wars of Religion, of Fascism, Nazism, Marxism. Though one may well regret it.

Or again—'I must see the men, I must see the things. I never govern myself, no rational man ever did govern himself, by abstractions and universals. I do not put abstract ideas wholly out of any question because I well know that under that name I shall dismiss principles.'

But this, too, seems rather a muddle. Presumably the emphasis is on '*govern*'. Yet to say 'no rational man' ever *governed* himself by abstractions and universals, merely begs the question. It means—'It anyone disagrees with my distrust of abstractions, he is not "rational".'

I suppose Burke meant that most generalizations are faulty and dangerous tools, though often useful; so that one should constantly check theory by practice (as Ibsen held in ethics). Burke had, in reality, a double standard—any policy, for him, was condemned either if it was unprincipled or if it was unpractical. But there were perhaps times when his opponents might not unjustly have complained that, when they urged practical measures, Burke would down them with principles; and when they pleaded principles, would deride them as unpractical 'metaphysicians'.

Take, for example, Rousseau's most famous sentence: 'Man is born free; and everywhere he is in chains'. This seems to me to deserve Burke's scorn of 'metaphysics'. For how is man 'born free', when he is born to be often the dupe of his senses, the slave of his passions, the plaything of his illusions, the victim of circumstance? Even the freedom of his will is disputable. What does it mean to say men have 'a right' to be free?[1] Is it more than a pompous way of saying that freedom appears more likely to further human happiness, health of mind, and progress? Men are born in bondage to Necessity; and it seems to me the business of the state to free them, as far as may be, from all external constraints that are not necessities.

[1] Mysticism about natural 'rights' can lead logically to such extravagances as those of the transcendentalist community founded in 1843 by the American A. B. Alcott; who banned not only animal food, woollen clothes, and leather shoes, but even the weeding of their crops. For, after all, the weeds had just as much *right* to grow. The experiment was brief.

Similarly with Rousseau's curious doctrine of the 'general will'. Rousseau was both a born rebel and yet afraid of his own rebelliousness; and so his political thinking veers between anarchy and repressiveness. But in talking of the 'general will', he seems to think of a community too much as if it were an individual; whereas really even an individual is more like a community—a welter of conflicting wills.

Similarly with all ideas of social contracts. There may have been something like a contract, at times, in feudalism. But often, between ruler and ruled, there has been no more semblance of a contract than between ant and ant-cow. One can only say that a decent constitution works *as if* there were a contract.

Yet Burke himself can talk of 'the great primeval contract of eternal society, linking the lower with the higher natures, connecting the visible and invisible worlds'. He can make emotional appeals to 'Nature' with that maddening eighteenth-century vagueness about the word which at times reminds one of Malory's Sir Percivale who, seeing a lion in battle with a serpent, helped the lion, 'for he was the more natural beast of the two'; or of the eighteenth-century lady who, when fashion replaced flowers by carrots and artichokes in the coiffure of Marie Antoinette (1785), exclaimed enchanted, that vegetables were so much more 'natural'. Here, as with his divine tactics, and marches of providence,[1] Burke seems himself as 'metaphysical' as the thinkers he condemns.

Still it remains, I think, fair to say that, especially in his best period, Burke's scorn for formulae, legal or philosophical, was healthy—part of a passion for common sense and common decency well befitting a friend of Johnson and contemporary of Hume. Here, indeed, his attitude was typically English. Unfortunately the English sometimes combine this healthy distrust for theories with a foolish obsession for rules and legalities; and Burke was at his best when he pointed out, though vainly, the folly of pedantically arguing whether on merely legal principles we had a right to tax America when in fact, legal right or no, the Americans would not pay, nor could we make them, or at least go on making them.

---

[1] Contrast Bentham's characteristic comment when things went provokingly wrong —'Just like Provvy!'; but compare his condemnation of the *Déclaration des droits de l'homme* as 'the *ne plus ultra* of metaphysics' (its articles, he said, were all either false, or unintelligible, or both).

Burke, in fine, with his sound distrust of doctrinaires, can be seen as the Apostle of Empiricism, the great Opportunist. So that he was often far wiser, I think, in criticizing political doctrines than in creating them.

Indeed, this son of the Age of Reason not only distrusted abstractions and universals; he had also, far more than most men of his time, a very reasonable distrust of reason itself. 'The more a man's mind is elevated above the vulgar, the nearer he comes to them in the simplicity of his appearance, speech,' (Burke hardly practised this) 'and even not a few of his Notions. He knows his reason very well and therefore he is suspicious of it.' 'Politics should be adapted, not to human reason, but to human nature, of which reason is but a part, and not the greatest part.' 'This sort of people are so taken up with their theories about the rights of man, that they have totally forgot his nature.' 'The nature of man is intricate. . . . When I hear the simplicity of contrivance aimed at and boasted of in any new political constitutions, I am at no loss to decide that the artificers are grossly ignorant of their trade. or totally negligent of their duty.' Like Pareto, Burke distrusted Utopian planners, because human beings in the mass are seldom rational, and often bad.

Further, Burke hates doctrinaires not merely for their blindness but also for their callous brutality. 'These philosophers consider men in their experiments no more than they do mice in an air-pump, or in a recipient of mephitic gas.' I think the sentence would be still better if it dropped its clumsy 'recipient of mephitic gas', and kept only the terse 'mice in an air-pump'. But its truth remains. I remember a conversation long ago at my College High Table between Lord Keynes and a foreign economist, on the liquidation of the *kulaks* in the Soviet Union. 'They are only,' argued the foreign economist, '5 per cent of the population.' 'But,' cried Keynes, 'they are eight million *people*.'[1] When human beings come to be thought of too much as percentages, the result is tyranny. Keen consciousness of that seems to me one of Burke's most lasting merits. Such truths may appear 'trite' (word beloved by mediocre critics); yet such truths are perpetually ignored, perpetually in need of restatement. Marx and other 'terrible simplifiers' have forgotten them. And mankind has paid.

[1] I will not vouch for the exact figures.

Hence Burke's irreconcilable quarrel with the Jacobins, and with all political pedants, doctrinaires, and fanatics. 'Circumstances (which with some gentlemen pass for nothing) give in reality to every political principle its distinguishing colour.' In short, politics should never be subjected to cast-iron rules and dogmatic absolutes. For there, too, is relativity. In fine, Burke preserves about what he calls 'metaphysics' in politics, a healthy scepticism not wholly unlike the scepticism of Hume about metaphysics proper.

To take a modern example. Nationalization is sometimes necessary; sometimes an advantage. In theory, it can seem rational and attractive. But, life and human nature being what they are, it does not always prove the magic panacea its zealots hope. Where the private *entrepreneur*, eager for wealth, cuts down expenditure, since it is he who pays, we sometimes get instead the bureaucrat, eager for power, who inflates expenditure, since the public pays. I have been a civil servant in war. And I have watched unscrupulous 'empire-builders' wantonly waste man-power, when man-power was short, and cry ceaselessly for bigger staffs, regardless of public expense; just because the bigger their staffs, the bigger their own importance, the quicker and loftier their own rise. Again, though the profit-motive can easily make men greedy, its absence can easily make them lazy. As the old Chinese proverb puts it—'One man will carry two pails of water for himself; two men will carry one pail for their common use; three will carry none for anybody's use.' Human nature is complicated.

Or again the doctrinaire's obsession that men are born equal, and should remain equal, may lead to George Orwell's state where cant proclaims that 'some men are more equal than others'. The cry in Lenin's day was that a man should lose himself in the mass. Yet the reddest days of the Russian Revolution never abolished first-class travel; even then the commissar travelled soft, and the peasant travelled hard; and to-day there seems to be more inequality in the U.S.S.R. than in the West. A few years ago, where an English subaltern got four times as much as a private, a Russian subaltern got a hundred times as much as a private. As another old Chinese proverb put it, 'not even the ten fingers can be equal in length'. Human nature is complicated.

Hence Burke's passion for liberty, which enables human nature freely to realize itself; for history, which teaches us what human nature is, and demands; for tradition and prescription and the venerable institutions of the past, which human nature has slowly and often unconsciously built up, more wisely than it knew, under the slow pressure of time and the long stress of circumstance. You cannot, he felt, build a constitution; as you cannot build an oak. Burke, at his wisest, looks before and after. He considers the long-term point of view, whereas most men, and most politicians, are short-sighted, and cannot see beyond yesterday, or beyond to-morrow. Burke remembered history: that is partly why history has remembered him.

At his best, he has moments not unworthy to recall the Antigone of Sophocles, in her noble vindication of those ancient and unwritten laws that short-sighted autocrats fondly dream they can override—

> It was not God that gave me such commandments,
> Nor Justice, consort of the Lords of Death,
> That ever laid on men such laws as these.
> Nor did I hold that in your human edicts
> Lay power to override the laws of God,
> Unwritten, yet unshaken—laws that live
> Not from today, nor yet from yesterday,
> But always—though none knows how first made known.[1]

To sum up, Burke's liberal side seems, though too limited, often admirable; but his conservative side (which more and more dominates his final phase), though sometimes wise, seems often arbitrary.

When Burke champions the liberties of America against English insolence; the liberties of Irish trade, Irish Catholicism, African negroes, or English Dissent against English greed or intolerance; the liberties of India against English rapine; the liberties of Members of Parliament against domineering constituents—then one can whole-heartedly applaud. Here his liberalism seems not only generous, but prophetically far-seeing, as he gropes forward towards

---

[1] *Antigone*, 450-7. Cf. Burke's actual words against Warren Hastings: 'We are all born in subjection... to one great, immutable, pre-existent Law, prior to all our devices, and prior to all our contrivances, paramount to all our ideas, and all our sensations, antecedent to our very existence, by which we are knit and connected in the eternal frame of the Universe, out of which we cannot stir.' (This too, however, grows rather 'metaphysical'; the real 'unwritten laws' seem to me those of human psychology.)

something like the British Commonwealth. For his plan for America was 'to mark the legal competency of the colony assemblies for their support of their government in peace, and for public aids in time of war'; and his plan for Ireland, as summarized by Dr Laurence, was to make her a sort of dominion that, 'with the entire and absolute power of local legislation, as she now enjoys it, should be bound in impartial questions of peace and war . . . to stand or fall with the fortunes of Great Britain'.

On this liberal side of Burke the most questionable element is perhaps his conviction that George III, in his first years as King, was pursuing a dark, nefarious, Machiavellian plot to subvert the British constitution; whereas the King's attempt to use his patronage and influence to support his ministers, instead of leaving that influence in the hands of some Whig peer like Newcastle, appears to have been perfectly constitutional. With the collapse of Jacobitism the distinction between 'Whig' and 'Tory' had grown ghostly. Politics had degenerated, rather, into an arena where not so much parties as gangs of politicians battled, not for principles, but for office and the spoils of office. Righteous indignation that the King too should use his patronage to uphold ministers he approved was perhaps as misplaced as the righteous indignation of Napoleon at the 'unfairness' of the Russians in burning Moscow. George III was to prove a muddle-headed, meddlesome disaster to England; but there seems little ground for Burke's picture of him as plotting to subvert ancient English liberties. King George was often a fool; but modern historians pronounce him to have been, on the whole, a quite legal fool.

In certain other directions, however, Burke's liberalism degenerated into a narrow and inadequate conservatism. In 1792 he opposed relief for the disabilities of Unitarians. For he had come to associate Dissent with Jacobinism. And this champion of freedom had long been intolerant towards free-thinkers. 'They are never, never,' he warned the Commons, 'to be supported, never to be tolerated.' And with his notions about the wickedness of even speaking to them he makes himself no less ludicrous than the 'great and in many respects good man' in Ireland at whom he smiles for demanding, in an advertisement for a blacksmith, that it must be a *Protestant* blacksmith.

In the struggle of Wilkes against Government and King, Burke's

Annual Register (1764) condoned the use of general warrants (where no individual was named for arrest) as 'nothing more than an irregularity'—'a loose office form, which had been constantly practised from the Revolution'. Now no doubt Wilkes *had* offended 'against decency and sober morals'. But that was not the point. Chatham and Camden seem to me far wiser than Burke in seeing what a menace general warrants could become. Indeed, it might be argued that more was really done for individual liberty in England by the cynic Wilkes than by the idealist Burke, who could accept general warrants just because he thought them sufficiently traditional.

Again, the reader who turns from Burke to the Hammonds' *Village Labourer* and *Industrial Labourer*, or even to the poetry of Goldsmith or Crabbe, is left wondering that, even allowing for the limitations of his time, he thought so little of that economic liberty from wage-slavery which remains far more important to the masses than even political liberty. Burke might wax righteously indignant over the extortion from the Americans of 3d. a pound on tea, or over the plundered peasantry of Hindustan; but he seems to have thought far less of the overburdened poor in his own country. Johnson was told by a former High Constable of Holborn that he underestimated in supposing more than a thousand wretches to die yearly in London of hunger or malnutrition. In some East End parishes the infant mortality is said to have reached at times 100 per cent. The mother of James Lackington, the bookseller, for years together worked nineteen or twenty hours a day to support her eleven children, since her drunken husband would not; sometimes she was still spinning an hour before childbirth. She was not unique. Weavers in Lyons might toil seventeen hours a day; but Burke's sympathies went out to Marie Antoinette.

This may seem the more strange because a passage in his early work does put the case of the poor with considerable vehemence.

> 'I suppose that there are in Great Britain upwards of an hundred thousand people employed in lead, tin, iron, copper, and coal mines; these unhappy wretches scarce ever see the light of the sun; they are buried in the bowels of the earth; there they work at a severe and dismal task, without the least prospect of being delivered from it; they subsist upon the coarsest and worst sort of fare; they have their health miserably impaired, and their lives cut short, by being perpetually

confined in the close vapour of these malignant minerals. An hundred thousand more at least are tortured without remission by the suffocating smoak, intense fires, and constant drudgery necessary in refining and managing the products of those mines. If any man informed us that two hundred thousand innocent persons were condemned to so intolerable slavery, how should we pity the unhappy sufferers, and how great would be our just indignation against those who inflicted so cruel and ignominious a punishment!'

But—stranger still—this passage from the *Vindication of Natural Society* (published 1756) is meant merely as an ironical *reductio ad absurdum* of Bolingbroke. For Bolingbroke had upheld natural against revealed religion, because of the abuses of the Church; and Burke is here retorting that one might as well uphold a state of nature against civilized society, on the ground that civilization, too, entails inevitable abuses. For him, with all their vices and failings, both revealed religion and civilized society remain the best that men can hope to find in this imperfect world. The opposite conclusion to Rousseau's.

But the victims of civilized progress might here, with some excuse, have found Burke a little too philosophic at their expense. Economics, indeed, he regarded as his speciality. At the beginning of his career, he says, he had decided that our greatness rested on our constitution and on our commerce. 'Both of these I have spared no study to understand, and no endeavour to support.'

All honour to his labours. Yet one may feel somewhat chilled by the frosty fatalism of his *Thoughts and Details on Scarcity* (1795). 'To provide for our necessities is not in the power of Government. . . . Numbers in their nature imply poverty.' Even a massacre of the few rich, 'would not give a bit of bread and cheese for one night's supper to those who labour.'

True, no doubt. And yet . . . After all, when one recalls Fox's gambling debts running into six figures, or the Duchess of Devonshire's approaching seven, or the remarks of airy plutocrats that one could manage to 'jog along' on £40,000 a year, there seems a touch of complacency about Burke's readiness to lay poverty and hunger on the broad shoulders of 'Divine Providence', and to emphasize that 'it is not in breaking the laws of commerce, which are the laws of nature, and consequently the laws of God, that we are to place our hope of softening the Divine displeasure to remove any

calamity under which we suffer'. One is too much reminded of four
ironic lines of Pope.

> 'God cannot love,' (says Blunt with tearless eyes)
> 'The wretch he starves,'—and piously denies.
> But the good bishop, with a meeker air,
> Admits, and leaves them, Providence's care.

Here, indeed, Burke seems to me at moments positively foolish.
He actually argues that agricultural wages will automatically be fair,
because 'in the case of the farmer and the labourer, their interests are
always the same, and it is absolutely impossible that their free contracts can be onerous to either party. . . . It is plainly more the farmer's interest that his men should thrive, than that his horses should
be well fed, sleek, plump, and fit for use, or than that his waggon
and ploughs should be strong, in good repair, and fit for service.'
A strange confidence, surely. As if the labourer, like the horse, were
the farmer's property!—as if, when his wage-slave died, the farmer
had to buy another, instead of simply hiring a new victim! And so
—after some equally curious praise of the poor man's gin as 'a medicine for the mind'—one reaches Burke's characteristic conclusion—
'My opinion is against an overdoing of any sort of administration,
and more especially against this most momentous of all meddling
on the part of authority: the meddling with the subsistence of the
people.' Poverty, in short, is an act of God. This is the sort of piety
that provoked Lenin's 'religion is the opium of the people.' Though
one might retort—'So is Leninism'.

Nor is it a sufficient excuse to say that everyone then thought like
Burke. They did not. 'In the name of God,' he writes to a correspondent in 1796, with that fondness for dragging in the deity which
seems to me one of the less admirable features of his political
thought, 'what is the meaning of this project of Mr Pitt's concerning the further relief of the Poor? What relief do they want, except
that which it will be difficult indeed to give, to make them more
frugal or more industrious? I see he's running for popular plates
with Mr Fox.'[1]

[1] And contrast Montesquieu: 'Quelques aumônes que l'on fait à un homme nu dans
les rues ne remplissent point les obligations de l'Etat, qui doit à tous les citoyens une
subsistance assurée, la nourriture, un vêtement convenable, et un genre de vie qui ne
soit point contraire à la santé.' (*Esprit des Lois*, XXIII, xxix.)

Poor Clare complained of Crabbe—unjustly, I think—that he wrote 'like a magistrate'. Clare might more reasonably have said it of Burke's last phase. And yet, personally, Burke was generous. He was always ready to help the needy and the beggared. At Beaconsfield he even went the perilous length of himself compounding pills for the local poor.

None the less, he seems far behind some of his own contemporaries in failing to see how much the explosion in France was due to economic oppression; in forgetting such enormities as the million or more ecclesiastical serfs still subject to the French Church in 1789. 'Of twenty millions of people supposed to be in France,' Jefferson wrote from Paris in 1785, 'I am of opinion there are nineteen millions more wretched, more accursed in every circumstance of human existence, than the most conspicuously wretched individual of the whole of the United States.' Exaggerated? Surely. But even so . . .

No doubt the tendency of men to grow more conservative with age is not merely because they usually grow more timid, and more indolent, and more opulent, than the young; it is also because it takes years of experience to realize fully how much more complicated life is than it looks; how unpredictable are both men and things; how feeble the reason remains in resisting the intoxication of emotions, both conscious and unconscious. The young see better the dangers of going too slowly; the old see better the dangers of going too fast.

In his energy, Burke after sixty was younger than his years; but his mental attitudes had become very old—too like the type of old gentleman who has acquired the simple conviction that all changes are invariably for the worse—'tampering', as Burke called it, 'the odious vice of restless and unstable minds'. Perhaps, indeed, everyone past forty should remember Burke as a constant warning.

Whether Burke was right in his policy of war and no compromise, whether Revolutionary France was as impossible to 'appease' as Nazi Germany, I do not know. But even supposing Burke's policy to have been right, and his propaganda necessary, his tone seems to me wrong—too violent, too hysterical, too fanatical. With the conservatism of a man of sixty he combined the vehement extremism of a youth of twenty.

'In his robust and hopeful prime,' says Acton, 'he was as much opposed to the theory of Progress as when the glory of Europe was extinguished for ever'; and again—'Burke had no conception of the evils of class government, being a defender of antiquity.' (Though here, in fairness, I think one should add—'except in Ireland'.) And so it seems hard to deny that Burke became, before he died, not only a die-hard, but a mystical die-hard—which seems a little absurd. 'The awful Author of our being is the Author of our place in the order of existence; and . . . having disposed and marshalled us by a divine tactick, not according to our will, but according to His, He has, in and by that disposition, virtually subjected us to act the part which belongs to the place assigned us.'

For the Almighty, substitute Marxism, as Marxists are apt to do, and a Marxist orator might say as much—and as little. If one is a determinist, and for 'the Author of our being' substitutes 'the laws of existence', Burke's statement may be ultimately true. But Burke was not a determinist; and, for all practical purposes, his assertion seems to come near asserting the divine right of the *status quo*. It is too much in tune with that edifying hymn—

> The rich man in his castle,
>   The poor man at his gate,
> God made them high and lowly
>   And ordered their estate.

A possible religion; but one should hardly call it after the teacher who told of the needle's eye, and of Dives and Lazarus.

If all the world's happenings are a 'divine tactick', and history is only 'the known march of the ordinary providence of God',[1] one might logically infer it useless, even wrong, to resist even such 'scourges of God' as Attila or Genghiz Khan. Such reasoning recalls the argument the Spanish Inquisition successfully brought against blasting the rocks of the Tagus—that if God had meant the Tagus to be navigable, He would have made it so; or the argument brought against drainage to combat cholera—that if God in His goodness meant us to have cholera, it is impious to thwart Him. The only

---

[1] Contrast Gibbon: 'History, which is indeed little more than the register of the crimes, follies, and misfortunes of mankind.' Both views seem to me extreme; but Gibbon's less so.

logical conclusion would be complete quietism—which was the very last thing Burke wanted. Indeed, as a guide to practical policy it seems hardly more helpful than proclaiming, 'as the old hermit of Prague, that never saw pen and ink, very wittily said to a niece of King Gorboduc, "That that is, is" .'

Politicians who talk about Providence, easily become provoking. It is merely a method of asserting one is right, by calling an infallible witness who, one knows, can never appear. There was force in Labouchère's comment that he would not mind Gladstone's habit of keeping a trump-card up his sleeve, if only he would not pretend the Almighty had put it there. Yet the temptation seems often irresistible. There was once, according to C. R. Fay, a Cambridge Vice-Chancellor who protested against the running of certain excursion-trains thither, on the ground that 'such a proceeding would be as displeasing to Almighty God as it is to the Vice-Chancellor of the University of Cambridge'. And I can remember a Labour candidate who sent round election-leaflets stating that he and his party 'stood for the Kingdom of God'; to which one could only murmur that it seemed a little greedy to stand for Cambridge as well.

It is this side of Burke that makes me wonder if his great reputation as a political philosopher is really deserved.[1] At times he seems to me, as his reasonableness declines, to typify that general decline of eighteenth-century good sense, in the closing years of the period, into the twilight of Romanticism; where, no doubt new nightingales begin to sing, but there emerge also hordes of bats and owls. Burke on taxing America had typified at moments the eighteenth-century mind at its best—impassioned good sense. But the Burke of the seventeen-nineties is, for me, a degeneration from the Burke of the seventeen-seventies, as Rousseau is a decline from Montesquieu. Chesterfield had been too cold; Burke becomes too heated. The dry light of reason grows blurred with the damp vapours of emotionalism. But of course that, if true, makes Burke, historically, a very interesting type.

Consider a few more of his dicta. 'The individual is foolish; the multitude, for the moment, is foolish, when they act without deli-

---

[1] It should be added, however, that this side of Burke remains still impressive to some modern minds. See, for example, Russell Kirk, 'Burke and the Philosophy of Prescription' in *Journal of the History of Ideas*, XIV (1953), 365-80.

beration; but the species is wise, and, when time is given it, as a species it always acts right.' But is this true? What of dinosaur and dodo? *Their* species seem to have gone wrong somewhere. Where are Neanderthal Man, and the Hittites, and the Mayas, and the Incas?

'Never was there a jar or discord between genuine sentiment and sound policy. Never, no, never did Nature say one thing and Wisdom say another.' But what does 'Nature' really say? Only 'Wisdom' can really hear her. One is left, surely, with tautology.

'We must all obey the great law of change. It is the most powerful law of nature, and means perhaps of its conservation. All we can do, and that human wisdom can do, is to provide that the change shall proceed by insensible degrees.' And again—'A state without the means of some change is without the means of its conservation.' It is certainly a relief to find this high-priest of tradition admitting that everything cannot always remain absolutely static. But do such statements help much? It is dangerous to go too fast—like Turgot, or the Emperor Joseph, of whom the great Frederick drily observed that he always took the second step before the first; it is also dangerous to go too slow, to make changes too little and too late—like the France of the old régime. Such generalities do little towards solving any specific problem.

What, for example, of the fundamental problem of democracy? 'In all disputes,' Burke had said in earlier years (1770), 'between them and their rulers the presumption is at least upon a par in favour of the people. . . . The people have no interest in disorder.' (But sometimes they think they have.) He had been aware, too, of the insidious temptations exerted by power and privilege—'all men possessed of an uncontrouled discretionary power leading to the aggrandisement and profit of their own body have always abused it' (1770). No doubt in his earlier utterances 'people' was far from meaning 'proletariat'. But with growing age there seems to grow also his deep distrust of the 'swinish multitude'. In 1776, when the crown gained the London mob, he concluded that 'one should put as little trust in them as in princes'. And by 1790—'a perfect democracy is the most shameless thing in the world. As it is the most shameless, it is also the most fearless. No man apprehends in his person that he can be made subject to punishment.' If men like hairdressers or working tallow-chandlers, he says in the *Reflections*, are allowed to rule 'either individually or collectively', then 'you are at war with nature'.

It is not surprising, therefore, that Burke opposed electoral reform, when Fox wanted annual parliaments, and the Duke of Richmond manhood suffrage. Very possibly they were going too fast. On the other hand, when the constituency of Old Sarum, deserted since the Reformation, could consist of a rubicund old gentleman, returning two members, while Sheffield, Birmingham, and Manchester returned none; when more than three hundred members of a House of Commons numbering less than six hundred were returned by just over a hundred and sixty persons (including, of course, many peers), one may well ask if Burke was not carrying rather far the English passion for venerable anomalies. But not only did he think the system 'perfectly adequate'; he even thought (1769) it would be 'more in the spirit of our constitution . . . by lessening the number to add to the weight and independency of our voters'! The fewer, the easier, one would have thought, to bribe; a curious avenue to 'independency'!

I suppose that Burke's main feelings were two—first, one must not 'tamper' with the venerable oak of the British Constitution, consecrated by immemorial traditions—let it continue its slow and secular growth; secondly, while it was good that popular opinion, at crises, should be able to boil over, it was desirable to keep it at the bottom of a very deep pot, so that boiling over should be extremely difficult, and extremely rare. It may well be true that much caution was needed in enfranchising the terribly uneducated masses of eighteenth-century England; still one has a feeling that Burke was too inclined, when asked by reformers for a little bread, to offer only a venerable and mossy stone.

What, then, of aristocracy? In earlier years Burke had declared himself no friend to it; viewing it, at most, with 'a cold and decent respect'. Throughout his career he must often have suffered, like Cicero, and like Brougham, as a man of self-made distinction trying to work with men of inherited pride and wealth. And right at the end of his life the Dublin attorney's son could put a Duke of Bedford firmly in his place, with no respect at all. But it was only human that this secretary of Lord Rockingham, daily mixing with noble Whigs, should come by degrees to feel differently. For here, too,

was a group of British oaks, 'green-rob'd senators of mighty woods'. And so he grew to stress the importance of a nation's élite, its 'natural aristocracy'. He may, too, have done a good deal to make some noble persons of his day more public-spirited. And yet one may feel a certain excess of deference in that letter to the Duke of Richmond (1772) where he says of men like himself—'we belly into melons that are exquisite for size and flavour,[1] yet still are but annual plants, that perish with our season, and leave no traces behind us. You, if you are what you ought to be, are in my eye the great oaks[2] that shade a country, and perpetuate your benefits from generation to generation.'

We have changed all that, too. Aristocracies are to-day as obsolete as cavalry. And yet, in fairness, one should remember how many great names in English history have been noble; how much wiser, in some ways, was the Congress of Vienna than the Treaty of Versailles; how much less sense, even to-day, is often talked in the House of Commons than in the House of Lords.

But, when all is said, if it is political philosophy one wants, I should have thought there was far less to be learned from Burke than from Montesquieu, or de Tocqueville, or Marx. To what do Burke's general principles amount? Respect tradition. But how *much*? Change slowly. But *how* slowly? Recognize that inequality, in wealth and in status, is inevitable. But how *much* inequality? With such generalities most men, except rabid revolutionaries and levellers, would agree: but about the really difficult problem—their practical application—men continue passionately to disagree. Finally we are told to regard history as a 'divine tactick'; but since in that case Robespierre and Marat are as much part of the 'divine tactick' as Washington or Burke, how are we helped?

What survives from it all? A salutary distrust for political theories (which did not always prevent Burke from propounding political

[1] Not a very happy image?

[2] Burke had a Druid's passion for oaks, with their ancestral dignity and imperceptible growth. Cf. for example, from *Reflections on the Revolution*, 'because half a dozen grasshoppers under a fern make the field ring with their importunate chink, whilst thousands of great cattle reposed beneath the shadow of the British oak,' (it must have been a large one) 'chew the cud and are silent, pray do not imagine that those who make the noise are the only inhabitants of the field.' Even in denying to Boswell that Croft's *Life of Young* was a good imitation of Johnson, Burke reverts to his favourite tree—'it has all the nodosities of the oak without its strength.'

theories himself); a salutary distrust of hasty reformers who uproot long matured traditions and prod sleeping dogs; a salutary detestation for all despotisms, whether of monarchs, or parties, or mobs.

In our time the world is divided between democracies which Burke would have dreaded and revolutionary despotisms that he would have abhorred. Which will prevail, no one knows. The despotisms are odious, but dangerous; the democracies more decent, but in some ways depressing. Can they cope with the increasing complexities of life? When one picks up a popular newspaper, or turns on a popular wireless programme, one may sometimes wonder if it is not fantastic that minds crude enough to take pleasure in such things should be asked to decide the ever more intricate problems of modern politics. Democracy, under such conditions, does not seem a good sort of government—merely the best of a very bad lot. Only, since government is a necessary evil, it remains at least a vital advantage that the governed should be able to change their governors peaceably, before 'the never-ending audacity of elected persons' grows insufferable. Other forms of government seem often at least as stupid; and often much more wicked. But to go further and ask that one should throw one's hat in the air for poor Demos, is rather too much.

Nor can we know how long Demos will reign. The nineteenth century seemed to see the triumphal progress of democracy; but, over much of the world, the twentieth has turned to autocrats, or the rule of oligarchic parties. Possibly the modern world is growing too complex for democratic government; which, in any case, can only work where the common man has more common sense and sense of compromise than the masses often have.

I repeat—for ideas can only hope to spread by constant repetition—that my dream would be rather an aristocracy of human beings, with a proletariat of machines (which cannot suffer), in a vastly less populated world. Modern humanity suffers from galloping elephantiasis. The finest human qualities are endangered, because the size of populations increases, and ought to be diminished; the size of states increases, and ought to be diminished; the size of cities increases, and ought to be diminished. Vast communities lead to small individuals; and the real worth of any community lies in the worth of its individuals. We have forgotten what Plato and Aristotle saw, that the best societies should not be too large. Vast democracies cannot keep the virtues of democracy—they become antheaps; still less can they keep the virtues of aristocracy. Ibsen was no snob; but it was Ibsen who told the artisans of Trondheim: 'An aristocratic element must come into our political life, into our parliament, and into our press. . . . I have in mind an aristocracy of character and mind and will. It is that alone that can make us free.' Burke might well have agreed. But all this, if it ever happened, could take another five centuries; perhaps with a period of technocratic barbarism in the interval. Indeed, if the human mania to propagate goes on unchecked, no one can say what worse barbarisms might not intervene in a world over-populated past all control.

But, to return to Burke and the eighteenth century, I do not really see why he is still hailed as a great political thinker—one whose name hereafter, it was recently said, 'may eclipse those of Rousseau and Bentham and Marx'. I think he should be honoured, rather, as a far-sighted and long-term political opportunist, whose strongest principle, when he was wisest, was his scepticism about all theoretical principles.

In practical politics, on the other hand, his intuitions were sometimes keen-eyed. Where so many others were blind, he saw the American Revolution, not as a storm over tea-cups, but as a tempest that could be met only by a generous liberalism. Where so many others were blind, he saw the French Revolution, not as the dawning Heaven of starry-eyed fellow-travellers, like the young Wordsworth and Coleridge, but as the red morning of a civil and religious war for the civilized world. 'They made,' he says truly of the Revolutionary extremists, 'a schism in the whole universe; and that schism extended to almost everything, great and small.' And his words seem strikingly applicable to modern 'Communism' also, when he gives warning that the Revolution's 'hostile amity can be obtained on no terms that do not imply an inability hereafter to resist its designs. . . . It is with an armed doctrine that we are at war. To us it is a Colossus which bestrides our Channel. It has one foot on a foreign shore, the other upon British soil.' He saw, too, very clearly what was really formidable about French Jacobins, as about Russian 'Communists'—that though they were 'full of levity, arrogance, and presumption, without morals, without probity, without prudence', yet they had one quality 'to make them terrible even to the firmest minds'—'one thing, one thing only,—but that worth a thousand—they have energy'. 'Their imagination is not fatigued with the contemplation of human suffering through the wild waste of centuries added to centuries of misery and desolation.'

Again, in the *Reflections* of 1790, he already foretold Napoleon, when Napoleon was only an unknown youth of twenty-one: 'the person who really commands the army is your master; the master (that is little) of your king, the master of your assembly, the master of your whole republic';[1] though here the prescience of that clever woman, Catherine of Russia, was still vivider, when in the next year she wrote to Grimm—'Quand viendra ce César?'—'Si la Révolution Française prend en Europe, il viendra un autre Gengis ou Tamerlan la mettre à la raison.'

Naturally, his intuitions were also often at fault. He was wrong in seeing George III as a schemer for absolutism like Louis Napoleon; but he was right, at least, in seeing also that this royal meddler was a calamitous menace.[2] He was fantastically wrong in seeing Warren Hastings as a man for whom 'Money is the beginning, the middle, and the end of every kind of act'; but he was right is seeing also that British rule in India had led to monstrosities that must be checked.

Secondly, it can justly be pleaded that, even when he was wrong, he did much to raise the general tone of English politics, from a cynical Machiavellianism to something with at least a little more idealism and more conscience. It seems something of a paradox that the individualistic Burke should have been the man to persuade individualistic aristocrats to accept something of party-discipline,

---

[1] But cf. Montesquieu: 'Sitôt que l'armée dépendra uniquement du corps législatif, le gouvernement deviendra militaire.'

[2] The mulish obstinacy of George III comes out well in his own words to Pitt (1797)—'I never assent till I am convinced that what is proposed is right, and then I keep them' [*sic*] '—I never allow that to be destroyed by after thoughts which on all subjects tend to weaken, never to strengthen, the original proposal.' Unlike Wellington, George III did not know when to retreat. He found it hard to change his mind, because he had not enough mind to change. Contrast Wilberforce's praise of Pitt 'for magnanimity which made him ready to change his measures when he thought the good of the country required it, though he knew he should be charged with inconsistency on account of the change.'

in an age when politicians had so largely and so long fought for themselves as anarchically as medieval barons; and, in a Parliament of unstable and opportunist gangs, should have welded the Rockingham Whigs, through years of frustration, into an Opposition with certain principles. Contrast Henry Fox to Rockingham—'You think you can but serve the country by continuing a fruitless Opposition. I think it impossible to serve it at all except by coming into office.'[1]

Ironically enough, Burke was himself to split the party he had done so much to make, over the French Revolution. But that too was for principles. And what Burke had done for principles before and during the Revolution in America, Charles Fox continued to do during the Revolution in France.

Speeches like Burke's, even if they often bored the House, must have helped to make political thought and conduct less squalid and self-seeking, both inside and outside Parliament. One can understand his bitterness when what he felt should be a crusade against Jacobinism, degenerated, as crusades are apt to do, into grabbings of territory by our continental allies, of colonies and sugar-islands by ourselves. 'A war for the Scheldt!' he cried. 'A war for a chamberpot.' The phrase illustrates that crude extravagance which is one of his blemishes. But one can understand.

And yet, though Burke seems to me distinguished rather for practical insight than for theoretical profundities, even his practical effectiveness was constantly frustrated by two defects. First, he seems more concerned to confute than to convince; to triumph than to persuade. He would make a great speech, and find that its own reward; without considering enough whether he was really forwarding to the utmost, in practice, the success of his policy, and his party, in the House of Commons. Yet, after all, the object of political oratory is not to produce masterpieces, but to persuade and get things done.

Secondly, he seems to me to have defeated himself at times by a growing lack of moderation, balance, and restraint. Not long ago Mr G. M. Young[2], whose opinion on any subject is worth having, portrayed Burke as more of a wild man than it is conventional to

---

[1] Quoted in Winston Churchill, *History of the English-speaking Peoples*, III, 143.
[2] British Academy Lecture, 1943.

do. He even suggested that Burke's nearest counterpart in the eighteenth century was, despite all their differences, Rousseau. 'The wild beast of the desert,' he aptly quotes, 'shall also meet with the wild beast of the island: and the satyr shall cry to his fellow.'

The comparison would have moved Burke to fury. It could not be pressed far, without bursting. But it is hard not to feel that Burke might have been far more effective in practice—not if he had been less passionate; for his passion was the source of his energy—but if he had kept more control of it.[1] For repeatedly in his later years he would affect one far more if he said less.

For example—'In the long series of ages which have furnished the matter of history never was so beautiful and so august a spectacle presented to the moral eye as Europe afforded the day before the Revolution in France.'

Now, even if one likes the 'moral eye', one may find this rather astonishing. Poland had been torn asunder in 1772, and was waiting to be torn asunder again in 1793. The year 1788 saw George III mad, the squabbles of the Regency Bill, revolt in the Austrian Netherlands, war between Sweden and Russia, war between Turkey, Russia, and Austria. Burke's talk of 'beautiful and august spectacles' becomes chilling hyperbole.

Similarly when one is told that 'the unhappy Louis XVI was a man of the best intentions that probably ever reigned'; or that the French clergy of the old régime were, as 'we now know', 'the most discreet, gentle, well-tempered, conciliatory and pious persons who in any order probably existed in the world', not even the iteration of 'probably' leaves most of us with any feeling of probability whatever.[2] Nor does much seem gained by fulminating at the Prince de Conti as 'this mean, stupid, selfish, swinish, and cowardly animal'. Even supposing the Prince *was* all that, this is a naive way of making anyone believe it. Burke forgot that the deadliest bites come from

---

[1] Cf. his early notebook (ed. H. V. F. Somerset), 'The Character of a Good Man': 'his imagination is lively, active, vigorous, quickly taking fire, and generally too powerful for an understanding fitted rather to conspire with it in its excesses than to restrain it.'

[2] Familiar enough is the comment of Louis XVI himself, when Loménie de Brienne was recommended for Archbishop of Paris—'Il faudrait au moins que l'archevêque de Paris crût en Dieu'. And see, for example, the Memoirs of Mme de Boigne.

creatures whose blood is cold—or at least seems so.[1]

Such violences damaged in Burke not only the politician but also the artist. It is time to consider him in this light too.

In some quarters Burke's art, like his thought, has been extolled with what seems to me a touch of Burke's own extravagance. Mackintosh and Montalembert could couple him with Shakespeare; Macaulay, with Milton. Hazlitt and Leslie Stephen thought his prose unsurpassed. Matthew Arnold, launching into a type of superlative that seems to me almost always foredoomed to folly, called him 'our greatest English prose-writer'. How can a rational mind draw up such orders of merit? There are too many different kinds of prose, with different requirements; too many different kinds of reader, also with different requirements. Still, all this makes an impressive chorus of acclamation for Burke's literary powers.

About Burke as orator, the verdict of the past becomes much more critical and conflicting. Remarkable he clearly must have been. His rise from Irish obscurity to the most famous place among English orators speaks for itself. And the enthusiasm of some of his hearers for some of his speeches was unstinted. Even his maiden speech impressed even Chatham. Mrs Montagu could write, during the debates on the Stamp Act, 'Mr Burke spoke divinely, yes divinely, don't misunderstand me, and report he spoke as well as mortal man can do, I tell you he spoke better.' Hearing him on American Taxation, Lord John Townshend exclaimed—'Heavens! what a man this is! Where could he acquire such transcendent powers!' Even the calm Malone could write of his 'most masterly manner' and 'most consummate art'; even the critical Gibbon, himself a target of Burke's economical reforms, deeply admired his speech on the subject—'I can never forget the delight with which that diffusive and ingenious Orator was heard by all sides of the House'. We are told that, on the use of Indians in the American war, he drew tears from the whole Commons—that his denunciations of

---

[1] It is worth contrasting the considered judgement of the wise and moderate de Tocqueville: 'Some good people have tried to rehabilitate the *Ancien Régime*. I judge it by the feelings it inspired in those who lived under it, and destroyed it. I see that all through the Revolution, cruel as it was, hate for the old régime outweighed all other hates; and that throughout the dangerous vicissitudes of the past sixty years the fear of its return has outweighed all other fears. That is enough for me.' It is enough for a good many of us.

Hastings, at one point, 'did not leave a dry eye in the whole assembly'. Which means, I suppose, that quite a lot of people wept. To Mrs Siddons, at the Hastings trial, he seemed to outdo the stage itself: Mrs Sheridan he threw into a fit. True, eighteenth-century ladies swooned easily. Sheridan on Hastings threw Mrs Siddons herself into a swoon; and one may recall the two characters in Jane Austen's *Love and Freindship* who 'fainted alternately' on a sofa. Whether or no any rational person would wish to produce all this weeping and swooning, the evidence is clear that Burke's oratory had effectiveness of a certain kind in a high degree.

And yet there is evidence also for serious defects. First, his manner was ungraceful. He was handicapped by a harsh voice, an Irish brogue (though *that*, in some, can be charming), ungainly gestures, and wobbly spectacles. Already at Trinity, Dublin, his faults of utterance had been noted. The minutes of its Historical Club record (April 28th, 1747): 'Burke receives thanks for the matter of his oration' (to the Genoese) 'but not for the delivery of it.' And this deficiency seems never to have been wholly overcome. Moore speaks of Burke's 'genius', with its 'superb plumage, glittering all over with the hundred eyes of fancy'; yet this peacock's gait, he adds, was 'heavy and awkward, and its voice seemed rather to scare than attract'.

All this becomes very surprising, when we consider the vital importance, to the orator, of delivery—which Demosthenes thought the most important thing of all. For, most mysteriously, in the mouth of a skilful speaker the driest, deadest leaves can seem transformed to a glitter of fairy jewels of speech. Manner can be far more important than matter. We may recall how the young Demosthenes himself, going home in gloom after an unsuccessful speech to the Athenian assembly, was followed by the actor Satyrus, who bade him declaim some passage of Sophocles or Euripides, then repeated the same passage himself with such skill of expression and gesture that it was utterly transformed. However it remains all the greater tribute to Burke's matter that it could triumph despite his manner.

Secondly, he was too excitable. He did not, said Rogers, 'do himself justice as a speaker: his manner was hurried, and he always seemed to be in a passion.' Indeed, he too often *was* in a passion; so that his friends might have to drag him down by his coat-tails. The story is familiar of his crowning a denunciation of Jacobinism by flinging on the floor of the House a dagger like a carving-knife; only to have this sublime effect made ridiculous by the ironic voice of Sheridan, inquiring 'Where's the fork?'

Such hysteria could lead to lapses not only from sense, but also from taste. In 1788, for example, Burke stormed at Pitt for maintaining that George III, though mad, was still unquestionably on the throne. Pitt, he said was 'making a mockery of the King, putting a crown of thorns on his head, and a reed in his hand, and dressing him in the purple to cry "Hail, King of the British".' Both as politics and as art, the parallel was felt to be itself almost crazy. Burke also sickened the House by discharging volumes of information compiled from lunatic case-histories to show that, even if the King recovered, he would be capable of any enormity, even murder. No wonder he was shouted down. This was no sane way to discuss madness. He was glibly talking of things he could not possibly know. And the motive was no more creditable than the result. For this righteous indignation was really inspired by the eagerness of the Opposition to see their patron, the future Prince Regent, hoisted speedily into the saddle, so that he might haul them up after him.

Nor was this an isolated lapse of taste.[1] Burke could treat the eighteenth-century House of Commons to imagery so coarse that even those strong men were left silent.

There are indeed two types of orators, as of actors—those who are themselves swept away by emotion; and those who are not. Both types can triumph. Hitler could work multitudes into a frenzy by working himself into one, smashing innumerable spectacles behind his back in the process. Yet success is also gained by cold-blooded orators, like Shakespeare's Mark Antony; or even like Horatio Bottomley in the First War, who would cast an appraising eye over the assembled thousands, weighing whether they were numerous

---

[1] Cf. what seems to me a touch of crudity in Burke's remark to Hannah More in 1788 on the multitude of books about the dead Johnson—'How many maggots have crawled out of that great body!' It recalls the comment of the Attic orator Demades on rumours of Alexander's death—'Were he dead indeed, by now the whole world would have smelt of his corpse.' Such epigrams may get themselves remembered; but not always to the credit of their authors. Even the unsqueamish Wilkes found in Burke's oratory a want of taste—a tang of whisky and potatoes. (Boswell's *Johnson*, iv, 104.)

enough to be worth his stock purple-patch on 'the Prince of Peace'.

This cooler type of actor or orator is far more reliable. Those who lose themselves in their parts may sometimes be tremendous; but sometimes they may get badly lost, on days when inspiration fails, or they are off colour, or something disconcerting occurs.

Thirdly, Burke was prolix. We hear of him speaking for five hours. True, others have done it. Palmerston on a famous occasion spoke for five hours; Mr Khrushchev has spoken for six. (And one need not count filibustering senators in U.S.A.) But such feats seem ridiculous; so does any system that permits them. The object of speaking is to convince. But such verbosity exhausts rather than convinces; overwhelms rather than persuades. It is less oratory than vanity. Lord Abinger was wise, I feel, in refusing at the bar to exceed half an hour in his final speech—after that, 'if I drive into the heads of the jury important matter, I drive out matter more important that I had previously lodged there'. Unfortunately few men love brevity; many, the sound of their own ideas. That can often be seen at public dinners, which are apt to be spoilt for the speakers, because they are going to speak; and for everyone else, because they cannot stop speaking.

'Is the House up?' a member asked George Selwyn, whom he met leaving the Chamber. 'No. But Burke *is*.' My sympathies go to Lord North who, when reproached by some orator for being asleep, wearily replied—'I wish to God I were.'

Fourthly, Burke seems to have been not only too prolix, but also too profound; not only too long, but also too deep, too philosophical, too elaborate. Just as his literature tended to be too oratorical, his oratory tended to be too literary. Hence he was often better to read than to hear. Baron Erskine was once so bored by Burke that he crept along under the benches to escape; yet afterwards he thumbed the published speech to pieces. Burke's oration on the Nabob of Arcot's debts was thought by Pitt and Grenville not worth a reply; yet, printed, it roused the public. This defect too did not escape the keen smile of Goldsmith when he twitted his friend and fellow-Irishman—

Who, too deep for his hearers, still went on refining,
And thought of convincing, while they thought of dining.

These seem the four main charges brought (whether justly or no) against Burke's genius as orator—lack of grace, lack of restraint, lack of brevity, lack of simplicity. It was these, at least, that made many members think him a bore, cough him down, call him 'the Dinner-bell'. Not only was Fox more effective in debate; it was Sheridan's speech on the Begums of Oudh that men remembered as the most astonishing of Parliamentary speeches; it was to hear Sheridan's impeachment of Warren Hastings that English society bought seats at even fifty guineas apiece. Sheridan, indeed, once observed to Rogers—'When posterity read the speeches of Burke, they will hardly be able to believe that, during his lifetime, he was not considered as a first-rate speaker, not even as a second-rate one.' Sheridan may have been jealous; but neither he nor Rogers was a mere fool.

'Fox,' said Thurlow, 'speaks to the House of Commons, Burke speaks to himself.' And Flood shrewdly remarked of him to Lord Charlemont: 'He is always brilliant to an uncommon degree, and yet I believe it would be better he were less so. . . . Fox . . . makes use of Burke's speech as a repertory, and by stating crabbedly two or three of those ideas that Burke has buried under flowers, he is thought almost always to have had more argument.'

Horace Walpole in his *Memoirs* is more explicit still (and, I suspect, not far wrong):

> 'He was so fond of flowers, that he snatched them, if they presented themselves, even from Ovid's *Metamorphoses*. . . . Aiming always at the brilliant, and rarely concise, it appeared that he felt nothing really but the lust of applause. His knowledge was infinite, but vanity had the only key to it;[1] and though no doubt he aspired highly, he seemed content when he had satisfied the glory of the day, whatever proved the event of the debate. This kind of eloquence contented himself, and often his party; but the House grew weary at length of so many essays. Having come too late into public life, and being too conceited to study men whom he thought his inferiors in ability, he proved a very indifferent politician—the case of many men I have known, who have dealt too much in books or a profession.'

Here Boswell, for once, agrees with Walpole. After hearing

---

[1] This at least seems highly exaggerated.

Burke in the House, 'it seemed to me however that his Oratory rather tended to distinguish himself than to assist his cause. There was amusement instead of persuasion. It was like the exhibition of a favourite Actor.'

Finally there is Hazlitt's concurring verdict, that Burke was really 'out of place in the House of Commons'. 'Chatham's oratory was calculated to make men *act*; Burke's to make them *think*.'[1]

Perhaps these supposed blemishes should be regarded as mere spots on the sun. Whether we should like Burke's speaking to-day, is another question. We might find him too flowery. (Even in his own day, Hume commented that there was a great deal of flower, a great deal of leaf, and little fruit.) Personally I doubt if I should have found him nearly as impressive as Churchill. But that may be partly a personal antipathy to certain sides of Burke's character—his mysticism, his emotionalism, his exaggeration. And of course a ruthless realist might ask (as Stalin asked 'How many divisions has the Pope?')—how many votes did Burke ever turn?[2] The true answer might be chilling; though the question itself would be too narrow. All the same one asks oneself at times if Burke's thirty years in Parliament was not really a waste and a mistake—if his pen was not mightier than his tongue—if Goldsmith's shrewd innocence was not right yet again when he talked of Burke's giving up to party what should have been given to mankind. However Burke's power as a speaker is merely of historic interest—we cannot hear him; but we can still read him, and the living issue is his power as a writer. This raises the whole question of the place of oratory in literature.

It is not perhaps a very high place; to-day, particularly, after half a century of political phrasing and mouthing, many may feel inclined to echo Verlaine's cry—'take Eloquence, and wring its neck'. But let us not underestimate its powers. Oratory must be one of the oldest of the arts; and must for ages have been one of the most important. The invention of writing dealt it a serious blow: the invention of cheap printing was a blow still more serious. Yet even in our

---

[1] There is a useful summary of contemporary views on Burke's oratory (perhaps a little too favourable) by D. C. Bryant ('Burke's Speaking' in *Studies in Honor of F. W. Shipley*, St Louis, 1942.)

[2] There is interest in Walpole's comment on a speech by Lord Mansfield on *Habeas Corpus*: 'Perhaps it was the only speech that, in my time at least, had real effect; that is, convinced many persons.'

scientific age oratory has proved strangely potent.[1] Without his gift for it Lenin might not have gained domination in Russia. Hitler's power of whipping Germans to mass-frenzy has left its lasting scar on history. Nor let us forget Churchill's telling answers to that frenzy.

As artist, the orator enoys certain advantages. He wields a high potential of emotion. He excites his audience, and is in his turn excited by them. They are present in pulsating flesh and blood before him; while the writer must sit alone in the cold silence of his study.

Again, oratory often enjoys a high degree of actuality. It is usually concerned with matters that interest multitudes, perhaps urgently. There is less risk of that pedantry and unreality which make deserts of many books.

On the other hand, oratory is a dangerous and seducing art. Its business is to persuade crowds. But crowds have less intelligence, and less taste, than even their average as individuals. The orator sets out to shepherd herds of dumb animals. Because the minds of his hearers are partly stupid, partly stupefied, he is tempted to be, not intellectually honest, but sophistical; because their taste is partly vulgar, partly vulgarized, he is tempted to be crude; because he may himself become infected with crowd-psychology, because he is speaking and cannot stop, like a writer, to reconsider, and because he often knows that his words will not stand in black and white to witness against him, he is tempted to inexactitude, exaggeration, flamboyance—to seeming rather than being—to the arts of cheapjack, charlatan, and mountebank. The orator finds it hard not to become an actor.

Hence the discredit which in England at least—more than in Scotland or abroad—has firmly attached itself to the word 'rhetoric'. Still more contemptuous are the associations of the adjective 'rhetorical'. Plato's views are, to me, often unattractive and unconvincing; but I share his deep-rooted distrust of orators.

There is a further drawback to oratory. Political speakers have largely to deal, as some modern writers fondly imagine themselves in duty bound to deal, with matters of the moment. But precisely

[1] With television, of course, oratory may regain still more of its ancient power—whether for better or for worse, is another matter.

what has the most interest for contemporaries may have the least appeal to posterity. To-day's new bread is delicious; but within a few months it will normally have become stale, mouldy, nauseous. The lapse of a year can turn the liveliest actualities into the most unreal of fantasms. The orator is doomed to be often as ephemeral a may-fly as the journalist who toils day after day to write what nobody will want to read next week. Those who are always up-to-date, grow very quickly out-of-date.

Here, indeed, Burke partly escapes because he was concerned with historic events of lasting significance; and also because he kept his eyes less on transient details than on wider, more durable issues.

When read, oratory, like drama, can partly lose and partly gain. The graces of elocution and action are lost.[1] The herd-excitement of a tense audience is lost. The prolixities and repetitions entailed by the need to make stupid hearers understand, grow more offensive. So, usually, does the humour—for oratorical humour tends to be facile and popular. So do the hyperboles and sophistries and inexactitudes.

On the other hand, many speakers (like Burke himself) are not particularly graceful; just as many poets simply do not know how to read their own poetry. Here the silent reader gains. Prolixities, too, may become a little less tedious in print, because men can read faster than they can talk—they can even skip. Profounder excellences, on the other hand, can be more fully taken in.

In this contrast between public performance and private reading oratory seems not unlike drama. The lighter type of play—*The Merry Wives* or *The Alchemist* or *She Stoops to Conquer*—often improves in the theatre. Humour that seems thin on the page can be carried off by the 'business' of competent actors, and the contagious laughter of an audience. But more serious drama, like *Agamemnon* or *Hamlet* or *The Master Builder*, is often better to read. So with oratory. The serious Burke often succeeded better in print.

---

[1] Cf. Garrick:

> Nor Pen nor Pencil can the Actor save;
> The Art, and Artist, share one common Grave!

I think, however, the reader may find that Burke often gains markedly by being read *aloud*.

Yet even so the tediums and exaggerations of rhetoric tend to remain. Most of us, I think, would sooner read the histories of Herodotus or Tacitus than the orations of Demosthenes or Cicero; or the narrative of Thucydides than his speeches. If you would come to know the real Chekhov or Pirandello, you must look, I think, to the intimacy of their short stories rather than to their plays. At all events I cannot read Burke with the zest that quickens the pages of Johnson or Goldsmith, Hume or Montesquieu.

Further, oratory is a dangerous trade. Its bad habits are apt to grow engrained. Even when, in the years of his old age and the French Revolution, Burke turned from speaking to writing, his writing remained oratorical. At moments I ask myself if he might not have written better if he had never spoken at all. True, the best pages of his speeches on America or India are eloquence so magnificent that they should perhaps silence such cavils. Perhaps.

Consider, for example, a famous passage in the *Letters on a Regicide Peace* about the French reception of a British overture: 'I pass by all the insolence and contumely of the performance as it comes from them. The present question is not how we are to be affected with it in regard to our dignity. That is gone. I shall say no more about it. Light lie the earth on the ashes of English pride.' With that blank verse (I do not mind its being blank verse) the paragraph, for me, should have ended. But it does not. It drags on into anticlimax—'I shall only observe upon it *politically*, and as furnishing a direction for our own conduct in this low business.' How bumbling and how dull!

The question whether English dignity was really dead—whether calm reasonableness in the face of arrogance can dishonour anyone, need not for the moment be considered; merely the question of Burke's art. I think he lacked terseness. Even the epitaph he wrote on Garrick (1779) was rejected as too long. It *is*. He should have read Icelandic sagas.

Indeed, as an artist, no less than as a statesman, his great defect seems to me excess—an insufficient sense of measure. This can also be seen, I feel, in the humorous parts of his work. With more humour, he might have had more sense of proportion; with more sense of proportion, he might have had more humour. But, as things are, he trifles ponderously. Even passages that succeeded at the time appear tedious and laboured now.[1] Take, for example, his speech of February 1778 on the British employment of Red Indians against the colonists (already denounced in the previous November by Chatham): 'Suppose the case of a riot on Tower Hill. What would the keeper of His Majesty's lions do? Would he not leave open the dens of the wild beasts, and address them thus: "My gentle lions, my humane bears, my tender-hearted hyenas, go forth against the seditious mob on your mission of repression and retribution; but I exhort you as you are Christians, and members of a civilized society, to take care not to hurt man, woman or child."'

This passage is said to have left Lord North 'almost suffocated by laughter'; but it seems elephantine beside the deadly irony of Franklin on the same bitter theme.[2]

Rather better—indeed, famous—is Burke's persiflage in his speech of 1780 on 'Oeconomical Reform' and the obstacles opposed to it by mouldy anachronisms and sinecures—'Lord Talbot attempted to reform the kitchen; but such, as he well observed, is the consequence of having duty done by one person, whilst another enjoys the emoluments, that he found himself frustrated in all his designs. On that rock his whole adventure split—His whole scheme of oeconomy was dashed to pieces; his department became more expensive than ever;—the civil list debt accumulated—Why? It was truly from a cause, which, though perfectly adequate to the effect, one would not have instantly guessed;—It was *because the turnspit in the king's kitchen was a member of parliament.* The king's domestic servants were all undone; his tradesmen remained unpaid, and became bankrupt—*because the turnspit of the king's kitchen was a member of parliament.* His majesty's slumbers were interrupted, his pillow stuffed with thorns, and his peace of mind entirely broken,—

---

[1] Perhaps Burke laboured on his style at times too much. Charles Butler who visited him in 1791 records that every page of his manuscripts, and again of his first proofs, was so corrected as to be 'almost a blot'. Tom Paine was told by a Piccadilly bookseller, with regard to the *Reflections on the Revolution*, that Burke 'had revised some of the sheets, six, seven, and one nine times!' True, such relentless labour by a writer is sometimes just what gives a sense of delightful ease to the reader. But that appearance of effortless grace which Chekhov once commended to Gorky seems to me very rare in Burke. (An interesting rough sketch of his for parts of the *Reflections* has been published, from the Fitzwilliam-Burke papers, in the *Durham University Journal*, XLV (1953), 114-9. Other revisions in *English*, II, 324-40.)

[2] P. 244.

because the king's turnspit was a member of parliament. The judges were unpaid; the justice of the kingdom bent and gave way; the foreign ministers remained inactive and unprovided; the system of Europe was dissolved; the chain of our alliances was broken; all the wheels of government at home and abroad were stopped;—*because the king's turnspit was a member of parliament.*'

This too has been extolled as a masterpiece of persiflage; but, I think, too charitably. Because it is too exaggerated, my confidence in it fails; because it is too prolix, my patience.

Further, Burke's art tended to be not only excessive in words, in emphasis, in vehemence but also, I feel, excessive in ornament—especially as his style grew more purple with age. He once laid it down as a principle that a key-passage should contain three things—a thought, an image, and a sentiment. This seems partly obvious. For if the passage contained no thought, it could hardly be intelligent; if it contained no feeling, it could not be art; it is only his stress on the third ingredient—imagery—that interestingly marks in Burke the prose-poet. But I still feel that his images, too, tend to grow over-elaborate. Take, for instance, the close of that passage which by his own account cost him most labour (which need not, of course, make it his best—far from it). It comes in his reply to the Duke of Bedford's attack on his pensions—that *Letter to a Noble Lord,* which quite reasonably points out that it was folly for a Duke of Bedford, fat with the public grants lavished on his ancestors, to attack Burke, the champion of private property; to play Philippe Egalité; and to flirt with confiscatory Jacobins.

'Such are *their* ideas; such *their* religion, and such *their* law. But as to *our* country and *our* race, as long as the well compacted structure of our church and state, the sanctuary, the holy of holies of that antient law, defended by reverence, defended by power, a fortress at once and a temple,[1] shall stand inviolate on the brow of the British Sion—as long as the British monarchy, not more limited than fenced by the orders of the state, shall, like the proud Keep of Windsor, rising in the majesty of proportion, and girt with the double belt of it's kindred and coeval towers, as long as this awful structure shall oversee and guard the subjected land—so long the mounds and dykes of the low, fat Bedford level will have nothing

[1] *Templum in modum arcis.* Tacitus of the temple of Jerusalem.

to fear from all the pickaxes of all the levellers of France. So long as our sovereign lord the king, and his faithful subjects, the lords and commons of this realm—the triple cord, which no man can break; the solemn, sworn, constitutional frank-pledge of this nation; the firm guarantees of each other's being, and each other's rights; the joint and several securities, each in it's place and order, for every kind and every quality of property and dignity—As long as these endure, so long the Duke of Bedford is safe: and we are all safe together—the high from the blights of envy and the spoliations of rapacity: the low from the iron hand of oppression and the insolent spurn of contempt. Amen! and so be it; and so it will be,

Dum domus Aeneae Capitoli immobile saxum
Accolet; imperiumque pater Romanus habebit.'

Strange how tastes have changed! To-day a man would no more write a pamphlet so rhetorically than he would compose a leading-article in rhyme, or sing in the House of Commons.

But, even allowing for changes of taste, the pomp seems to me a little hollow, the art a little too unconcealed. One recalls the days when Burke had been less enthusiastic about 'our sovereign lord the king'; and as for the English poor being so free 'from the iron hand of oppression and the insolent spurn of contempt', that is not quite the impression we gain from some contemporary writers, such as the young poet so generously helped a few years before by Burke himself—George Crabbe.

Burke's style in passages like this has travelled far from Attic simplicity— at times, deep into Asia; and one may be more moved by the previous page where, in simpler, shorter sentences, Burke forgets some of his anger against the Duke in sorrow for his own dead son. 'The storm has gone over me; and I lie like one of those old oaks which the late hurricane has scattered about me. I am stripped of all my honours; I am torn up by the roots, and lie prostrate on the earth! There, and prostrate there, I most unfeignedly recognize the divine justice, and in some degree submit to it. But whilst I humble myself before God, I do not know that it is forbidden to repel the attacks of unjust and inconsiderate men. The patience of Job is proverbial. After some of the convulsive struggles of our irritable nature, he submitted himself, and repented in dust and ashes. But even so, I do not find him blamed for reprehending, and with a considerable degree of verbal asperity, those ill-natured neighbours of his, who visited his dunghill to read moral, political, and economical lectures on his misery. I am alone. I have none to meet my enemies in the gate. Indeed, my Lord, I greatly deceive myself, if in this hard season I would give a peck of refuse wheat for all that is called fame and honour in the world.' (There, I feel, Burke should have closed his paragraph; but there are still thirteen lines more, far less effective.)

And even this rings a little too elaborately. I am not sure that Johnson did not know better how to answer noble lords. Indeed, looking back over the world's literature, one may wonder if there is not often more real eloquence to be found in poets and novelists than in the orators themselves—when, for example, Clytemnestra greets the returning Agamemnon; or Antony rouses his rabble in the Forum; or Milton's devils hold debate in Pandemonium. Here, for example, is a petty robber-baron, far remoter from us than Burke, far more ignorant, far less public-spirited; protesting his right, not to a pension, but to a slave-girl whose very possession I suppose moralists would pronounce immoral. And yet how the words of Achilles ring out and stab home![1]

> What gained I then from the travail whereto my soul was steeled?—
> From hazarding my life upon the battlefield?
> As a bird that brings each morsel that ever she finds, to fill
> The beaks of her unfledged nestlings, and fares herself but ill,
> So have I too watched sleepless, many and many a night,
> And filled my days with bloodshed, matching myself in fight
> With desperate men defending the wives they left at home.
> Twelve cities have I sacked now, with my ships, beyond the foam,
> And in the fertile marches of Troy eleven more;
> Many a costly treasure I plundered there, and bore
> To Atrīdes, lying easy by the swift ships of our host—
> He took them, and gave some few away, and kept the most.
> Yet the gifts he gave to honour the other chiefs and kings,
> At least are not snatched from them! But her whom I loved he wrings
> From me alone of Achæans. So be it! Let him take

Iliad, IX, 321-45, 375-92, 401-9; *Greek Poetry for Everyman*, 32-4.

His pleasure, lying by her! Yet why do the Argives make
War, then, on Troy? What made the son of Atreus bring
Our people hither, if not fair Helen's ravishing?
Is it only the Atrīdae, of all men born on earth,
That love their wives! Ah no! Any man with heart of worth
Loves the woman he makes his own—as *I* held dear,
With all my heart, Brīsēis, though I won her with my spear.
But now that he has deceived me and grasped his gift again,
Let him not tempt me further. I know him. His words are vain. . . .
He has wronged me, he has tricked me, he shall not fool me still
With words—let once suffice him! Let him run now, at his will,
To ruin! Since Zeus in His wisdom has surely crazed his wit.
I loathe his gifts; and his greatness—I care not a straw for it!
Ten times his wealth he can offer, or twenty times—in vain!—
Ay, twenty times the treasure that he has, or hopes to gain—
Nay, all the wealth that enters Orchómenus' treasury,
Or comes to Thebes in Egypt, of all the towns there be
The richest (for a hundred are its gates, and from each one
With chariots and horses two hundred warriors run).
Not even with gifts like the dust, like the sand in multitude,
Shall King Agamemnon have power to melt my mood,
Until he has paid to the utmost for the wound he dealt my pride.
Nor yet will I take the daughter of Atreus' son for bride;
Not though she vied in beauty with the golden Queen of Love,
And with flashing-eyed Athene in handicraft she strove—
Not even so would I wed her! For her husband let him try
Some Argive that better suits him, one kinglier than I. . . .
More worth than all is life to me—than all the gold
Men say the fair-set city of Ilios used to hold
Ere came the sons of Achaea, when peace lay on the land;
Or all the hoards that, guarded by his stone-built threshold, stand
In the hall of the Archer Apollo, by Pytho's craggy steep.
For a man may plunder cattle and drive fat flocks of sheep,
And chestnut steeds, and tripods, with gold a man may gain;
But life!—no sword can gain it, to buy it is in vain
For ever, once the spirit between man's lips is fled.

That, even through the mists of translation, seems to me supreme
eloquence. It is spoken through no hollow pompous mask. The
sympathy it wakens is spontaneous and instantaneous: I do not have
to make an effort to sympathize. It comes keen and clear, across

three thousand years, as the sea-wind off the Hellespont, or the cry of the wild birds from Mount Ida—not like the squeak of a quill in a shuttered study.

It may be said that the comparison is unfair. But, for me, unfair or not, it insists on making itself. And I doubt if it is really unfair. Consider this account from a contemporary witness, neither politician nor poet, but still a woman with taste and perception, of the impression made by Burke. Fanny Burney is describing his opening speech against Warren Hastings: 'When he came to his two narratives, when he related the particulars of those dreadful murders, he interested, he engaged, he at last overpowered me; I felt my cause lost. I could hardly keep on my seat. My eyes dreaded a single glance towards a man so accused as Mr. Hastings; I wanted to sink on the floor, that they might be saved so painful a sight. I had no hope he could clear himself; not another wish in his favour remained.'

Then a striking change. 'But when from this narration Mr. Burke proceeded to his own comments and declamation—when the charges of rapacity, cruelty, tyranny, were general, and made with all the violence of personal detestation, and continued and aggravated without any further fact as illustration; then there appeared more of study than of truth, more of invective than of justice; and, in short, so little of proof to so much of passion, that in a very short time I began to lift up my head, my seat was no longer uneasy, my eyes were indifferent which way they looked, or what object caught them; and before I was myself aware of the declension of Mr. Burke's powers over my feelings, I found myself a mere spectator in a public place, and looking all around it, with my opera-glass in my hand!'

How convincing! What an interesting lesson in style! I feel the same about writers like Carlyle or Ruskin, as well as about Burke and oratory. Passion is vital—but, for art, the passion should be, at its wildest, still controlled. Burke lacked that control; just as Byron's more romantic verse lacked it. But Byron's superb letters, and much of his later verse, do not lack it—and how they gain! For, in the long run, passion without a strong sense of fact and a keen sense of irony is apt to become a deadening bore. The moral?—beware of hysteria and histrionics; prefer understatement; and flee prolixity like the plague.

When Gibbon's first volume appeared in 1776, Burke told Reynolds that he much disliked its style, as very affected, mere frippery and tinsel. Gibbon's is doubtless no very natural style; yet it keeps somehow the air of being very natural to Gibbon; and one may vastly prefer it to the floridities of the later Burke. Gibbon seems serenely being himself; Burke appears trying—straining—to impress.

It is also curious that the *Annual Register's* review of Rousseau's *Émile*, perhaps by Burke, taxes Rousseau with what seems to me Burke's own besetting sin: 'He never knows where to stop. He seldom can discover that precise point in which excellence consists, where to exceed is almost as bad as to fall short, and which every stop you go beyond, you grow worse and worse. He is therefore frequently tiring and disgusting by pushing his notions to excess; and by repeating the same thing in a thousand different ways.'

More and more, for Burke at his best, I come back to those speeches on America which are less violent, ornate, tormented, still content with justice, sense, and truth—which, in fine, are still eighteenth-century and not yet Romantic. But in his later manner there seems to me a touch of the extravagance of Beckford's Fonthill Gothic. I prefer the simpler grace of Palladio, or the simpler strength of Norman Romanesque.

Lastly, Burke as a man. His intellectual eminence often deeply impressed his hearers, in conversation as well as in his speeches; though his letters seem to me stilted, stiff, and tedious.[1] He found no Boswell; and *our* Boswell, for some reason, is more apt to extol Burke's brilliance than to illustrate it. Still it remains extraordinary how the Tory Johnson reiterated to the end his praises of this 'Whig dog'. He knew, he said, only two men 'who had risen considerably above the common standard—Lord Chatham and Edmund Burke'. 'His stream of mind is perpetual.' 'No wonder he is the first man in the House of Commons for he is the first man everywhere.' 'What I most envy Burke for is his being constantly the same. He is never what we call humdrum.' 'If Burke should go into a stable to have his horse dressed, the hostler would say—"we have had an extra-

---

[1] The *Times Lit. Sup.* for 30/12/49 published two short notes from Johnson to Burke. They are trifling in subject and importance; yet even these few lines exhibit a virile, common-sense brevity that brings home, I feel, precisely what Burke lacked.

ordinary man here".' 'That fellow calls forth all my powers; were I to see Burke now, it would kill me.'

Johnson's only reserves were, as we have seen, about Burke's wit —"tis low, 'tis conceit',[1] and about his emotional unbalance in politics. 'But,' said Boswell in 1783, 'they represent him as actually mad.' ' "Sir," said he, "if a man will appear extravagant as he does, and cry, can he wonder that he is represented as mad?" '[2]

Grattan, again, spoke of Burke as 'the best talker he had ever known'. 'Like the fabled object of the fairy's favours,' commented Wilberforce, 'whenever he opened his mouth, pearls and diamonds dropped from him.' And Mackintosh pronounced that Gibbon might have been taken from a corner of Burke's mind without anything being missed. One may think this mere idiocy. But its historic interest remains.

Reynolds, again, to the engravings of his portrait of Burke appended Milton's lines on the loyal Abdiel—

> So spake the fervent Angel, but his zeal
> None seconded, as out of season judged,
> Or singular or rash ... unmoved,
> Unshaken, unseduced, unterrified,—
> His loyalty he kept, his love, his zeal.

But Burke, with a fine modesty, insisted on their deletion.

Posterity has at times been no less rapturous. Montalembert called Burke and Shakespeare the two greatest Englishmen; Macaulay once judged Burke 'the greatest man since Milton'.

All this is powerful evidence. Yet I remain unconvinced. Of

---

[1] Cf. p. 131; and Mrs. Thrale's account of Lord Mulgrave's saying at her table, 'So, Burke, you riot in puns now Johnson's away!' 'Burke changed colour and looked like death.' Judging from one of the specimens recorded by Boswell, when Burke, being placed at table next a ham, said 'Now I am Hamburgh' (Ham-Burke), one would have sighed for Johnson's return. Yet the man who loved bandying such idiocies with Boswell could see 'no merit' in *The Beggar's Opera* (it shocked him).

Maybe, of course, the modern contempt for puns is itself merely a fashion. After all, Lamb and even Shakespeare revelled in them. One should not be intolerant. But, even as puns, Burke's efforts seem to me usually poor. (For other horrible examples, see D. C. Bryant, *Burke and his Literary Friends*, pp. 61, 63-4.)

[2] Buckle, indeed, explained away Burke's final phase of anti-Jacobin vehemence on the simple theory that he actually went mad. But Burke, like Brougham, had always been over-excitable; and his hatred of the French Revolution was not really inconsistent with his defence of the American.

Burke's powers as a talker, from the specimens preserved, I have a lingering doubt whether he was not one of those who impress hearers less by what they say than by something hypnotic in their tone. No doubt his knowledge and memory may have been encyclopedic, like Macaulay's.[1] But if we had as much of Burke's talk as we have of Coleridge's, I suspect that—rightly or wrongly—I should find it, like Coleridge's, overrated, disappointing, and immensely inferior to Johnson's.[2]

On Burke the politician, as contrasted with Burke the statesman, verdicts are highly contradictory. There is, on the one hand, the tribute of the Duke of Richmond, 'Burke, you have more merit than any man in keeping us together.' There are, on the other hand, judgements like that of Horace Walpole—'Of all the politicians of talents I ever knew, Burke had the least political art'; or the comment of Fox, after Burke's death, 'After all, Burke was a damned wrong-headed fellow, through his whole life jealous and obstinate.' True, this was when Fox and Burke had quarrelled over France. And if one finds significance in Burke's failure ever to be given any higher office than that of Paymaster-General, it can be pleaded that this is explicable by the reserve of English aristocrats towards a comparatively plebeian Dubliner. But I suspect that this plea is inadequate—that his colleagues felt also a rooted distrust for this figure who might be a genius, but was so difficult, wayward, temperamental. Fox's view is strikingly supported by what Morley quotes as the reply of 'the late Lord Lansdowne'[3] to the question why Burke never reached cabinet-rank—'Burke! He was so violent, so overbearing, so arrogant, so intractable, that to have got on with him in a cabinet would have been utterly and absolutely impossible.'

It was not that Burke lacked party-zeal—on the contrary. One could wish that it had not made him oppose Pitt's scheme for freeing Irish trade in 1785, or his commercial treaty with France,

[1] They were not, naturally, infallible. Burke could mispronounce the Latin word *vectigal* in the House, with the 'i' short; so that Lord North (with an Etonian knowledge of classical quantities) was roused from his slumbers to cry 'For God's sake, *vectīgal*, Mr Burke!' A very eighteenth-century episode.

[2] 'His manner in conversation,' said Malone (who could defend even Burke's wit), 'were it not for the great superiority of his talents and knowledge, would be disagreeable.' (Burke, though generously modest towards Johnson, seems to have been, or become, in general a bad listener.)

[3] Presumably the third Marquis (1780-1863), Shelburne's son.

really because they were Pitt's; or Fox's motion to repeal the disabilities of Dissenters in 1789, because Burke had come to dislike Dissenters' politics. The dead Goldsmith had said it long ago—

And to Party gave up what was meant for Mankind.

But perhaps Burke was rather a great partisan than a good partyman. The violence which could hurl daggers on the floor of the House, or a gilt volume of Navy Expenditure at the Treasury Bench, taking a candle with it on its way, made him a formidable enemy; but they made him also a distrusted ally.

It is dangerously easy to be glib about national characteristics. But perhaps Burke is better understood if visualized always as a certain type of emotional Anglo-Irishman intruded into our more phlegmatic, easy-going English world. We have seen how, though nobly disinterested in many ways, he remained entangled with his own rather squalid Irish clan. 'Burke,' wrote Elliot as late as 1793, 'has now got such a train after him as would sink anybody but himself:—his son who is quite *nauseated* by all mankind; his brother who is liked better than his son, but is rather offensive with animal spirits and with brogue; and his cousin, Will Burke, who is just returned unexpectedly from India, as much ruined as when he went many years ago, and who is a fresh charge on any prospects of power that Burke may ever have. Mrs Burke has in her train Miss French, the most perfect *she-Paddy* that ever was caught. Notwithstanding these disadvantages, Burke is himself a sort of *power* in the State. It is not even too much to say that he is a sort of *power* in *Europe*.'

Certainly the Burke household must have been an odd place, if one can trust Mrs Thrale's descriptions of it as living 'among Dirt, Cobwebs, Pictures, and Statues'—while a negro servant carried tea about with a cut finger wrapped in rags—in short, 'Misery and Magnificence'. ('Burke,' she also says—much more surprisingly, 'was the first man I had ever seen drunk, or heard talk Obscaenely.')

With this touch of Irish Bohemianism went also a strain of Irish vehemence. Fanny Burney describes how delightful Burke still remained in the nineties, so long as he kept off politics; but 'his irritability is so terrible on that theme that it gives immediately to his face the expression of a man who is going to defend himself from murderers'.

I do not think Fanny Burney exaggerated. This fanatical horror which haunted Burke's last years followed him even to the grave. He sternly refused the request of Fox for a final interview of reconciliation; and his body was not laid under its marble slab in Beaconsfield Church, but in a lead coffin elsewhere in the building, for fear it might one day be treated by Jacobins as the Restoration treated the dead Cromwell. A more balanced character would not have thought the danger, even if it existed, worth the fuss. Far wiser the Socrates who smiled at Crito's anxiety over such trifles.[1]

I must own that there are other types of Irishman that I much prefer—the gentle irony of Goldsmith, or the calm, dry irony of Wellington, who seems never to have lost half an hour's sleep even when he had to meet Burke's 'murderers' next day on the open field of battle.

Yet, in fairness, one must remember also the Irish generosity in Burke—how one of the first things he did with his wealth was send the young Irish artist Barry to study in Italy; how he lavished money and kindness on French émigrés, and even on the tiresome Mme de Genlis who, as Burke's guest (in 1785?), so hated the least light in her bedroom that a carpenter had daily to nail boards over every chink; how he dared to defend homosexuals from judicial murder; how, amid the political excitements of 1781, he yet found time and energy to rescue the despairing Crabbe, who, rejected by peers and publishers, by North and Shelburne, Dodsley and Becket, had written Burke a last appeal, then walked all night up and down Westminster Bridge—how Burke got *The Library* published, introduced the young poet to Fox, Reynolds, and Johnson, and had him made curate of Aldborough, then Chaplain to the Duke of Rutland.

If Burke, with his passion for chivalry and the glorious traditions of the past grew at times almost as mad as Don Quixote; if he too sometimes tilted at windmills; still, like Don Quixote, he was nobler and more generous than many calmer and more prudent men. By nature an intellectual and an artist, he yet refused, like the great

---

[1] It is fair to add that Burke expressed this strange wish on July 6, 1797, only three days before he died; so that his mind *might* have been failing. (See B. D. Sarason in *Notes and Queries*, 200 (1955), 69-70.) But Windham found him in full command of his faculties on July 5; and even on the evening of July 8 he had Addison read to him, and discoursed on the grim political situation.

Greeks, to withdraw to sigh in shades; he took his part in the battle for human liberty.

At moments he recalls the Scot Carlyle—with all their differences, there is in both a tendency to hysteria, a self-defeating exaggeration, an excessive inclination to see, wherever convenient, the hand of the Almighty; a pity, yet deep distrust, for the masses; a contempt for the more Philistine boasts of so-called 'Progress'; a passion for what was best in the past; and a passion for righteousness. Probably neither of them would have governed England as well as that completely opposite type, the cynical, jolly Robert Walpole, (who, long before Burke, had sensibly refused to tax America). Yet there is always a tendency for party-politics and international politics to grow too cynical, too Machiavellian. Burke at his best stood, on the one hand, for principle against the Machiavellians; on the other, for practical good sense against the fanatical doctrinaires.

That seems to me his finest claim. In judging Burke it is vital to avoid that exaggeration into which Burke himself was too prone to fall. Gladstone's 'almost divine man' seems to me excessive; Burke was often all too human. Macaulay's 'greatest man since Milton' seems to me likewise excessive; and as excessive in the opposite direction is Macaulay's other dictum—'he generally chose his side like a fanatic, and defended it like a philosopher'. 'Generally . . . like a fanatic' is surely too strong. Macaulay was juster, I think, in a third verdict—'His reason, like a spirit in the service of an enchanter, though spell-bound was still mighty. It did whatever work his passions and his imagination might impose.'

But perhaps the most vivid picture of this Romantic orator comes from the youthful memories of a Romantic poet—Wordsworth.

> Like a hero in romance,
> He winds away his never-failing horn;
> Words follow words, sense seems to follow sense;
> What memory—what logic! till the strain
> Transcendent, superhuman as it seemed,
> Grew tedious even in a young man's ear. . . .
>
> I see him,—old, but vigorous in age,—
> Stand like an oak, whose stag-horn branches start
> Out of its leafy brow, the more to awe
> The younger brethren of the grove.

Wordsworth's praise is not uncritical; it is itself not beyond criticism. For my ear does not much enjoy 'the *more* to *awe*'; and 'the younger brethren of the grove' seem rather anaemic descendants of eighteenth-century convention. None the less, that 'stag-horn oak' towers up in the memory. Burke, lover as he was of imagery, and of historic oaks, might not have been ill-pleased.

BENJAMIN FRANKLIN

Inventas aut qui vitam excoluere per artis,
Quique sui memores alios fecere merendo.

VIRGIL

Men who made life fairer by the arts they brought to
birth,
Whom their fellows yet remember for their service and
their worth.

Ce bon-sens perfectionné, qui est bien plus rare que
l'esprit, et presqu'autant que le génie.

GIBBON

'I, BENJAMIN FRANKLIN, of Philadelphia, printer, late Minister Plenipotentiary from the United States of America to the Court of France, now President of the State of Pennsylvania'—so begins the will drawn up by the old statesman in July 1788, two years before he died.

'Printer . . . Plenipotentiary . . . President'—the wording is typical. Franklin had too much good sense to conceal the inky fingers with which his long career had begun. And he was too human not to feel a just pride in that long ascent from printer to President; too genuine to disguise the just pride that he felt. He had, indeed, left his lasting imprint on the Western Hemisphere. Yet, unlike most great men, and many successful men, he had also succeeded in being happy. Johnson would not have repeated a single week of his own life, not though an angel offered; but Franklin would, he said, have been willing to run through his again—wishing, if possible, to have· an author's privilege of emending certain *errata*; yet ready for a repetition, even were that denied.

Perhaps he lacked imagination; perhaps he would have refused, after all, had it really been possible to live over again. Yet he must have thought what he said; for Franklin was honest. And to have got so much zest from a life of over eighty years is perhaps still more remarkable than for a tallow-chandler's son to have disarmed the lightning, and checkmated a king.

Here, indeed, is a typical sage of the Century of Sense and Prose —yet free from its endemic melancholy, its hypochondria, its spleen. Franklin was not quite as unpoetic as the young Bentham, who watched him on that dramatic day in 1774 when the quiet American was baited in the Cockpit by Wedderburn before ministers and Privy Councillors. Franklin could enjoy the verse of Thomson and Cowper; he could turn out verses of a kind himself; yet his mind remained essentially prosaic, and his strength is the strength of firm-based prose.

Indeed, contemplating his life, one may suspect, like Jane Austen, that *too* deep an absorption in poetry does not often bring much happiness—pleasure, no doubt; at times, even joy; but, perhaps, not much lasting happiness. Poetry can console, enchant, ennoble; it can transfigure the world with the magic of moonlight; but its greatest lovers are seldom the most cheerful or most practical of men—as Franklin *was*.

Nor, though it was his early ambition to become a prose stylist, did Franklin greatly care about even prose literature, or art, for their own sakes. 'And, for one,' he writes, 'I confess, that if I could find in any Italian travels a receipt for making Parmesan cheese, it would give me more satisfaction than a transcript of any inscription from any old stone whatever.' Flaubert might have thought this a perfect gem of bourgeois fatuity.

But at least Franklin was as plain-spoken and downright as his name. And since the world has far more art than any lifetime can cope with, but infinitely less honesty and intelligence than it urgently needs, I am not on that account disposed to disparage him.

Nor did Franklin feel much, apparently, for the loveliness of Nature. It is characteristic that he employed Wordsworth's Derwentwater, not as a theme for poetic feeling, but as a surface to cast oil on, in an experiment for calming troubled waters.[1]

Yet one should not exaggerate Franklin's lack of the imaginative. The kind of imagination that shows itself in whimsical humour, in graceful wit, in vivid apologue and illustration, was his to a high degree. Only he remained essentially an efficient, extroverted person, who preferred to any other art the art—some might say, the craft—of living; perpetually curious of new truths, fundamentally impatient of the vague, the rapturous, the futile. Johnson, no doubt, thought him a Whig dog of the most vicious kind; but Franklin, though far calmer, saner, more practical, remains far nearer to Johnson than to ethereal souls like Shelley. Which type one prefers is a matter of private feeling and judgement; one may be glad that mankind, in its infinite variety, can produce both.

Franklin's two great loves were Science and America. Both are present in Turgot's famous line on him—

Eripuit caelo fulmen, sceptrumque tyrannis.[2]

(He snatched from Heaven the lightning, the sceptre from tyrants' hands.)

---

[1] No less typically, Franklin used to tell how an English farmer was once so astounded by his calming of troubled waters with oil, that the man threw himself at the miracle-worker's feet, and asked what he should believe. 'What you have seen', was the curt reply, 'and nothing else.'

[2] In a variant form, 'mox sceptra tyrannis'.

Franklin's modesty at once disclaimed this hyperbolic praise —the lightning, he said, still fell; and he was only one among thousands who helped to break the power of George III. Still that epigram keeps more truth than many. To-day, indeed, Franklin might be less wholly happy about those two great causes. Science, since then, has grown too strong, and too mixed a blessing; and the United States have perhaps grown too big—not, indeed, for the defence of Western freedom, but for their own well-being. Yet, on balance, he might still be content.

But Franklin himself remains of more than historic interest. For he is also a standing example of a man of good will, who laboured fruitfully for the lives of his fellows, and for his own as well. Saints have often been slightly foolish or perverse; one may prefer sages. And Franklin was a sage. He found happiness, as it is best found, by health of mind and body, by activity in the service of others, by a versatility which preserved him from our modern disease of specialist's cramp. Printing, commerce, public service, diplomacy, mathematics, electricity, meteorology, astronomy, geology, ethnology, education, physics, chemistry, agriculture, medicine, hygiene, navigation, aeronautics, cookery[1]—even this does not exhaust the long list of his activities.[2] He recalls the happy versatility of the Renaissance. To-day his work is long since done, his discoveries obsolete; yet from the life of Benjamin Franklin there is still, I think, much to be learned.

The ancestral stock of this most typically English American came, like Washington's, from the very heart of England—Ecton above the Nene, five miles east of Northampton. No less appropriately, his ancestors for generations had been practical farmers or village blacksmiths. Franklin's father, Josiah, (b. 1658), the youngest of four sons, became a dyer; but, after migrating in 1683 to Boston, New England, changed to a tallow-chandler. (His famous son was likewise to prefer light to colour.) Josiah too, in his far smaller way, was noted among his neighbours for solidity of judgement and love of experiment; for instance, he is said to have successfully tried the

---

[1] See *Benjamin Franklin on the Art of Eating*, ed. G. Chinard (Princeton), 1958.

[2] Among his other pieces of inspired commonsense was the invention of bifocal lenses for spectacles; and considerations on lead-poisoning, daylight-saving, the right-coloured clothes for hot climates, and (against all the prejudices of his day) the value of fresh air.

transfer of fish-spawn from one river to another. By his first, English wife he had seven children; by his second, from Nantucket, 'a discreet and virtuous woman', he had ten more—seventeen offspring in all, ten of them boys. Benjamin (born January 17, 1706) was the eighth child of the second brood, and the youngest son (as his fathers had been for four generations before him).

At seven came the familiar episode of the whistle, when he exposed himself to the mockery of his family by wasting his savings to pay too much for that joyous source of noise;[1] thus rediscovering for himself the principle of La Rochefoucauld—'la souveraine habileté consiste à bien connaître le prix des choses'. Hence, we are told, his lifelong refusal 'to pay too much for my whistle'. One may, indeed, doubt such lifelong influences; just as one may doubt whether Mérimée's lifelong determination never to be duped really came from that moment in childhood when, going out of the room after a scolding, he overheard his father say, laughing, to his mother—'*Pauvre petit*, he *does* think we are angry!' Such trifles seem not so much to mould a temperament as to reveal it. Probably the saturated solution would, sooner or later, have crystallized anyway. Still it is interesting thus to catch a glimpse of the first crystal.

At eight the boy was sent, for less than a year, to a grammar school; but, independent to the bone, he was to remain always a self-taught, self-moulded personality. Later he was to teach himself French, Italian, Spanish (and thence Latin), as well as German; just as he became a self-made writer, and a self-made scientist.[2]

Originally meant for the Church (as a kind of tithe, being the tenth son), at the age of ten he was taken instead into his father's tallow-business. But he disliked tallow, and wanted to go to sea. (His brother Josiah did, and was drowned.) In the end he was to have enough of the sea, with eight Atlantic crossings. But now his prudent father took him round to look at various trades—joiners, braziers, and so on. Finally at twelve, in 1718, he was apprenticed to his brother James, nine years his senior, as a printer.

No apprentice of Hogarth's was more industrious. He devoured

[1] This familiar tale (unlike the priggish legend of Washington's 'little hatchet', which appears unauthenticated) comes from Franklin himself.

[2] Those who wish to realize how self-made Franklin was, should glance at the strangely illiterate letters of his wife and his favourite sister, Jane Mecom. Both good women are almost capable of spelling 'wife'—'yf'.

books in his spare time, even during the other printers' mealtimes—
Bunyan, Xenophon's *Memorabilia*, Plutarch's *Lives*,[1] Defoe's *Essay
on Projects*, Cotton Mathers's *Essays to do Good*, Locke's *Human
Understanding*, Shaftesbury, Collins. He also tried writing as well
as reading—even writing verse. In this he gained a success, at twelve,
with two popular ballads; one on the drowning of a lighthouse-
keeper with wife and daughter, the other on the killing of Black-
beard the Pirate. But his father, like Ovid's, discouraged these
efforts with humorous warnings that 'verse-makers were generally
beggars'. Franklin, less poetic than Ovid, gave ear. 'So I escaped
being a poet, most probably a bad one.' Four specimen lines from a
manuscript elegy on a sister-in-law will make most readers inclined
to agree—

> Yet her sad Exit maugre my Resolves
> In Woe's profound Abyss my soul involves;
> With Sighs & Groans my lab'ring Bosom swells
> And down my cheeks Grief's mournful Stream impels.

But it is only fair to add that some of his later drinking-songs were
at least a good deal less abysmal.

> Then toss off your glasses and scorn the dull asses
> Who, missing the kernel, still gnaw the shell;
> What's love, rule, or riches? Wise Solomon teaches
> They're vanity, vanity, vanity still.

> *Chorus.*

> That's true!
> He knew!
> He'd tried them all through;
> Friends and a bottle still bore the bell.

Who could have imagined the sober Franklin in such a Sir-Tobyish
vein? He was indeed versatile!

He also wrote prose which his father more sympathetically
criticized for 'lack of order, clarity, elegance'. Finding an odd

---

[1] One of the most fruitful of ancient classics, from the Renaissance to the eighteenth
century. A pity that it now lies so little read.

volume of *The Spectator*, the young printer set himself methodically to master the art of style—taking notes of *Spectator* essays, then rewriting from them essays of his own. Sometimes he jumbled the order of his notes, so as to teach himself also the art of arrangement; sometimes he versified his original, then retranslated his verse back into prose. Occasionally he flattered himself that he had even hit on improvements. 'This encouraged me to think I might possibly in time come to be a tolerable English writer, of which I was extremely ambitious.' Nor in the issue was he disappointed. Addison, Bunyan, and Defoe were not his masters in vain. 'Prose writing,' he concluded in later years, 'has been of great use to me in the course of my life, and was a principal means of my advancement.' It was true.

Reading Franklin's prose, I do not think I should guess that Addison had been his master. Franklin's style seems more virile; and though at times it shows a likeness to Swift or Voltaire, it is to a kindlier Swift, a more staid Voltaire. Franklin has not their brilliance; but he remains always human, where Swift becomes at moments a hyena, Voltaire a monkey.

This apprenticeship in writing soon bore fruit. In 1721 James Franklin started *The New England Courant*.[1] In 1722 the sixteen-year-old Benjamin, realizing that contributions from a mere boy like himself would be scorned, began slipping anonymous articles under the office-door; beginning with a *Letter from Mrs Silence Dogood*. These proved a great success. Then in 1723, when James Franklin, through his newspaper's outspokenness, had got himself forbidden by the Boston authorities to continue it, he adopted the simple stratagem of transferring the paper to his brother of seventeen. One article of Benjamin's, on Honours, already reveals the future democrat—'Adam was never called Master Adam; we never read of Noah Esquire, Lord, Knight and Baronet, nor the Right Honourable Abraham, Viscount Mesopotamia, Baron of Canaan.' Presumably the Boston Council had no objection to this sort of attack on English

---

[1] The *Courant* conducted a violent campaign against small-pox inoculation, and Cotton Mather who supported it. The unfortunate minister even had a grenade thrown through his window at 2 a.m., with the legend 'Damn you, I will inoculate you with this; a pox to you!' Curious that the scientific Franklin should have begun his career by working for this rabidly anti-scientific journal. (Cotton Mather (1663-1728), Boston minister and author of 450 works, had been a believer in witchcraft in the seventeenth century, but became a champion of inoculation in the eighteenth.)

titles, which left their respectable selves in peace. The paper pros-
pered. But Franklin's authorship of the Dogood Papers came out;
and there was friction with the jealous James, who did not even
refrain from blows. So Benjamin quitted his brother's printing-
house; and since James then blocked his chances of employment
with the other Boston printers, the lad of seventeen pushed off to
seek work first in New York, next in Philadelphia (then with a
population of perhaps 10,000). The Quaker city was to prove better
suited than Boston to Franklin's tolerant temperament.

On the voyage he was tempted, though now a vegetarian, by the
appetizing odour of cod being cooked on board. Then, recollecting
that he had seen smaller fish taken out of bigger fishes' stomachs, he
reflected—'If you eat one another, I don't see why we mayn't eat
you.' 'So convenient a thing it is to be a reasonable creature, since it
enables one to find or make a reason for everything one has a mind
to do.' One thinks of that other young vegetarian, Shelley, who
with all his gifts could never have been so ironically light-hearted.
But one of the admirable things about Franklin is that, with all his
excellent eighteenth-century passion for sound sense, he never fell
into the folly of trying to be unreasonably reasonable; and with all
his model efforts at morality, kept always a saving sense of humour.

And so we see a dirty, unkempt youth, travel-stained from an unpleasant voyage, strolling through the streets of unknown Philadelphia and gnawing a large puffy roll, with another large puffy roll
under each arm. Someone else saw him, and laughed at the odd
spectacle—a girl standing at her father's door—Deborah Read, one
day to become Deborah Franklin. This too is typical of the homespun thread of realistic romance that runs through Franklin's years.

The lad got work with an eccentric, Mosaically bearded[1] printer,
Keimer; then, by his brightness, caught the attention of the effusive,
irresponsible governor of Pennsylvania, Sir William Keith; and was
by him encouraged to sail for London, buy the necessary type, and
set up in Philadelphia as a printer on his own. But this new patron
failed him, as Chesterfield failed Johnson; though Franklin took the
disappointment with much more philosophic calm. 'He wished to
please everybody'; runs his quiet comment on Keith, 'and, having
little to give, he gave expectations.' Reaching London in 1724 with

---

[1] *Leviticus*, xix, 27: 'neither shalt thou mar the corners of thy beard'.

only £12, Franklin found that the ship's mail-bag held none of Keith's promised letters of recommendation. However he could well recommend himself. He worked for a year and a half as a printer; wrote and printed (1725) a '*Dissertation on Liberty and Necessity*' (but Hume's field was not the more practical Franklin's); astonished his beer-swilling fellow-compositors, one of whom swallowed three quarts a day, by a sobriety that won him the nickname of the 'Water American'; and in July 1726 re-embarked for America with one Denham, a merchant who had been attracted by Franklin on the outward voyage, and now proposed to take him into service as clerk. Two months before, in May 1726, a very different young foreigner had sailed up that same estuary of the Thames—Voltaire. Not till fifty-two years later, in 1778, were he and Franklin to meet and embrace at last, as figures of world-fame, amid the ecstatic plaudits of Paris. Franklin was unromantic: but his life was not always that.

Six months after their return to America, Denham died; Franklin went back to printing, under Keimer; and in 1728, at twenty-two, set up independently. Next year Keimer failed; and Franklin, buying Keimer's *Pennsylvania Gazette*, became master of a paper, as well as a press, of his own. The year after that, in 1730, the prosperous young tradesman married.

Before leaving for England he had become engaged to Deborah Read; but absence failed to make the heart grow fonder. He wrote only once to her from London, and she married a potter, Rogers; however, her marriage proved unhappy and, hearing that Rogers had a previous wife still alive in England, Deborah left him. The returned Franklin pitied her loneliness and melancholy; and in September 1730 he took her to wife, though without church-ceremony or extant legal record. For there was no proof, either that a previous Mrs Rogers had really existed to nullify Deborah's first marriage, or that Rogers himself was, as reported, now dead in the West Indies.

Deborah was a sturdy, resolute woman—she appears once to have described herself as 'a hedgehog'. But her letters display an incredible illiteracy, that suggests little education, and not very much intelligence. The marriage does not give me the impression of having been *deeply* happy—few marriages are; but (like most things in Franklin's life) to have been quite reasonably and solidly so. 'Keep your eyes wide open before marriage,' says Franklin's Poor Richard, 'half-shut afterwards.' One may doubt if Deborah Read could stir his imagination as, in later years, Catherine Ray did, or Polly Stevenson, or Madame Helvétius, or Madame Brillon. Still there is a charmingly human touch about a postscript of his in 1756, reproaching Deborah for not writing—'P.S. I have *scratched out the loving words*, being writ in haste by mistake, when I *forgot I was angry*.' And to the end of her life, though of its last eighteen years her husband spent fifteen away in England, she remained in his letters 'Dear Child'. On the other hand I feel that a really devoted wife would not have been deterred from joining her husband in England, even by dread of the eighteenth-century Atlantic. And shortly before her death in 1774 Franklin gently complains to her that 'it is now nine long months since I received a line from my dear Debby'.

She bore him a son Francis and a daughter Sarah. But little Francis died at four, from smallpox (1736); and anyone who is tempted to think Franklin unfeeling, might pause to consider his reference thirty-six years later to his lost child, 'whom I have seldom seen equalled in every thing, and whom to this day I cannot think of without a sigh'.

But at the time of his marriage the situation was complicated by the birth, in this same year 1730, or the next, of a natural son by an unknown mother—William Franklin, the future loyalist, and governor of New Jersey.[1] Franklin was perhaps sometimes a prig, but never a prude; all his life a moralist, but never a Puritan.

'About this time I conceiv'd the bold and arduous project of arriving at moral perfection.' Franklin drew up a list of virtues—1. Temperance; 2. Silence; 3. Order; 4. Resolution; 5. Frugality; 6. Industry; 7. Sincerity; 8. Justice; 9. Moderation; 10. Cleanliness; 11. Tranquillity; 12. Chastity; 13. Humility. 'I made,' he continues, 'a little book, in which I allotted a page for each of the virtues. . . . I determined to give a week's strict attention to each of the virtues successively . . . marking every evening the faults of the day.' This would make a course of thirteen weeks, to be repeated four times in

---

[1] Who was in his turn to have a natural son in England (1760); who was in *his* turn to have a natural son in France (1785).

the year. In practice, he found that he succeeded in diminishing his black marks, before he finally tired of the experiment—as most men would, if they ever began it. Few of us, indeed, would ever make it. There is about it an air of the ridiculous. One recalls the Memnon of Voltaire—'Memnon conçut un jour le projet insensé d'être parfaitement sage. Il n'y a guère d'hommes à qui cette folie n'ait quelquefois passé par la tête.'

True, Franklin realized that such perfection could be only relative—'a man in this life cannot be so perfect as an angel. . . . But that a man is not capable of being so perfect here as he is capable of being here is not sense.' But, better still, before we can smile at Franklin, he has already smiled at himself. Humility, he says, was added to his list only by an afterthought, 'a Quaker friend having kindly informed me that I was generally thought proud; that my pride showed itself frequently in conversation; that I was not content with being in the right when discussing any point, but was overbearing and rather insolent.' And then, with returning irony, he observes: 'I cannot boast of much success in acquiring the *reality* of this virtue, but I had a good deal with regard to the *appearance* of it.'

Indeed, with Franklin this disarming humour is always breaking in; as when another Quaker solemnly consulted him—'Friend Franklin, thou knowest everything. Canst thou tell me how I am to preserve my small beer in the backyard? My neighbours, I find, are tapping it.' To which the sage cheerfully replied: 'Ah, put a barrel of old Madeira by the side of it.'

As for humility, joking apart, it is perhaps a virtue of which the appearance—in other words, courtesy—is really more valuable than the reality. Its excellence, one may feel, has been overlaboured by Christian ethics; there may be more sense, and honesty, in Aristotle's ideal of the 'high-souled man' who neither overrates nor underrates his own worth, but sees things as they in fact are. Is there really much virtue in self-deception?

In any case Franklin's diplomatic career would have been a good deal less successful, had he not thus effectively schooled himself to seem unassuming. By reading about Socrates he had become himself too clever a master in the Socratic art of entangling opponents in their own line of argument—a form of dialectic that can become no less exasperating than effective—as Socrates found to his mortal cost.

But Franklin did cure himself of such irritating disputatiousness. 'Persons of good sense, I have since observed, seldom fall into it, except lawyers, university men, and men of all sorts that have been bred at Edinburgh.' (He forgot Hume.) And again, 'You can always employ your time,' he wrote, years afterwards, to Ingenhousz, 'better than in polemics.' This was, in fact, an exaggeration; for political polemics formed a vital part of Franklin's own career. Still he did train himself to beware, when controversy became inevitable, of that foolishly dogmatic tone which is the common vice of argument. As a controversialist he may be often less striking than Swift, Johnson, Burke, or Macaulay; but he is often far more persuasive, largely because he remains so undogmatic. 'This mode,' he comments, 'which I at first put on with some violence to natural inclination, became at length so easy, and so habitual to me, that perhaps' (note 'perhaps') 'for these fifty years past no one has heard a dogmatical expression escape me.'

But it was one of Franklin's qualities not to be content to better himself without trying also to better the world about him. In 1727 he founded a secret club[1] of twelve, the 'Leather-apron Club' or 'Junto', for which he drew up, in 1728, a typically practical set of questions, which all members were to read over and consider on the morning before each weekly meeting. Could they report anything of interest in the book they had last read?—any new story, 'agreeable for telling?'—any recent business-failure or success, with reasons?—any recent cases of good or bad conduct, or of illness and treatment, for comment?—any deserving strangers, or beginners, and possible means of helping them?—any chance for the club to do public service?—any occasions for change of laws, or defence of liberty?—had any member need for assistance in some plan of his own, or against injury received, or for making some desired acquaintance?

Members had also to produce queries in morals, politics, or natural philosophy; and to read one essay each every three months. Once a year they dined. From the Junto Franklin himself gained help in his own printing-business; through it he was able to start a successful subscription-library for Philadelphia (to which Franklin

---

[1] Five years later, in 1732, he became also a Freemason; and Masonry seems to have played a part of much importance in his life.

appropriately gave Montaigne's *Essays* and a reprint of *Magna Charta*); and also a volunteer fire-brigade.

Again, it was in the Junto that Franklin first discussed the question of reintroducing a paper currency for Pennsylvania. Then he published a pamphlet in favour of it (1729). Last of all, when the scheme was carried against opposition in the Assembly, he received the profitable job of printing the notes. A most happy ending.

For Franklin (it becomes hard to remember, after so much wisdom, that in 1729 he was still only twenty-three) had his own way to make; and made it, like Wellington, by the simple process—though much less simple than it sounds—of applying good sense to the circumstances of the moment. He had, in particular, to gain the confidence of shrewd citizens, who might well distrust his raw youth. And so—

> 'I took care not only to be in *reality* industrious and frugal, but to avoid all appearances to the contrary. I drest plainly; I was seen at no places of idle diversion. I never went out a-fishing or shooting; a book, indeed, sometimes debauch'd me from my work, but that was seldom, snug, and gave no scandal.'

(As so often, when Franklin is in danger of seeming too much the prudent prig, there comes the redeeming jest.) Finally, 'to show that I was not above my business, I sometimes brought home the paper I purchas'd at the stores thro' the streets on a wheelbarrow'. For he was not only a printer, but also a bookseller and stationer, who further sold, at times, wares as diverse as chocolate, lampblack, coffee, mustard, mackerel, spectacles, cloth, lottery-tickets—and slaves!

After Keimer's exit to Barbados, Franklin still had another rival-printer to cope with—the postmaster, Bradford, who did Pennsylvania's government-printing. But Franklin hit on the device of re-printing an address from the Assembly to the Governor with an accuracy much superior to Bradford's official version, and sending it to members of the Assembly; as a result, in 1730 Franklin was voted printer for Pennsylvania. This ruse was only fair warfare; for Bradford, as postmaster, had jealously forbidden his carriers to carry Franklin's *Pennsylvania Gazette*, although they carried Bradford's own *Mercury*.

In 1732 Franklin struck out a new line—as astrologer. The

colonies, as yet, offered little market for books; but there *was* a ready sale for almanacs. In December 1732, Franklin published his *Poor Richard*, an almanac for 1733 ('Poor Richard' being supposedly an astrologer, Richard Saunders, wed to a shrewish wife, Bridget, 'his duchess'). Franklin's rival, Andrew Bradford, had long published an *American Almanac* by one Titan Leeds. Now 'Poor Richard', re-calling Swift's baiting of Partridge, humorously prophesied the death of the competing Titan Leeds, for October 17, 1733. But he also provided abundant humour of his own. And for the next quarter of a century Franklin proceeded to pour out through his almanacs a stream of simple, practical adages, partly collected and partly invented—but always characteristic.

As one would expect, 'Poor Richard' is a realist, not a romantic.

> 'A little house well filled, a little field well tilled, and a little wife well willed, are great riches.'

But—

> 'Keep your eyes open before marriage, half shut afterwards.'

Sometimes Franklin's slightly cynical shrewdness recalls the Greek peasant-poet Hesiod.

> 'Love your neighbour, yet don't pull down your hedge.'

> 'Fish and visitors smell in three days.'

> 'A countryman between two lawyers is like a fish between two cats.'

> 'Cut the wings of your hopes and hens lest they lead you a weary dance after them.'

> 'The most exquisite folly is made of wisdom spun too fine.'

> 'None preaches better than the ant, and she says nothing.'

> 'The worst wheel of the cart makes the most noise.'

At moments there rises prophetically the voice of the future democrat—

> 'The King's cheese is half wasted in parings; but, no matter, 'tis made of the people's milk.'

But another utterance is curiously unprophetic—

> 'The first mistake in public business is the going into it.'

For Franklin was to spend most of his future life in nothing else.

Some of his maxims, on the other hand, are more generous—and he was himself to live up to them.

> 'The brave and the wise can both pity and excuse, when cowards and fools show no mercy.'

> 'Defer not thy well-doing; be not like St. George, who is always a-horseback and never rides on.'

> 'Serving God is doing good to man, but praying is thought an easier service, and therefore more generally chosen.'

Poor Richard, in fine, is only a La Rochefoucauld in homespun; yet he remains no unworthy citizen of the Century of Sense.

'Philistine!' Arnold might have murmured; and Carlyle (who once observed, before a portrait of Franklin, 'There is the father of all the Yankees') might have growled something about 'Gigmanity'. But to judge so would be narrow. Throughout *Poor Richard* the gaiety of the humorist relieves, even if at times a little crudely, the prudence of the moralist.

> 'Ignorant men wonder how we astrologers foretell the weather so exactly, unless we deal with the old black devil. Alas, 'tis as easy as — For instance, the star-gazer peeps at the heavens through a long glass. He spies perhaps Virgo (or the Virgin); she turns her head round as it were to see if anybody observed her, then crouching down gently, with her hands on her knees, she looks wistfully for a while right forward. He judges rightly what she is about, and having

calculated the distance and allowed time for its falling, finds that next spring we shall have a fine April shower. What can be more natural and easy than this?'

Too frivolous to be worth recording? Perhaps. But I am trying to paint Franklin as truthfully as possible—as Cromwell wished to be painted, warts and all. Bunyan and Addison might have looked a little askance at such persiflage in their literary disciple; but Franklin was one of those bluff, jesting characters who set out resolutely to make the world better without any wish to dream it, or themselves, better than they really are. What, indeed, would Victorian prudery have thought of Franklin's surreptitious piece, *Advice to a Young Man on the Choice of a Mistress* (1745)? He counsels marriage. 'A single man . . . is an incomplete animal. He resembles the odd half of a pair of scissors.' 'But if you will not take this counsel,' then he recommends an elderly rather than a young mistress, for a variety of reasons; some of them highly prosaic. For instance, the elderly know more of the world. They talk better. There is less harm done. 'And lastly, they are so grateful! Thus much for my paradox. But still I advise you to marry directly.'

As with Franklin's ethics, and his humour, so with his religion. It was broad. He believed in a Creator who had made men immortal; wished them to serve one another; and would deal justice hereafter. 'With most of the present Dissenters in England', he had some doubts of Christ's divinity; though he thought Christian ethics the best. So he wrote in the last year of his life, in answer to an enquiry about his beliefs from the President of Yale; and added optimistically that, 'having experienced the goodness of that Being in conducting me prosperously through a long life, I have no doubt of its continuance in the next, without the smallest conceit of meriting it'. Pascal would have been appalled by such calm complacency; but this simple creed seems to have sustained Franklin through his long career. For, after a youthful phase of determinism and disbelief in immortality, his tenets seem to have changed little. Indeed he does not give the impression that his thoughts were much occupied with such topics. It was, in fact, not a very religious sort of religion.

Typically enough, when Franklin encountered 'enthusiasm' in the shape of Whitefield (1739), he became a most helpful friend, but not in the least a convert. His interest in Whitefield's oratory took, on the contrary, a characteristically scientific turn.

> 'Being among the hindmost in Market Street, I had the curiosity to learn how far he could be heard, by retiring backwards down the street towards the river; and I found his voice distinct till I came near Front Street, when some noise in that street obscured it. Imagining then a semicircle, of which my distance should be the radius, and that it were filled with auditors to each of whom I allowed two square feet, I computed that he might be heard by more than thirty thousand. This reconciled me . . . to the ancient stories of generals haranguing whole armies, of which I had sometimes doubted.'

Whitefield, in short, had converted Franklin—to Thucydides!

True, Franklin could also be touched by Whitefield's preaching —though less vividly than Lord Chesterfield.[1] He attended a sermon with some copper in his pocket, three or four silver dollars, and five pistoles in gold.

> 'I silently resolved he should get nothing from me. . . . As he proceeded I began to soften, and concluded to give the coppers. Another stroke of his oratory made me ashamed of that, and determined me to give the silver. And he finished so admirably that I emptied my pocket wholly into the collector's dish, gold and all.'

But this was philanthropy, not faith. Whitefield prayed for Franklin's conversion; but gained from Franklin only the dry comment that Whitefield 'never had the satisfaction of believing that his prayers were heard'.

But it is time to return to Franklin's increasingly public and scientific career. In 1736 he became, and till 1751 remained, Clerk of the Pennsylvania Assembly. In 1737 a rival candidate was put forward by one of the Assembly. Franklin's reply was simply a polite letter to the hostile member, asking to borrow a rare book in his possession; thus making him a friend for life. 'He that has once done you a kindness will be more ready to do you another than he whom you yourself have obliged.' What could be more characteristic? So began a public service of fifty-two years.

---

[1] When Whitefield, it is said, once pictured in a sermon a blind man tottering on the brink of a precipice, Chesterfield became so carried away at the climax as to spring from his seat with the cry—'By God! he's gone!'

In 1737 Franklin became also Postmaster at Philadelphia. In 1740 he invented a much improved stove, and most generously refused the offer by the Governor of Pennsylvania of a patent for it. In 1743–4 he helped to found the American Philosophical Society, with similar interests to the Royal Society in England. In 1745 he received from Peter Collinson, a Quaker mercer in London, an account of electric experiments. Next year he was busy experimenting himself.

For a time, in 1747, he was interrupted by public danger. Pennsylvania was threatened by French and Indians. The colony's Quakers and Germans remained lethargic. And it was left for the ever resourceful Franklin to write a pamphlet, *Plain Truths*, and form an Association which ultimately raised over 10,000 volunteers. In 1748 he went to New York to get artillery from the governor, Clinton. 'He at first refused us peremptorily.' But at dinner with his council 'there was great drinking of Madeira wine'; and the Governor gradually mellowed to a loan of six cannon; then of ten; finally of eighteen!

But that same year came the Peace of Aix-la-Chapelle. And Franklin, aged forty-two, hoped, ironically enough, to be able to retire from printing, and devote the rest of his life to tranquillity and science. He had made a private competence; he had become public printer for Pennsylvania, Delaware, New Jersey, and Maryland; he had set up subordinate printers at ten different places in the colonies. He had done public service in helping to found a library,[1] a fire-brigade, a city-watch, a militia, the American Philosophical Society. He was soon to add to the number a hospital, a fire-insurance company, and an academy from which grew, eventually, Pennsylvania University. His long life of eighty-four years was now at its mid-point. But instead of well-earned repose and privacy the next forty years were to be one long record of toilsome public labour, rewarded by world-fame. Franklin, however, with his calm penetration probably thought the sense of successful service a better reward than the fame. Rest he was to find only in extreme old age, and death.

Still, for a few years, from 1746 to 1752, he was able to turn his mind to electricity. In 1749 he made a battery; and in 1750, meaning

---

[1] 'The mother,' as he says, 'of all the North American subscription libraries, now so numerous.'

to electrocute a turkey, nearly electrocuted himself.[1] 'The greatest
known effects of common lightning', he came to think, might be
exceeded by linking up enough electric bottles. 'So we are got beyond the skill of Rabelais's devils of two years old, who, he humorously says, had only learnt to thunder and lighten a little round the
head of a cabbage.'

In 1749 Franklin had written down twelve reasons for identifying
lightning with electricity—a view previously put forward as early
as 1708. It now remained to prove it experimentally. In 1751 Johnson's editor, Edward Cave, published Franklin's *Experiments and
Observations on Electricity*. In May 1752 d'Alibard at Marly succeeded in drawing electricity from the sky with a forty-foot iron
rod. In the following June, probably, Franklin made his own famous
experiment of sending a kite up into a thundercloud and drawing
sparks with his knuckle. He was luckier than the Swede, Rickmann,
who a twelvemonth later, in 1753, killed himself at St Petersburg
with an experimental rod. In this same year 1752 Franklin received
honours from the King of France, and a gold medal from the Royal
Society. But no wreaths ever turned that solid head of his. Franklin
was never ridiculous, because he never remained solemn. 'The
Tatler,' he wrote to Jared Eliot, 'tells us of a girl who was observed
to grow suddenly proud and none could guess the reason, till it
came to be known that she had got on a pair of new silk garters. Lest
you should be puzzled to guess the cause, when you observe anything of the kind in me, I think I will not hide my new garters under
my petticoats, but take the freedom to show them to you in a paragraph of our friend Collinson's last letter' (which describes the
honours conferred).

Equally admirable was Franklin's readiness to admit scientific
errors, and to publish imperfectly confirmed hypotheses, if they
might be useful—'it being of more importance,' he wrote to Collinson, 'that knowledge should increase, than that your friend
should be thought an accurate philosopher'.[2]

[1] One of the lighter electrical diversions of Franklin and his friends was to electrify
a little metal crown above an engraving of the king—the loyal current would shock
anyone who dared to touch. Still remote were the days when Franklin was to turn a
current far stronger, but less loyal on to George III.

[2] For an estimate of Franklin's scientific eminence (he has too often been thought
of as merely a brilliant dabbler), see I. B. Cohen, *Franklin and Newton* (1956),

So came the lightning-conductor. It was, years after, to save Franklin's own house. At first of course, as with inoculation against smallpox and with sanitation against cholera, there were pious owls who suggested that the scientific innovations of this new Prometheus were thwarting the will of God. In 1754 Ebenezer Kinnersley, Baptist minister and electrical scientist, had to explain in Philadelphia that lightning-conductors were *not* irreligious. However, reason prevailed; and the most orthodox churches of Christendom learnt to protect themselves against fire from Heaven by this contrivance of an American heretic.

But once more public affairs claimed him. In 1753 Franklin gained the appointment, with William Hunter, of 'Deputy Postmaster and Manager of all His Majesty's Provinces and Possessions on the Continent of America'. It was, in fact, fantastic as it would then have seemed, a first step towards Franklin's managing His Majesty's Provinces and Possessions to the exclusion of His Majesty.

From 1754 to 1756 he was visiting post offices in the northern colonies, in Maryland, and in Virginia. From a Pennsylvanian, he was fast becoming an American; and his drastic re-organization of the postal service in the colonies proved a foundation for building also their political union. Already in 1751 he had published in his *Gazette* the first of his attacks on English injustice. Why should the colonies be vexed with transported English felons dumped on them? The grievance is obvious; but the humour of its expression is pure Franklin. England, he argues, is plagued with felons, America with rattlesnakes; why not reciprocity?

> 'In the spring of the year, when they first creep out of their holes, they are feeble, heavy, slow, and easily taken; and if a small bounty were allowed per head, some thousands might be collected annually and transported to Britain. There I would propose to have them carefully distributed in St. James's Park, in the Spring Gardens and other places of pleasure about London; in the gardens of the nobility and gentry throughout the nation; but particularly in the gardens of the prime ministers, the lords of trade, and members of Parliament, for to them we are most particularly obliged.'

But Franklin, though he might justly resent this particular abuse, was not yet in the least anti-English. His vision foresaw, on the contrary, a union of the colonies as part of a united empire, with that representation at Westminster without which taxation by the English Parliament was, to him, injustice. And for this united empire there lay open a splendid future, since the New World offered room for a population doubling itself every twenty-five years. Indeed, had Franklin's dream come true, the centre of gravity of the British Empire would long since have shifted to the United States.

In 1754 Franklin's *Gazette* published a cartoon (perhaps drawn by him) which showed the colonies as a snake chopped in eight pieces, with the motto 'Join or die'. And he vainly proposed a first Plan of Union at the Albany Congress. But if one obstacle to American expansion lay in English conservatism, there was now a more pressing danger from French enterprise, which threatened to encircle the colonies, and head off their extension to the west, by spreading south from Canada to Louisiana through Ohio. So in 1754 opened the American prelude to the Seven Years War (1756–63); with it Franklin's varied career widened to include a chapter of soldiering. General Braddock, a veteran of sixty, arrived from England. When he explained to Franklin his confident plan for taking Fort Duquesne (Pittsburgh), then marching by Niagara on Frontenac (Kingston), the prudent American warned him against Indian ambuscades. 'He smiled at my ignorance and replied: "These savages may, indeed, be a formidable enemy to your raw American militia, but upon the King's regular and disciplined troops, Sir, it is impossible they should make any impression."' Franklin said 'no more'. Who was a mere Postmaster-General to dispute with a real General?

Braddock, as it happened, had similar warnings from a young American officer called Washington; who was present when his warnings were bloodily justified, and learnt thenceforth not to overestimate the effectiveness of English regulars in American wildernesses.

But what Franklin could do, he did. When Braddock found colonial feeling tepid, and could raise in Maryland only twenty-five wagons for his 'supply-service', Franklin quickly produced from Pennsylvania no less than one hundred and fifty four-horsed wagons and two hundred and fifty-nine pack-horses, by giving his own bond to compensate the owners if they were lost. After Braddock's disaster that commitment threatened to involve Franklin in a liability for close on £20,000. For in July 1755, near Fort Duquesne, the English general lost half his army and his own life, exactly as Franklin had warned him.

Braddock died with the words, 'We shall better know how to deal with them another time.' Wolfe did know better. But this same professional contempt for colonial troops was one day to bring far worse catastrophes in the War of Independence, now just twenty years ahead.

Meanwhile Pennsylvania itself seemed in danger. Franklin drew up a militia act which passed the Assembly. He sat as head of a committee appointed by the Assembly to manage its funds for defence. And he published, in his *Gazette*, *A Dialogue between X, Y, and Z concerning the Present State of Affairs in Pennsylvania*.

> '*Z.* For my part I am no coward, but hang me if I'll fight to save the Quakers.
>
> *X.* That is to say, you won't pump ship, because 'twill save the rats, as well as yourself.'

Such Johnsonian concreteness the dullest could understand.

Then, laying down his pungent pen, Franklin led a successful expedition to restore the colony's defences, where they had been breached by an Indian massacre of the Moravian villagers at Gnadenhuetten. When the chaplain of the force complained that the men neglected prayers, 'I said to Mr Beatty, "It is perhaps below the dignity of your profession to act as steward of the rum; but if you were to deal it out, and only just after prayers, you would have them all about you." ' It worked; and everyone was satisfied. As usual with Franklin, good sense and good humour had found out the way. He built three forts, and returned.

But such unfailing competence meant no rest for its possessor. It now led him across the Atlantic.

The 'proprietors' of Pennsylvania, in succession to their father, its founder, were Thomas and Richard Penn. They appointed, and tightly controlled, its governors; and growing friction had resulted from their narrow refusals to have their own estates taxed, even when the whole colony was in peril. In early 1757 Franklin was appointed by the Assembly to plead their case in England. His first crossing of the Atlantic, in 1724, had been as a poor printer; his second, in 1757, was as representative of Pennsylvania. Not for five years was he to return home.

But before he could leave he was to suffer again from that British nonchalance and superciliousness which did so much in these years to fling away the colonies. The Earl of Loudoun was now C.-in-C. America. Despite the fuming of passengers, the chafing of merchants, and the consumption of sea-stores, the three London packets were not allowed to weigh anchor because 'his lordship's letters were not ready; and yet whoever waited on him, found him always at his desk, pen in hand'. Here in the flesh was Poor Richard's St George, always a-horseback, yet never riding on. Not for six weeks was Franklin free to sail; not till July 1757 did he reach London, by way of Stonehenge.

The next five years in England were not all labour. Franklin contrived to travel—to Cambridge, to Oxford, to his ancestral Ecton, to Birmingham, Coventry, and Liverpool, to Edinburgh, St Addrew's and Glasgow, to Belgium and Holland; and he contrived, as usual, to charm, and to make friends. 'I never saw,' wrote Strahan, the publisher of Johnson, Hume, and Gibbon, to Deborah Franklin, 'a man who was, in every respect, so perfectly agreeable to me.' It is, indeed, a little extraordinary that this Yankee, whom one might have imagined cutting a very provincial figure, should have fitted so easily into that critical English society of George III, just as he fitted later into the critical French society of Louis XVI. Indeed, he fitted so well that when, at the end of these five years, Strahan pressed him to settle down in England for good, Franklin was seriously tempted.

Meanwhile he did Pennsylvania's business. It was in vain that he met Penn's sons, the 'proprietors', who viewed him as a dangerous trouble-maker. One dramatic moment of antagonism he has recorded. Franklin pleaded that William Penn had granted to Pennsylvania all the powers and privileges of a free assembly. Thomas Penn replied that by the royal charter his father had no powers to do so. In that case, said Franklin, the first settlers were deceived. Thomas Penn retorted that, if so, it was only their own fault—'the royal charter was no secret'.

'And that he said with a kind of triumphing, laughing insolence, such as a low jockey might do when a purchaser complained that he had cheated him on a horse. I was astonished to see him thus meanly give up his father's character, and conceived at that moment a more cordial and thorough contempt for him than I ever felt for any man living, a contempt that I cannot express in words, but I believe that my countenance expressed it strongly, and that his brother who was looking at me, must have observed it.'

Franklin controlled himself, and went. But it is a vivid moment. Some, as I have said, see in the eighteenth century a cynical, apathetic Ice-Age of Reason, only melted into life by the Romantics. But the kind of controlled passion that gets things done—the best kind of passion, to my mind—lived in their best men no less—perhaps more—than in most of ours. Franklin was genial, sceptical, indulgent, tolerant; but for him, as for any decent person, indulgence and toleration had abrupt limits.

He now proceeded again to use his pen; until by propaganda and persistence he finally gained, in 1760, the approval of the Privy Council's Committee for Plantation Affairs, and the royal assent, for taxation of the Proprietors' lands.

But now Franklin was fast becoming, not merely the agent of Pennsylvania, but the voice of the American colonies. In 1760 he published a pamphlet, *The Interest of Great Britain Considered with Regard to her Colonies and the Acquisitions of Canada and Guadeloupe*. There were some in England who thought a sugar island more desirable than a Canadian wilderness. Against this view Franklin held up the prospect of a glorious expansion whereby the English in America would one day outnumber those at home; while at the same time he tried to reassure the English in England that, even though in a few centuries there might be a hundred million Americans, they would still be mainly agricultural—not manufacturing rivals, but a vast market for English manufactures. As for the danger that the colonies might unite to rebel, he pointed out that not even the menace of French and Indian attack had sufficed to unite them. 'When I say such an union is impossible, I mean without the most grievous tyranny and oppression.' 'The waves do not rise but when the winds blow.' It is possible that this pamphlet really contributed towards the retention of Canada; anyway, at the peace of 1763, Canada was retained. And it may be recalled how Montcalm had predicted that, with the fear of a French Canada withdrawn, the English colonies would one day withdraw themselves from England.

Indeed, William Burke, in urging that it would be better to keep some West Indian islands, had pressed this very point—that a French Canada would be a useful check on the British colonies. That may have been true; but it was hardly wise to say in print. Franklin countered with one his terse, ironic analogies—'A modest word this "check" for massacring men, women and children. . . . Instead of using Indian massacres to check our colonies let me propose a method less cruel—the Egyptian policy (Exodus, Chap. 1). Let an Act of Parliament thus be made enjoining the colony midwives to stifle in the birth every third or fourth child.' Here is Swift's *Modest Proposal* revived—but without Swift's gloating ferocity.

To consider whether Montcalm's prophecy would have been realized even without British high-handedness, is vain guessing; but perhaps the shrewdest prophet of all was Pratt, the future Lord Camden, in a talk with Franklin still earlier (1757). The Americans, Pratt had said, would one day claim independence. Franklin protested that the idea had never entered their heads; nor would it, 'unless you grossly abuse them'. To which Pratt shrewdly answered: 'Very true, that is one of the main causes I see will happen, and will produce the event.'

Franklin's own secret dream was rather, I take it, that the colonies would eventually supersede England, as the centre of an empire such as his contemporaries lacked the vision to foresee. 'I have long been of opinion,' he wrote to Lord Kames in 1759, 'that the future grandeur and stability of the British Empire lie in America; and though, like other foundations, they are low and little seen, they are nevertheless broad and strong enough to support the greatest political structure human wisdom ever yet erected.' But for English folly, it might have been so; or there might have come, I suppose, an *English* War of Independence.

In August 1762 Franklin sailed from Portsmouth for home. He had not, even now, wholly abandoned Strahan's idea of his settling in England—if only he could coax Deborah across the Atlantic. After all, it was natural enough that he should feel more appreciated, and find more that was congenial, in the more civilized Old World. 'Of all the enviable things England has,' he wrote to Mary Stevenson, 'I envy it most its people. Why should that petty island, which compared to America is but like a stepping-stone in a brook, scarce enough of it to keep one's shoes dry; why, I say, should that little island enjoy in almost every neighbourhood more sensible, virtuous, and elegant minds than we can collect in ranging a hundred leagues of our vast forests?' He saw that the balance would one day be redressed—'we shall come to think of the embellishments'. Yet even in our own century there have been Americans who still felt Franklin's leaning towards the Old Country.

However, though the next year, 1763, at last brought peace, there was no long peace for him. Its summer saw an Indian war, followed in December by a butchery of some twenty friendly Indians near or in Lancaster by Presbyterian fanatics calling themselves the Paxton Boys. A band of several hundreds moved on Philadelphia to seek further Indian victims. In January 1764, Franklin's honest indignation at this early example of Lynch-law produced his *Narrative of the Late Massacres in Lancaster County*—'Do we come to America to learn and practise the manners of barbarians?' Then, practical as ever, he put down his pen to organize another Association, for defence of the Moravian Indians in Philadelphia. Within twenty-four hours, so he wrote to Fothergill, 'your old friend was a common soldier, a councillor, a kind of dictator, an ambassador to a county mob, and, on his returning home, a nobody again'.

But more sinister shapes were rising above the horizon. In the spring of 1764 came talk of the Stamp Act. As usual, Franklin hit straight on the vital point with the vital phrase. 'What you get from us in taxes,' he wrote to Collinson, 'you must lose in trade. The cat can yield but her skin.' He did not as yet add that the cat might prove a tiger, and sell its skin dear.

At the same time there arose fresh financial quarrels between the Pennsylvania Assembly and the Proprietors' governor, now John Penn, a grandson of the founder. Franklin decided that the Proprietors were hopeless. Pennsylvania ought to pass from them to the crown. In October 1764 he was chosen by the Assembly to plead this course in England; that December he saw again the cliffs of the Isle of Wight. He thought he had come for a few months; in reality, it was for ten years—the first half of his twenty years' fight for American independence.

Two months later, in February 1765, the mule-headed Grenville brought in the Stamp Act. Even Franklin, while deploring it, had not foreseen the fury of the explosion that followed in the colonies —riots, a Stamp Act Congress, the cutting of trade with England by half. Like Montaigne, he found himself, for his moderation, attacked by extremists on both sides. His American enemies accused him of being bought by the ministry; and caricatured him as listening to the Devil, who whispers 'Thou shalt be Agent BEN for all my Realms.' His Philadelphia house was in danger of being burnt; and the resolute Deborah had to fortify and garrison it herself.

In July 1765 Grenville was replaced by the more reasonable Rockingham. And Franklin worked hard at winning English public opinion, in opposition to the lawyers (who saw the question legalistically), the landowners (who wanted lighter taxes), the placemen (who regarded America as a place for jobs), and the King (who felt any resistance to be infringement of his prerogative). Franklin's own plan was that the colonies should, like Scotland, send members to Westminster; or else that there should be a common council in the colonies from which financial contributions should be asked when needed.[1]

In February 1766 came Franklin's famous examination before the House of Commons, sitting as a committee. His replies to questions, both by friends and by enemies, were a personal triumph; and reports of the proceedings were published not only in London, but at Boston, New London, New York, and Philadelphia (in German and English), and even at Strasbourg (in French). Next month, the Stamp Act was repealed. And so strong was still the feeling of loyalty, at least in many Americans, that three hundred gentlemen of Philadelphia agreed to wear suits of British manufacture on the King's next birthday, giving their old homespun clothes to the poor. But that good will was soon to be frittered away by fresh governmental follies.

Franklin himself, despite his victory, had by now grown more pessimistic. In May 1766 he wrote, of American representation in Parliament, that the English would not grant it while the Americans would still accept; and when the English at last were willing, the

[1] For inner fluctuations in Franklin's mind about American taxation see V. W. Crane, *Benjamin Franklin and a Rising People* (1954), ch. vi.

Americans would be so no longer. And, with his unfailing gift for picturesque illustration, he recalled the legend of the brazen head that Friar Bacon made, to reveal the means of guarding England with a brazen wall—how Friar Bungay, set to watch till the head should speak, slept at his post—how the head cried in vain 'Time is', 'Time was'—and how Bungay woke only to hear 'Time is past'. 'An explosion followed that tumbled their house about the conjurers' ears.' The prophecy was only too exact.

Throughout, Franklin's own principles on American taxation were simple, clear, and, it seems to me, reasonable. Legally, he held, the English parliament had no more right to tax America than to tax Hanover. Both America and Hanover were subject to the King, not to Parliament. In any case, whatever the legalities, it did not make common sense for a statesmen like Townshend to impose taxes which might yield £40,000 a year, at the risk of a war costing thousands of times as much. Right at the end of his life, when the fatal war had been fought and won, the old Franklin still persisted (September 20, 1787)—

> 'I am confident that Canada might have been purchased[1] from France for a tenth part of the money England spent on the conquest of it. And if, instead of fighting with us for the power of taxing us, she had kept us in good humour by allowing us to dispose of our own money, and now and then giving us a little of hers, by way of donation to colleges, or hospitals, or for cutting canals, or fortifying ports, she might have easily drawn from us much more by our occasional voluntary grants and contributions than ever she could by taxes.'

And then follows the usual homely illustration in the style of Poor Richard—'Sensible people will give a bucket or two of water to a dry pump.' The history of the Second British Empire seems to me strong evidence that Franklin was right. It is something to our credit that this lesson was learnt in the end; though not till too late in our dealings with Ireland. But if a little more of Franklin's good sense had existed in the English King, Lords, and Commons, that lesson might have been learnt at smaller cost than the loss of an Empire.

[1] As Louisiana *was* purchased from France in 1803.

Meanwhile, however, Franklin found much to enjoy in his stay; while he became, as years passed, agent also for Georgia, New Jersey, and Massachusetts. He visited Germany in 1766, France in 1767 and 1769; and though in May 1767 the irresponsible Charles Townshend had introduced his fatal taxes on American imports of gloves, paint, paper, and tea, that autumn Franklin was still so loyal as to write, after his gracious reception at Versailles, 'No Frenchman shall go beyond me in thinking my own king and queen the very best in the world, and the most amiable.' 'I fancy,' he had remarked at the beginning of his journey, 'that intriguing nation would like very well to meddle on occasion, and blow up the coals between Britain and her colonies; but I hope we shall give them no opportunity.' Little he guessed that ten years later he would himself reappear in Paris as principal bellows.

In this same month of September 1767, the fatal Lord North succeeded Townshend. In the following January Franklin produced a new piece of propaganda in the *London Chronicle—Causes of American Discontents before* 1768. Why, he asked, should America have to import Portuguese wine, oil, and fruit exclusively by way of England? Why should a few British merchants be able to prevent nine colonies from issuing paper currency? Why should Americans be prohibited from making themselves hats, nails, or steel? In spite of such provocations America was still loyal. 'But this unhappy system of politics tends to dissolve those bonds of union and to sever us for ever. Woe to the man that first adopted it!'

But that autumn (October 1768) eight warships and two battalions were sent to make Boston pay its customs; though the Wilkes riots of that year should have warned authority how hard it was to deal with popular tumults, even on a minor scale, and even at home. Franklin's enemies campaigned against him in the press, and tried to make him resign his postmastership—but failed, 'I being deficient in that Christian virtue of resignation'.

Year by year, the drift towards Niagara quickened. In January 1770 the stupid and passionate Hillsborough, Secretary of State for the colonies, refused to recognize Franklin's appointment as its agent by Massachusetts; in March 1770 North carried the repeal of all Townshend's duties except that on tea, which was retained only by North's deciding vote in the Cabinet (against his own better

judgement) in deference to his royal master. So the English persisted in squandering an empire for three pence on a pound of tea. English governments could not realize that, for the colonies, the amount of taxation had become a trifle compared with the principle that the colonies should not be taxed; though for themselves the principle that the colonies *should* be taxed had become so important that they were ready to lose millions of pounds in enforcing it.

On the same day as North's fatal vote, March 5, 1770, came the 'Boston Massacre'—five men killed by British troops firing on a crowd. Writing in May to the Boston Committee of Correspondence, Franklin predicted more repression leading to riots, more riots leading to repression; 'and the bloody struggle will end in absolute slavery to America or ruin to Britain by the loss of her colonies: the latter most probable, from America's growing strength and magnitude'.

In 1771, he visited Dublin, then Edinburgh (where he stayed with Hume); contrasting the abject poverty he saw on his journey with the prosperity of New England. The same year brought the beginning of his famous *Autobiography*, of which the first part (nearly half) was written while he was the guest of the liberal Bishop of St Asaph at Twyford near Winchester. In 1773 appeared in France *Les Oeuvres de M. Franklin*; and in England his pamphlet-eering pen was now busy with two last efforts to inject a little reality into British brains—*Rules by Which a Great Empire May Be Reduced to a Small One* and *Edict by the King of Prussia*. 'A great empire,' says the first, 'like a great cake, is most easily diminished at the edges.' And the principles for doing it are drawn straight from British practice—forgetfulness that the colonies were founded at their own expense; jealousy of their growth; suspicion of their loyalty; the choice of greedy governors, and indifference to complaints against them; contempt for voluntary contributions, and imposition of novel taxes, accompanied by the claim 'that your power of taxing them has no limits; so that when you take from them without their consent one shilling in the pound you have a clear right to the other nineteen'. To these recipes were added infringements of personal liberties; dissolution of provincial assemblies; misuse of the British navy for vexatious interference with American shipping, in enforcement of vexatious customs-duties; and misuse of the British army to burden the colonial populations, instead of defending them.

The *Edict by the King of Prussia*, not surprisingly, sold even better; some simple readers were actually hoaxed into supposing it a genuine document of Frederick's. The King of Prussia was represented as claiming that England was, in origin, a German colony, settled by 'Hengist, Horsa, Hella, Uff, Cerdicus, Ida and others'; and had in the recent war been defended by German arms against France—for which Prussia could justly claim compensation. Therefore duties should now be laid on British exports and imports; all shipping to and from Britain should call, for search, at Königsberg; no iron, no hats should be manufactured in Britain; and all Prussian criminals not hanged should be transported to Britain, 'for the better peopling of that country'.

Yet at the same time as Franklin's pen stabbed at the pretensions of the mother-country, it preached conciliation to Americans; urging them to bear 'a little with the infirmities of her government, as we would with those of an aged parent'.

But neither satire nor conciliation could alter the arbitrary arrogance of English authority, or the conceited nonchalance of much English public opinion. Perhaps Pitt's victories in the Seven Years War had gone too much to our heads; in any case there was the traditional English superciliousness. 'Every man in England,' Franklin had complained to Lord Kames in 1767, 'seems to consider himself as a piece of a Sovereign over America; seems to jostle himself into the throne with the King, and talks of "our subjects in the colonies".' But the English were not to talk so for much longer. In December 1773, a couple of months after Franklin's two pamphlets, came the Boston Tea-party.

Almost simultaneously in London the British Government made a determined attempt to tip overboard Franklin himself. The trouble had long been brewing. The governor of Massachusetts, Thomas Hutchinson, and the lieutenant-governor, his brother-in-law Andrew Oliver, were both Americans. At the end of 1772 there were put into Franklin's hands certain letters written by both men to England in 1767–9, supporting firm repressive measures against the colonies. He was shocked that Americans should be guilty of what seemed to him such treachery; but at the same time the discovery lessened his resentment against the English government; and so, hoping that it might similarly lessen resentment in Massachusetts, he sent the letters to Cushing, of the Committee of Correspondence in Boston, with instructions that they might be shown to certain trusted persons, but not copied nor printed.

Now Franklin's motive was peace-making. And it is easy to be wise in retrospect. But one may wonder if here he showed his usual prudence. These letters were high explosive. He stipulated, indeed, that they should be shown by Cushing only to five persons he specified, 'with a few other such gentlemen as you may think fit to show them to'; but such vagueness was very poor security. By June 1773 the letters had caused so much gossip that Samuel Adams thought fit to read them to a secret session of the Assembly. Then they slipped into print. Then the Assembly petitioned the King to dismiss Hutchinson and Oliver from office. Franklin had meant to pour water on the flames: but he had poured oil.

The letters were originally written in 1767–9 to one Thomas Whately, who served under Grenville and North. They were lent to Grenville, who lent them to some third person. But in 1770 Grenville died; in 1772 Whately died; and by some channel still unknown the letters had reached Franklin. In December 1773, when Franklin's part in the business was as yet a secret, William Whately, brother of the dead Thomas, accused a certain John Temple of the leakage. The controversy passed into the public press; then on to the duelling-ground, where Whately was wounded. Franklin still lay low. But, hearing that the duel was likely to be repeated, on Christmas Day 1773 he honestly and humanely stated in the *Public Advertiser* that Thomas Whately and John Temple were both wholly innocent of sending the letters to Boston. The act had been his alone.[1]

Franklin had offered himself as the lightning-conductor; now the lightning fell—with a heavier charge than he looked for. He received private warnings that he would lose his place as Deputy Postmaster-General; that he might even exchange it for a place in Newgate Prison. The King had referred the Massachusetts petition, for the removal of Hutchinson and Oliver, to the Lords Committee

---

[1] The mystery is deepened by a later claim on Temple's part that he *had* been privy to the whole affair. But Temple was then pleading for compensation from the state of Massachusetts; and Franklin appears to have ignored his statements.

of the Privy Council for Plantation Affairs. After a preliminary meeting of this Committee on January 11, 1774, a full hearing was appointed for the 29th. Just before that, news reached London of the Boston Tea-party. The atmosphere grew more electric still.

That Eve of St Charles the Martyr, 1774, saw an unprecedented concourse of thirty-six privy-councillors in the Privy Council chamber at the Cockpit—appropriate name for the occasion. Among them sat the Archbishop of Canterbury and the Bishop of London; the Duke of Queensberry and eight earls, including the disreputable 'Jemmy Twitcher', Lord Sandwich; nine other peers, including the clever but imprudent Lord North; and others such as Charles Jenkinson, leader of the 'King's Friends', and Sir Jeffrey Amherst, conqueror of Louisburg and Fort Duquesne. The liberal Lord Camden, warned what was coming, did not come. Among the spectators were other names more distinguished still—Burke, Priestley, Shelburne, the young Bentham. Franklin, for the Massachusetts Assembly, was represented by Dunning (proposer six years later of the famous motion on the increasing influence of the Crown) and by John Lee. For the governors of Massachusetts there appeared the Solicitor-General, the canny, shifty, foul-mouthed Wedderburn,[1] hereafter Lord Chancellor and Earl of Rosslyn, to whom belonged the dishonours of the day. The councillors sat at a long table; the spectators stood; the old Franklin, in a suit of Manchester velvet, stood also, facing the councillors, on the left of the fireplace at the room's end. The scene might have made a fine historical painting, in the days when painters did not disdain to be also historians, and had not yet withdrawn themselves, like deities, into the clouds.

[1] Alexander Wedderburn, later Lord Loughborough, (1733–1805) began as an advocate in Edinburgh (1754), but in 1757 transferred himself, more successfully than poor Boswell, to the English bar. With the rise of Bute (1760) this fellow-Scot rose also. Yet in 1768 he supported the anti-Scottish Wilkes. In 1771, deserting to North, he became Solicitor-General; in 1780, Chief Justice of the Common Pleas; in 1793, Lord Chancellor. 'As for Wedderburn,' wrote Junius, 'there is something about him which even treachery cannot trust.' Nor was Churchill kinder—

> Mute at the bar, and in the senate loud,
> Dull 'mongst the dullest, proudest of the proud,
> A pert, prim prater of the northern race,
> Guilt in his heart, and famine in his face.

Still let it also be remembered that he helped to get Johnson his pension.

In theory, the business of the day was to pass judgement on the Massachusetts petition; in practice, it became a judgement on Franklin, as the criminal agitator who had set a peaceful province aflame. He had, thundered Wedderburn, got hold of private correspondence 'by fraudulent or corrupt means for the most malignant of purposes; unless he stole them from the person who stole them'. The Solicitor-General called on the Privy Council 'to mark and brand this man, for the honour of this country, of Europe, and of mankind'. Then, for this was a classical age, he quoted Plautus— 'homo trium literarum'.[1] And, having quoted ancient comedy, he passed to modern tragedy—to the African villain of Young's *Revenge*, who boasted:

> 'I forged the letters; I disposed the picture;
> I hated, I despised, and I destroy.'

This 'wily American', Wedderburn continued, had been so carried away by his ambitious fantasies as to behave as if he were ambassador of 'a Great American Republic', free to hire spies and buy intelligence. And Wedderburn foolishly suggested that Franklin was a self-seeker, hoping to be made governor of Massachusetts himself, in place of Hutchinson.[2]

For nearly an hour this tirade thundered on—and it may be remembered that Franklin was now a man of sixty-seven, Wedderburn only forty. Of all the Privy Councillors present, only North, it is said, had the decency and dignity not to join in the jeering laughter and applause. The scene left Bentham stunned, and Priestley horrified. Burke, himself no mean expert in violent invective, thought Wedderburn 'beyond all bounds and measure'. Yet Franklin, by temperament neither submissive nor over-patient, had learnt the lesson of his Quaker friend long ago—he could avoid the appearance of arrogance. But he could also avoid the appearance of misplaced humility. His lips were still sealed as to the source whence

---

[1] 'A man of three letters'; i.e. *fur*, 'thief'.

[2] A little later Franklin was accused by 'Sagittarius' in the *Public Ledger* of plotting for a 'GREAT AMERICAN COMMONWEALTH' of which 'the GREAT and LEARNED DOCTOR was to be the REGULATOR and DICTATOR! The old dotard thought he saw himself as the founder of empires and the father of kings.' 'The old dotard' was to succeed as a founder of empires better than the writer dreamed.

he got the letters. Neither excuse nor recrimination would serve him before that hostile audience. There was only one right course in his predicament—and he took it—immobile and impassive silence. Through his counsel, Dunning, he declined to be examined. The Committee voted the Massachusetts petition 'groundless, vexatious, and scandalous'. Next day Franklin was dismissed from the office of Deputy Postmaster-General.

The same day at breakfast he told Priestley that he had no regrets for what he considered one of the best actions of his life. He had indeed come out of it with dignity. But since his object had been and still remained reconciliation, I find this attitude, if he really held it, a little strange. No doubt, the righteous indignation of Wedderburn at the use Franklin had made of the Hutchinson letters was probably cant; for Wedderburn is unlikely to have been ignorant that Franklin's own letters were repeatedly opened by the British government. But Franklin's use of those letters had in fact brought nearer, not peace, but the sword. The clash may have been inevitable. But the miscalculation remains.

Wedderburn's foolish triumph, however, is not ill summed up in an epigram of Horace Walpole's—

> Sarcastic Sawney, swol'n with spite and prate,
> On silent Franklin poured his venal hate.
> The calm philosopher, without reply,
> Withdrew, and gave his country liberty.

For peace, however, Franklin continued to work, though with increasing hopelessness, for over another year. In answer to the Boston Tea-party, the Government closed the port of Boston, made General Gage governor of Massachusetts, and remodelled its constitution. In reply a colonial conference met at Philadelphia. Franklin on his side wrote to America urging compensation for the tea— 'the India Company are not our Adversaries'; and pleading that a boycott of British goods was far better tactics than rioting and disorder. 'By the Boston Newspapers there seem to be among us some violent Spirits, who are for an immediate Rupture. But, I trust, the general Prudence of our Countrymen will see, that by our growing Strength we advance fast to a Situation in which our Claims must be allow'd.'

That restraint would perhaps have been the best policy to pursue to the end. But this would be expecting too much of the sagacity of ordinary men. Indeed, Franklin himself became suspected in America of lukewarmness. In England, however, he was now consulted by Lord Chatham and Lord Howe. Yet month by month the gap was widening. The Ministers were so anxious to save their faces that they lost their heads.

In November 1774 a new Parliament was elected; but court-influence and political prejudice ensured that it was no wiser than the old. For the opening session Franklin wrote, though he did not publish it, an imaginary speech from the throne. Instead of the real George III, both headstrong and weak in the head, there speaks in it an imaginary George with eyes opened at last. Let not Parliament believe that an American conflict would be the easy rout of a mere rabble.

'If you undertake this job it will cost you at the least farthing a good round sum of forty or fifty millions; forty or fifty thousands of your constituents will get knocked on the head; and then you are to consider what the rest of you will be gainers by the bargain even if you succeed. The trade of a ruined and desolated country is always inconsiderable, its revenues trifling; the expense of subjecting and retaining it in subjection certain and inevitable.'

'You must know this is not the first time that the Serpent has been whispering in my ear, Tax America. Cost what it will, make them your hewers of wood and drawers of water. . . . But if I were to give you a word of advice it should be to remind you of the Italian epitaph upon a poor fool that killed himself with quacking. *Stava bene, per star meglio, sto qui.* That is to say: I was well, I would be better, I took physic and died.'

Unfortunately, there were too many fools in England duped by braggarts like General Clarke, who undertook with a thousand British grenadiers 'to go from one end of America to the other, and geld all the males, partly by force and partly by a little coaxing'. In January 1775 the petition of Congress was left to lie on the table of the House of Commons; in the Lords, Chatham's proposal to withdraw troops from Boston could muster only eighteen votes against sixty-eight (including twenty-four bishops). And next month when Chatham proposed his plan of reconciliation, Sandwich took the opportunity to attack Franklin, who was leaning on the bar of the House, as inspirer of the scheme and 'one of the bitterest and most mischievous enemies this country had ever known'. As when he stood before Wedderburn, Franklin kept his countenance 'as immovable as if my features had been made of wood'. But Sandwich was not, like Wedderburn, to go unanswered. Chatham retorted with a tribute to 'one whom all Europe held in high estimation for his knowledge and wisdom, and ranked with our Boyles and Newtons; who was an honour not to the English nation only but to human nature'. Before such praise Franklin's features found it harder to keep their impassivity.

But Chatham's bill, said Franklin, 'was treated with as much contempt as they could have shown to a ballad offered by a drunken porter'. These 'hereditary legislators', in his opinion, 'appeared to have scarce discretion enough to govern a herd of swine'.

The story of these years has, indeed, some of the quality of a nightmare, even to the modern reader who watches in impotence as their folly unfolds. And yet elected legislators can be as blind as Chatham's Lords. In the years before Munich Neville Chamberlain's compact majority drifted as dully as North's down a course that might have proved still more disastrous, while Churchill's warnings went as unheeded as Chatham's; with the difference only that the men of Munich did far too little, where their eighteenth-century predecessors did far too much. George III had indeed become a king; but only to lose an empire. It is ironic to think that, could we have exchanged crowned fools with France, the world might have been spared both American and French Revolutions, and all the misery they cost. For Louis XVI was an inert fool who would never have raised the American storm; while George III, though a meddler and muddler, showed himself in the Gordon Riots at least a resolute person in the face of mobs.

To the end Franklin still fought on against the inevitable. In February 1775 he undertook, at the risk of ruin, to guarantee on his own responsibility compensation for the Boston tea, provided that the Massachusetts Acts were repealed. But the Government representatives who negotiated with him could not go far enough

to meet him; though they went foolishly too far in offering him personal advantages which he could only regard as bribes, and therefore contemptible. Indeed, he had now come to consider the whole political system of England so corrupt that his own earlier wishes for closer union had seriously weakened—'it seems to be Mezentius' coupling and binding together the dead and the living'. Yet he saw the coming conflict with anguish. In March 1775, reading aloud American newspapers for Priestley to make extracts for the English press, he was at moments blinded by his tears. Next day he left for Portsmouth. An incongruously calm voyage was used by him to write the inner history of his vain negotiations—and to experiment with dropping thermometers in the Gulf Stream. Politics pass: science endures. But while he stemmed that smooth Atlantic under the April sun, already the first blood flowed among the lanes of Lexington.

After that, the deluge; the sluice-gates stood wide for the slaughter, not only of the American Revolution, but also of the consequent French Revolution, and of Napoleon.

As soon as he landed in May 1775, the old man found himself in the thick of new activities. He was chosen deputy to the Second Continental Congress at Philadelphia; and though he often slept at its meetings (as will surprise no one accustomed to public speaking), he was made member also of all important committees. Of both him and Washington, Jefferson noted that he never heard them speak more than ten minutes at a time.[1] They confined themselves to the points that really mattered. In July 1775, after Bunker's Hill, Franklin became President of the Committee of Safety for the defence of Pennsylvania, busy with the manufacture of pikes and *chevaux de frise*; and also Postmaster-General. That July the last petition from Congress to the King was not even presented by Lord Dartmouth; in August a royal proclamation declared the Americans to be rebels. Franklin's blood did not boil easily; yet there were moments when it boiled now.

'Mr Strahan,' he wrote that July (1775) to his old friend, the famous publisher, 'You are a Member of Parliament, and one of that Majority which has doomed my Country to Destruction.—You have

[1] Contrast Burke.

begun to burn our Towns, and murder our People.—Look upon
your Hands!—They are stained with the Blood of your Relations!—
You and I were long Friends:—You are now my Enemy,—and
I am
                              Yours
                                   B. Franklin.'

I like the old sage the better because he could be so passionate;
but I like him better still because, even in passion, he remained a
sage. Having usefully relieved his feelings by writing this letter, he
after all refrained from sending it.[1] His friendship with Strahan
survived.

In October 1775, to the more sympathetic Priestley, Franklin
could point out with calmer triumph that one hundred and fifty
Yankees had been killed at a cost of three millions (£20,000 each!);
and, in the same period, 60,000 born!

None the less, having lost his wife, the old Franklin now in effect,
lost also his only son. For William Franklin took the opposite side,
becoming president of the Associated Loyalists of New York.[2]
From 1776, he spent more than two years in prison. Franklin was
reticent about his private sorrows; but 'nothing has ever hurt me so
much'.

In that spring of 1776, despite his seventy years, Franklin served
on an arduous, but ineffectual mission to raise the French of Canada
against England. The autumn brought him a mission to the French
of France, which was to have very different success, and to employ
perhaps the most famous and most effective years of his whole life.
For a fourth time, in October 1776, he saw the shores of the New
World fade to westward; and now he was facing the risks not only
of the sea (his frail vessel was lost on her return voyage), but also of
the English navy and an English prison. But again his scientific side
found occupation in the Gulf Stream. Accompanied by William
Temple Franklin, the natural son of his natural son, in December
1776 he landed at Auray. That same month Lord Stormont, report-
ing from our Paris Embassy to Lord Weymouth on the old man's

[1] It was, however, later printed by the periodical, *Affaires de l'Angleterre et de
l'Amérique*, to which Franklin contributed during his stay in France.
[2] It may be relevant to recall that illegitimate children are apt to bear their fathers a
secret grudge.

arrival, added: 'In a word, my lord, I look upon him as a dangerous engine, and am very sorry that some English frigate did not meet with him by the way.' Few tributes could be so sincere.

Franklin had spent ten years in England trying to prevent the American Revolution from happening; he was now to spend eight in France securing its success. The time of life between seventy and eighty, when most men are dead, or have suspended animation, brought *his* greatest triumph.

Yet his task remained full of delicacy and difficulty. Vergennes, though sympathetic, had at first to tread with extreme wariness for fear of embroiling France with England. Then there were the financial difficulties of both France and the colonies. Franklin spent much of his time either begging money from the French till he blushed, or remonstrating with Congress for expecting him to meet drafts that he was at his wits' end to pay. Then there were difficulties with colleagues, especially with Arthur Lee, who hated him, wanted to displace him, and suspected him of embezzlement. There were innumerable adventurers who pestered him to serve in America where, even if they were capable of being useful, Congress might have difficulty in using them. And there were English spies—such as Edward Bancroft, who lived for a time in Franklin's own household, and communicated intelligence by bottles left in a hole of a tree near the Tuileries. Indeed, I get the impression that, as over the Hutchinson letters, Franklin was too negligent of security. Finally, there was a sheer weight of business—diplomatic, financial, commercial, naval—that might have broken a far younger man. As he wrote of himself to the President of Congress in 1788, 'though he has always been an active man, he never went through so much business during eight years, in any part of his life, as during those of his residence in France'. And by 1780 he was suffering from gout; by 1782, from the stone. For, as he philosophically put it, 'People who will live long, who will drink of the cup to the very bottom, must expect to meet with some of the usual dregs.'

Yet patience, good humour, and good sense, as always with Franklin, prevailed. In February 1778 was signed a treaty of amity and commerce; at which, it was told, Franklin wore the same blue Manchester velvet as when four years before he had stood in the Cockpit, as target for the shafts of Wedderburn.

> Ho! dogs of false Tarentum,
>   Is not the gown washed white?

Saratoga (October 7, 1777) had borne its fruit.

A month later (March 1778), with his colleagues, he was received at Versailles—not, like the rest, in court-dress, but wigless and swordless; and conspicuous with spectacles, white hat under arm, and white hair flowing free. That July the sails of d'Estaing appeared off the Delaware.

Peace was still five weary years away. But the end grew more and more inevitable, with the intervention of Spain in 1779, with the Armed Neutrality of the North in 1780, with Yorktown in 1781. Even when the news from the colonies was bad, Franklin would maintain American prestige by his smiling imperturbability; it is supposed to have been from his calmly repeated 'Ça ira' that the famous song of the French Revolution was derived. And still he found time for political satire. He probably wrote *The Sale of the Hessians*, a supposed letter from a Count de Schaumbergh delighting in reports of the number of Hessians killed, since each dead soldier meant British blood-money—'I am about to send you some new recruits. Don't economize them. Remember glory before all things.'

Further, Franklin was certainly responsible for the *Supplement to the Boston Independent Chronicle* (1782), printed by the private press he had set up at Passy. It purported to come from a New England captain who had seized eight packages consigned by the Seneca Indians to the English governor of Canada, and containing American scalps—those of eighty-eight women, one hundred and ninety-three boys, two hundred and eleven girls, and twenty-nine infants ripped from their mother's bellies. 'It is . . . proposed to make them up in decent little packets . . . one to the king . . . one to the queen . . . the rest to be distributed among both Houses of Parliament, a double quantity to the bishops.' This recalls Franklin's early, lighter-hearted jest on rattlesnakes; it does not add to Franklin's literary reputation; but it was apparently based on facts only too genuine, and was doubtless effective propaganda.

Pleasanter reading is provided by his instructions (1779) that any American armed ship meeting Captain Cook (who was by then already dead in the Pacific) should treat him and his company, not as enemies, 'but with all civility and kindness . . . as common friends to mankind'.

But perhaps nothing that Franklin did, or wrote, worked more for his country's cause than simply what he was, as a symbol in the eyes of a France now filled with new idealism; as an incarnation of the patriarchal simplicity of Rousseau's dreams, in a real man who was yet at the same time not a noble savage, but scientist and sage. Typical were the encounters in 1778 between Franklin and that Voltaire who had visited London almost simultaneously with him half a century before, and had now returned to Paris to die of an apotheosis. When they met in the Academy of Sciences, there was a general cry that the two venerable philosophers should exchange civilities. They grasped each other by the hand. But that was not enough. The tumult of enthusiasm persisted—'Il faut s'embrasser à la française.' The pair hugged and kissed. And the cry rose— 'Qu'il est charmant de voir s'embrasser Solon et Sophocle!' Again, when Voltaire gave his benediction to Franklin's grandson, it was with the words 'God and Liberty.' 'All who were present shed tears of tenderness.' It would be interesting to know Franklin's private thoughts of these amateur theatricals.

To us who have since seen too many New Jerusalems descend from Heaven only to prove Cities of Dreadful Night, that dawn in the closing eighteenth century, when young men like Wordsworth could find it, if only for a moment, Heaven to be young, seems ironically naïve. Human perfectibility!—the final triumph of reason and virtue!—from the modern young such credulity could win only a disgusted smile. Perhaps, even, we have swung too far in the opposite direction of disillusion. At all events the mood was real. And French industry was kept busy reproducing Franklin's likeness in busts, engravings, medallions, rings, and snuff-boxes.

His very simplicity, like Hume's, was a further source of success. Patriarchs *should* be simple. Franklin's French was, at first, so defective that at some meeting he was reduced to the expedient of applauding whenever Mme de Boufflers applauded—only to find that he had thus been led to clap loudest at praises of himself. But such stories made him, like Hume, seem only more charming; and, despite his age, he contrived in time to learn enough French to complete his conquests.

And so, though Franklin was no Rousseau, and far too realist to become a rapturist, yet this benevolent ancient, with the silver locks falling from beneath his cap of fur, could provide a paternal embodiment for the new hopes to cluster round. And though these hopes were by no means to found the New Jerusalem, they were not negligible in helping to found the United States.

Of course, as usual in politics, the true inner history of these years was less idyllic. Beneath the heaving, sunlit surface of emotional idealism ran under-currents and cross-currents of a chillier realism. Many in France warmly sympathized with the Americans: yet French policy did not wish to see the colonies *too* independent, or annexing Canada. Many in America were deeply grateful to France: yet American policy did not wish to grow *too* entangled with her—there were some who thought Franklin too French. And so, inevitably, each ally developed views and aims that were kept carefully secret from the other.

Such is the perpetual difficulty of politics, the constant clash between private and public morality (which tends to worry the Anglo-Saxon more than the Latin races). To his ideals the individual may sacrifice his interests; but the politician cannot sacrifice to his own ideals the interests of his countrymen. And so the diplomatic history of these years also has plenty of subterfuges and deceptions to make the cynic smile, and recall the disillusion of the aged Sophocles, two thousand years ago—

> Dear son of Aegeus, to the Gods alone
> There comes not near for ever Age or Death;
> But all things else all-mastering Time confounds.
> The strength of the fields grows faint, the body's strength,
> And old trust dies, and new distrust is born,
> And the same breath of friendship blows not long
> 'Twixt man and man, nor yet 'twixt land and land;
> But, be it soon or in slow lapse of years,
> Things loved grow bitter, then beloved again.

Which in its turn recalls the disillusion of Wordsworth—

> Earth is sick,
> And Heaven is weary, of the hollow words
> Which States and Kingdoms utter when they talk
> Of truth and justice.

Even in Franklin's own political thinking there remained needs and motives not always easy to harmonize—altruism, yet power-politics; native honesty, yet diplomatic cunning; pacifism, yet an expansionism looking north towards Canada and west to the Mississippi; desire for reconciliation,[1] yet resentment against the 'wickedness' of England, and implacability towards the Loyalists who, like his own son, had clung to her. Further, there were not a few Americans to whom Franklin himself became an object of suspicion, envy, or dislike.[2]

However, through all these difficulties, as so often before, common sense carried him. Franklin was not, like the English statesmen who provoked the American Revolution, a pedantic legalist—he was too practical. He would not have minded in 1769 the claim of Parliament to legislate for the colonies, provided it were never put in practice—'we shall consider it in the same Light with the Claim of the Spanish Monarch to the Title of King of Jerusalem'. He was not, like such typical eighteenth-century minds as Priestley or Condorcet, a Utopian, bemused with intoxicating optimism about human nature. He had shocked his simple sister by describing men as 'Devils to one another'. He had doubted in a pessimistic moment whether 'the Species were really worth producing or preserving'. Yet he was no cynicized Machiavelli. He held strongly that honesty, if not always possible in international politics, was usually the best policy. He was the reverse of Mazarin, of whom Don Luis de Haro shrewdly said that his great diplomatic fault was that he wished *always* to deceive. (The type is not extinct.) Asked what sort of ambassador we had best send to Paris after the War, Franklin replied 'a plain, downright, honest man'—'*finesse* might serve to gain a point at first but it afterwards would be found the longest & most difficult way of doing business'. So Wellington also thought. As for the constant clash of national interests, Franklin believed that they need not clash nearly so often as men assume; that two nations can frequently gain far more by seeking the advantage of both than the damage of each other; that one does not best grow rich by beggaring

[1] Cf. his suggestion, after the war, to David Hartley for 'a family compact between England, France, and America. America wd be as happy as the Sabine girls, if she cd be the means of uniting in perpetual peace her father and her husband.'

[2] The whole tangled situation is excellently analysed in G. Stourzh, *Benjamin Franklin and American Foreign Policy* (1954).

one's neighbour. In short, a policy of enlightened self-interest—with stress on the enlightenment. No doubt it would be excellent, could men acquire better hearts; but the world could become a great deal happier even if they only acquired clearer heads. For America his ultimate dream appears to have been an agricultural democracy. free from the corruption of great cities where, crawling and sprawling over one another, men grow venomous. Not even he could then foresee how quickly America would fill, from ocean to ocean.

Meanwhile, for Franklin himself these years in Paris became perhaps the most genial phase in all his long life. While performing his laborious duties, he had no intention of blacking himself all over to play Othello. Jealous rivals might judge him frivolous; but they achieved far less themselves. Never was he more human and more humorous. He had always felt the charm of feminine society. And now he admitted that 'the matter of genders had bothered him for sixty years, and at seventy-eight he still found the French feminines a plague'. But, after all, he was still young. 'Being arrived at seventy,' he explained, at seventy-four, 'and considering that by travelling further in the same road I should probably be led to the grave, I stopped short, turned about, and walked back again; which having done these four years, you may now call me sixty-six.' And so it came about that never had he flirted so gaily.[1]

The two chief objects of his gallantries were Mme Helvétius and Mme Brillon. Madame Helvétius, widow of the optimistic *philosophe* (d. 1771) who fondly believed that education could do everything, was now in her sixties;[2] and, living (with ten dogs and eighteen cats) at Auteuil, she was a neighbour to Franklin at Passy. To her the aged Fontenelle had sighed—'Ah, Madame, if I were only eighty again!' Turgot had wished to marry her after the death of Helvétius (1771). And Franklin himself, how seriously one cannot tell, wished to marry her now. After her refusal he wrote to her that he

---

[1] Even, according to the *London Chronicle* of July 4-7, 1778, with Marie Antoinette. When he showed her some electrical experiment in the gardens of Versailles, the Queen was said to have asked if he did not fear the fate of Prometheus; to which he was supposed to have replied that he would indeed fear it, were it not that he saw unpunished a pair of eyes that had stolen far more fire from Jove than he, and did far more mischief than all his experiments.

[2] Born 1719; died 1800. 'Quoiqu' elle ne sût rien,' it has been a little unkindly said, 'et ne réflechît à rien de ce qu'elle disait, elle plaisait toujours et instruisait quelquefois.'

had dreamed he was in Elysium, where he met the late Helvétius who, it turned out, was now remarried there, and quite astonished to hear of the obstinacy of his widow on earth. Then entered the new Mme Helvétius, with the coffee. Who should she be but the late Deborah Franklin?—who calmly retorted, when he claimed her back—'J'ai été votre bonne femme quarante-neuf années et quatre mois, presque un demi-siècle; soyez content de cela. J'ai formé ici une nouvelle connexion qui durera à l'éternité.—Mécontent de ce refus de mon Eurydice, j'ai pris tout de suite la résolution de quitter ces ombres ingrates, et de revenir en ce bon monde revoir le soleil et vous. Me voici: vengeons-nous!'

But it was in vain that he baited his hook so fancifully; in vain that he replied, to her complaint of an omitted visit, 'Madame, I am waiting till the nights are longer'; in vain, that he enlisted the very flies in his house to intercede for him—they were so grateful to her for clearing away the spiders; would she not join the household for good? Mme Helvétius preferred to remain single; but when the time came, in 1785, for Franklin's return to America, she begged him to finish his days as her neighbour; and in 1787 he was still writing, reminding her, through the Abbé Morellet, of the thousand acres on the Ohio he had promised her if only she would cross to *his* side of the Atlantic.

Candour must record, on the other hand, that Abigail, wife of Franklin's colleague John Adams, has left an account of Mme Helvétius and her behaviour that is crude and even disgusting. But ladies are not always reliable witnesses about one another; and I suppose most centuries would be shocked by one another's manners, were they not, fortunately, unable to meet.

Franklin was equally, if not still more, attached to Mme Brillon, a younger woman, in her thirties, married to a much older treasury-official. She promised to become Franklin's wife in paradise, 'on condition, however, that you do not make too many conquests among the heavenly maidens while you are waiting for me. I want a faithful husband' (M. Brillon was not) 'when I take one for eternity.'

With similar playfulness (or, puritans might say, profanity), Franklin could write to her in his imperfect French: 'Il ne faut pas blamer la Providence inconsidèrement. Reflechissez combien de nos

Devoirs même elle a ordonné d'être naturellement des Plaisirs; et qu'elle a eu la Bonté de plus, de donner le Nom de Pechés a plusieurs afin que nous en jouissions avec plus de Gout.'

On another occasion, when she accused him of inconstancy, he laughingly replied it was 'plain as Euclid that constancy to several was more than constancy to one'.

Again, perhaps amid the peace-negotiations of 1782, after some small difference between them, he amused himself with drawing up a peace-treaty of a lighter kind.

'Article 1.

There shall be eternal Peace, Friendship, and Love, between Madame B. and Mr F.

Art. 2.

In order to maintain the same inviolably, Madame B. on her Part stipulates and agrees, that Mr F. shall come to her whenever she sends for him.

Art. 3.

That he shall stay with her as long as she pleases.

Art. 4.

That when he is with her, he shall be oblig'd to drink Tea, play Chess, hear Musick; or do any other thing that she requires of him.

Art. 5.

And that he shall love no other Woman but herself.

Art. 6.

And the said Mr F. on his part stipulates and agrees, that he will go away from Mme B.'s whenever he pleases.

Art. 7.

That he will stay away as long as he pleases.

Art. 8.

That when he is with her, he will do what he pleases.

Art. 9.

And that he will love any other Woman as far as he finds her amiable.

Let me know what you think of these Preliminaries. . . . I shall insist pretty strongly on the eighth Article, tho' without much Hope of your Consent to it; and on the ninth also, tho' I despair of ever finding any other Woman that I could love with equal Tenderness: being ever, my dear dear Friend,

Yours most sincerely
B. F.'

But behind these light-hearted interludes of social comedy the iron years of tragedy dragged on; and the same pen of Franklin as flourished and gambolled in romantic badinage, could at need assume a trenchant sternness.

When his daughter, for example, wrote from America begging, amid the financial stresses of the war, for vanities like black pins, lace, and feathers, she got no such parcels, but only irony in answer —'If you wear your cambric ruffles as I do, and take care not to mend the holes, they will come in time to be lace; and feathers, my dear girl, may be had in America from every cock's tail.'

Again, when goaded by the petulant Arthur Lee, Franklin could reply in a style where every sentence stings (though he may not have actually sent the letter):

'It is true I have omitted answering some of your letters. I do not like to answer angry letters. I am old, cannot have long to live, have much to do and no time for altercation. If I have often received and borne your magisterial snubbings and rebukes without reply, ascribe it to the right causes: my concern for the honour and success of our mission which would be hurt by our quarrelling, my love of peace, my respect for your good qualities, and my pity of your sick mind, which is for ever tormenting itself with its jealousies, suspicions, and fancies that others mean you ill, wrong you, or fail in respect for you. If you do not cure yourself of this temper it will end in insanity, of which it is a symptomatic forerunner, as I have seen in several instances.'

Equally pungent is a letter of 1780 to a Captain Landois who had exhausted Franklin's patience by his quarrels with the famous privateer, Paul Jones:

'I should not give you the pain of reading it if your Demand did not make it necessary. I think you, then, so impudent, so litigious and so quarrelsome a man, even with your best friends, that Peace and good order, and consequently the quiet and regular Subordination so necessary to Success, are, where you preside, impossible. These are matters within my observation and comprehension, your military Operations I leave to more capable Judges. If therefore I had twenty Ships of War in my Disposition, I should not give one of them to Captain Landois.'

Johnson himself could hardly have been more forcible.

Even King George did not escape this trenchant pen. Franklin had favoured pointed lightning-conductors; one Benjamin Wilson preferred blunt ones. With the American War this scientific question became political. The King replaced the sharp conductors on Kensington Palace by blunt; and tried to make Sir John Pringle support this view. Sir John, having rashly replied that natural laws were not changeable at the royal pleasure, lost by his frankness the posts of President of the Royal Society, and physician to the Queen, and was banished the court. To some correspondent, Franklin commented:

'The King's changing his *pointed* conductors for *blunt* is, therefore, a matter of small importance to me. If I had a wish about it, it would be that he had rejected them altogether as ineffectual. For it is only since he thought himself and family safe from the thunder of Heaven, that he dared to use his own thunder in destroying his innocent subjects.'[1]

But even the royal obstinacy had at last to accept the inevitable, which Eliott's successful defence of Gibraltar, and Rodney's defeat of de Grasse off Dominica, could only alleviate, not evade.

In March 1782, North fell. In April, meetings began between Franklin and an old retired merchant, Oswald, the emissary of Shelburne. Franklin, who had once urged the cession of Canada by France, now wanted it ceded by England. But this time he did not get his way. In November 1782 the preliminaries of peace were

---

[1] The episode produced a typical epigram of the day in England:
> While you, great George, for safety hunt,
> And sharp conductors change for blunt,
>   The nation's out of joint:
> Franklin a wiser course pursues,
> And all your thunder fearless views,
>   By keeping to the *point*.

signed by Franklin, Jay, and Adams, without informing Vergennes
—a lapse of courtesy between allies which it took all Franklin's tact
to smooth over.

Finally, in October 1783 was signed the Peace of Versailles. And
Franklin could turn his scientific attention to the new science of
aviation. 'What,' asked someone, 'is the use of a balloon?' 'What,'
retorted Franklin, 'is the use of a new-born baby?' He might have
been less happy, could he have foreseen wha a demonic force this
new infant of aviation would become, and how many human infants
it would one day cripple or kill.

But Franklin's thoughts were bent, on the contrary, towards
civilizing even war; and one of his last diplomatic acts before leaving
for home in 1785 was tso sign a treaty with Prussia, whereby, in the
event of war, merchant resident in either country were to be given
nine months to settle their affairs, then depart in peace with their
effects; privateers were to be abolished, and merchant-ships left un-
molested; and neither side was to interfere, in unfortified towns or
villages, with women, children, scholars, cultivators, artisans, manu-
facturers, and fishermen, or with their occupations; a very eighteenth-century contrast to 'Total War'.

A few days later, in July 1785, he left Passy amid the lamentations
of his French friends. Since his sufferings from the stone made
movement painful, for the journey to Havre the Duc de Coigny
lent a mule-litter of the Queen's; too late, Vergennes offered a royal
frigate for the voyage. At Southampton Franklin met his loyalist son
and, less coldly, old friends like the Bishop of St Asaph and his
family. Once again the voyage itself was made an opportunity for
scientific investigations. And hardly had he landed amid the bells
and cannon of a cheering Philadelphia than, despite his infirmities,
he found himself a member of the Pennsylvania Council; then
President of Pennsylvania; then member of the Constitutional
Convention.

He was, indeed, too old now to be very active in the Convention;
his opinion was often not the one that prevailed; but his final speech
of September 17, 1787, when the Constitution was ready for signa-
ture, embodied that moderate sense of compromise, that realistic
acceptance of imperfection, which had always marked, and made,
his long career.

'I confess,' he said (though the speech was read for him by another), 'that there are several parts of this Constitution which I do not at present approve, but I am not sure I shall never approve them; for, having lived long, I have experienced many instances of being obliged, by better information or fuller consideration, to change opinions even on important subjects which I once thought right, but found to be otherwise. . . . Most men indeed, as well as most sects in religion, think themselves in possession of all truth. . . . But' (and here rose a memory of that loved France he was not to see again) '. . . few express it so naturally as a certain French lady who in a dispute with her sister, said: "I don't know how it happens, Sister, but I meet with nobody but myself that is *always* in the right. . . ."'

'It therefore astonishes me, Sir, to find this system approaching so near to perfection as it does. . . . On the whole, Sir, I cannot help expressing a wish that every member of the Convention who may still have objections to it would with me on this occasion doubt a little of his own infallibility, and, to make manifest our unanimity, put his name to this instrument.'

It was not with this humorously resigned sense of the possible, and acceptance of the imperfect, that men were soon to speak in the assemblies of the French Revolution. But there are advantages in eighteenth-century reasonableness and scepticism. They are so much more economical of guillotines.

Franklin's work was done. 'For my own personal ease,' he said in 1789, 'I should have died two years ago.' For he was feeble and suffering. The 'dregs' of life were bitter. Still he took pleasure in the presence of his grandchildren round him, and in his daughter's readings of Johnson's *Lives of the Poets*. Johnson's vehemence had been in favour of burning American cities, and letting them 'enjoy their forests'; but now Johnson himself lay at peace, while the wisest of Americans enjoyed, instead, his immortal *Lives*.

On one thing at least both men had been agreed—the evils of slavery. Franklin had now become President of the Pennsylvania Society for its abolition. And, in March 1790, the old satirist was roused by an anti-abolition speech in Congress by one Jackson, of Georgia, to take up his pen once more, with the same mischievous, yet deadly irony of earlier years. He was reminded, he said, of a debate in Algiers of a century before,[1] on the lawfulness of piracy

[1] This, of course, was quite apocryphal.

against the Christians, and their enslavement. There, after a certain Sidi Mehemet Ibrahim had eloquently defended both practices, 'the Divan came to this resolution: "The doctrine that plundering and enslaving the Christians is unjust, is at best problematical; but that it is the interest of this state to continue the practice, is clear; therefore let the petition be rejected." And it was rejected accordingly.'

Less than four weeks after thus attiring Mr Jackson in a mock-turban, Franklin was dead; happy to escape further decrepitude, and the spectacle of that France which had saved America, now becoming a terror to Europe and to herself. The prophet of reason and realism had passed away; and a new age was dawning, with that sinister and angry red which romantics have often loved too well.

Why was it, then, that Franklin would have been willing, as we have seen, to live his life again, and Johnson not?

Johnson's career, like those of Boswell or Gray, leaves, I think, with all our admiration for their qualities, a certain sense of frustration that those qualities yet failed, so completely, to bring satisfaction or content. Whereas the careers of Franklin, Gibbon, or Hume, possess, on the contrary, a satisfying balance, an artistic completeness, that seem characteristically eighteenth-century.

One may say, of course, that the contrast was largely luck. But 'luck' means merely the unlikely convergence of certain trains of causation. And when, over a long period, men are consistently fortunate or the reverse, it generally means that they have an inward tendency to play well, or ill, the cards that life deals to them.

The differences in these six lives turn mainly on the presence or absence of health, mental and bodily; of good sense; of affection; and of effectiveness in serving others, as well as themselves.

In bodily health, Johnson and Gray were unlucky from birth. Boswell wrecked his. But Hume, Gibbon, and Franklin were more fortunate; though even they might have given the matter more thought (as Franklin confessed in his dialogue with the Gout). They loved the table too well. But it is a mistake to grow fat.

Mentally, Johnson, Gray, and Goswell all suffered from a neurotic melancholia, which made them often unhappy in this world, and made two of them unhappy about the next; in contrast to the natural gaiety of the other three. Happiness, indeed, depends more on temperament than on reason. Yet lack of practical good sense can produce circumstances where happiness becomes difficult, even for temperaments as gay as Goldsmith's.

Hume and Gibbon both played their cards prudently; but here perhaps Franklin stands out, as the very incarnation of prudence.

No doubt, he too could be led by violent feeling into follies. He too could commit his 'errata'; and pay too much, at times, for his 'whistles'. Yet without that warmth of feeling his prudence might have become repellent to others, boring to himself. On the other hand, he had none of that false shame about good sense as something somehow mean, ridiculous, or prosaic, which has made many men prefer to be foolish. Typical is the method of reaching a decision in difficult dilemmas which he propounded in a letter to Priestley—his 'moral or prudential algebra'. This consisted in taking a sheet of paper; dividing it into two columns, 'Pro' and 'Con'; filling one with the reasons for doing the thing in question and the other with the reasons against; and then cancelling those that seemed equal or, say, two reasons on one side against three slightly less weighty on the other; the advantage being that in this way one can consider two or more factors simultaneously, whereas the ordinary person thinks only of one at a time, and veers endlessly back and forth. I own that I have never tried this, any more than Franklin's scheme for reaching moral perfection. Perhaps one is too shy of being too methodical and mechanical. At all events, when one contrasts Franklin's ways with the catalogues of human imbecilities that make up half of every morning's newspaper, I find myself in warm sympathy with his cry of exasperation, provoked by the pig-headedness of certain Dover postilions—

> 'They added other Reasons, that were no Reasons at all, and made me, as upon a hundred other Occasions, almost wish that Mankind had never been endow'd with a reasoning Faculty, since they know so little how to make use of it, and so often mislead themselves by it, and that they had been furnish'd with a good sensible Instinct instead of it.'

In personal relations, Johnson was warm-hearted, but too dictatorial; Boswell, mercurial and philandering, became sadly conscious that in a self-defeating way he cheapened himself, and seldom won fondness without an admixture of contempt; Gray was caged in his own shyness. In contrast, 'le bon David' charmed even his enemies; Gibbon might fail Suzanne Curchod, but his physical grotesqueness did not impair the warm ties that bound him to his stepmother, to Deyverdun, to Lord Sheffield; and Franklin with his shrewd simplicity and his whimsical fondness won hearts not only in his own countries of America and England, but even in critical and aristocratic France.

Still, for happiness, love alone is, in the long run, seldom sufficient; there is need also for activity, preferably activity of some use in the world. For men are also gregarious, social creatures. Johnson, however, though he toiled heroically, was haunted by a guilty sense of idleness and waste. Boswell, though he kept his journals, frittered away his days. And Gray was thwarted by the niggardliness of his poetic inspiration; while the learning he piled on learning, like a miser's riches, was a means of killing his time rather than of enriching his life. He could acquire knowledge; but he could not impart it, living, nor keep it, dead. Gibbon, by contrast, did his job (though he did not like it much) as captain of Hampshire grenadiers; and was rewarded by being the better able to do his real job of reviving a dead Rome, and writing a history which survives all that modern research can find to correct in it. Hume, having done for philosophy the best service perhaps that can be done for it, by proving the futility of much of it, was not only an effective public servant, but also played a lasting part in diffusing tolerance and sense. And Franklin, as scientist, diplomat, patriot, and humanitarian, was probably the happiest of them all, in seeing, before he died, the new world he had largely created, and finding it good. Perhaps, even his balanced judgement was slightly carried away by the optimism of the time. 'Thank God,' he wrote to his French friend, Le Veillard, in 1788, 'the world is growing wiser and wiser: and as by degrees men are convinced of the folly of wars for religion, for domination, or for commerce, they will be happier and happier.' Le Veillard was to be guillotined.

But if Franklin became over-optimistic, this was for him a pleasant error. Possibly his hopes merely ante-dated a saner future: possibly they were only a kindly dream. But at least they lasted his time.

It may, of course, be felt that Franklin, despite his occasional rhyming, suffered from a certain lack of poetry. Yet, he enjoyed Thomson.

> 'Whatever Thomson writes,' says a letter to Strahan in 1744, 'send me a dozen copies of. I had read no poetry for several years, and almost lost the Relish of it, till I met with his *Seasons*. That charming Poet has brought more Tears of Pleasure into my Eyes than all I ever read before. I wish it were in my Power to return him any Part of the joy he has given me.'

And again as an old man in 1782, when 'the relish for reading poetry had long left me', he enjoyed Cowper's *Poems*, and read them all, some more than once. He had also strong, if simple, tastes in music; he himself played guitar, harp, and violin. His improvements in the harmonica[1] (musical glasses) may have been partly love of mechanics as well as of art. All the same there remains no tale of him more typical than that which tells how the town of Franklin, having taken his name, asked him to send them church-bells—and received instead a consignment of books; on the ground that 'sense is better than sound'. Some may have disapproved that sober jest; some will disapprove it still. But I shall not join them.

Franklin may be regarded, like Hume, as on the whole a prosaic person. And so to-day he is far less of an influence in the world than, say, Wordsworth. It is of the nature of scientific or political successes that time leaves them behind, superseded. On the other hand, it is easy to exaggerate this aspect. The literary forget how much poetry, also, dies of old age; and how tiny a fragment even of civilized populations cares a pin for poetry. Indeed, there may well be far more to-day who believe in astrology.

Again, there is more good poetry in existence than the world has time for. The supply has long exceeded the demand. For though time slowly gnaws even at poetry, it is a durable thing—like York Minster—which centuries do not make obsolete. Further, however much we owe, and go on owing, to a poet like Wordsworth, it is common enough for poets not to be in other ways the most admirable or attractive of men. I would far rather have the life of a Franklin than of a Wordsworth; I would far rather live with a Franklin than with a Wordsworth. I suspect, indeed, that Words-

[1] Mozart and Beethoven composed for it.

worth, like many of his fellow-bards, would have been most trying to live with.

Nor, even if Franklin seems prosaic, was his life without imagination. He had those imaginative gifts without which it is impossible to become either a scientific discoverer, or a far-sighted statesman; and his playful fancy was probably more effective at redeeming life, for him and his, from dulness, than even the poetic imagination of most poets.

And so there is not only fascination in following his passage through life, there is also a good deal to admire—his many-sidedness; his balance; his happy combination of speculative thought and practical action, which saved him from the irritable frustration common among men too exclusively theoretical or imaginative. 'I will disinherit you,' said Sydney Smith to his daughter, 'if you do not admire everything written by Franklin.' Sydney Smith was given to humorous exaggeration; but he was a man of sense.

It seems to me that our world might gain a good deal in well-being from a multiplication of Franklins. That is why I thought it not unreasonable to redress the balance of this series of literary portraits by calling in from the New World a figure far less literary, yet in some ways still more alive—the Socrates, the Timoleon, and the Archimedes of America.

A very different view, as might be expected, was taken by D. H. Lawrence.[1] Like Carlyle, he saw in Franklin 'the father of all the Yankees'; but, more vehement even than Carlyle, he saw the United States as a nation of dreary, futile, muck-raking dummies, hustling and bustling, ape-like, about a colossal cage. 'The pattern American' writes Lawrence, 'this dry, moral, utilitarian little democrat, has done more to ruin the old Europe than any Russian nihilist.' He is particularly outraged by Franklin's homely list of virtues; which he replaces by thirteen improved rules of his own—for example, 'Cleanliness. Don't be too clean. It impoverishes the blood.' This, if not science, is at least candour.

The gulf, of course, between types so opposite as Franklin and Lawrence remains unbridgeable. There can hardly be reconciliation between those who value, above all, 'fire in the belly' and those who value light in the brain. Lawrence liked to picture himself as a wolf

[1] *Studies in Classical American Literature.*

with red eyes, and as a dark forest full of multitudes of selves and strange gods, including the Holy Ghost; whereas Franklin, he thought, subconsciously hated Europe and set out to destroy it. Hence Lawrence's conclusion—'Let Hell loose and get your own back, Europe!' To this kindly wish I suppose Franklin might have replied with a smile that, like King George in 1775, Europe did 'let Hell loose' in 1914 and 1939—and only strengthened America. What Europe 'got back' is less apparent. As for 'subconsciously hating' that Europe in which he lived a quarter of a century, and several times considered settling for life, even were this pretty theory true, Franklin might have asked why it should be wicked for him to hate Europe, yet right for Lawrence to hate so much of America.

But the debate is idle. I suppose one should be grateful for the infinite variety of human nature—though I own I should not much lament a world without Lawrences. Too many Franklins—too many of any type—would grow monotonous. But the risk of many Franklins seems remote. I think we could do with a good many more.

CONCLUSION

How did life feel to those who had outlived this age 'qui venait de disparaître dans le flot de l'histoire, avec un bruit de soie, un murmure de chansons, et quelques grandes pensées'? How did it seem to older eyes as the new century advanced, its first decades daemonic with the intoxication of Napoleon and the Romantics; its skies darkened, here by the smoke of cannonades, there by the smoke of furnace-chimneys; its masses more and more regimented, here into the barracks of the new conscription, there into the factories of the new industrialism?

Perhaps, indeed, those who remembered the years before 1789 when, as Talleyrand told Guizot, it was possible to know 'la douceur de vivre', were yet in some ways less conscious of the contrast between eighteenth and nineteenth centuries than we. History seems much slower to live through than to read. Retrospect foreshortens. As Horace Walpole put it, the coffee-house wits of Pella may well have thought Alexander an unconscionable while a-conquering the world. Even revolutions take time. Month by month, year by year, one imperceptibly adapts oneself. Those who to-day can still recall another period when the world seemed comparatively civilized, before 1914, have long grown used to things that our grandfathers would have thought past endurance or even belief. The transformations we have lived through may perhaps likewise appear more abrupt and astonishing to our posterity than to ourselves.

Besides, between the settled life of the eighteenth century and the settled life of the nineteenth there intervened the great murky interregnum of the Revolutionary and Napoleonic Wars, blurring the full sense of the contrast; as two World Wars have blurred it for us.

Yet there come moments when we can glimpse the spirit of the old order in contrast and conflict with the new. They may be trivial, but none the less vivid, as when through the eyes of Harriet Martineau, for example, we catch a fleeting vision of Walpole's Miss Berrys (1762–1852, 1763–1852) as they appeared to the new England of the Reform Bill—two dear old ladies, still charming, but now half shocking, and most bizarre, with their rouge, their pearl-powder, their false hair, their usage (horrid to Evangelical ears) of such startling profanities as 'Oh Christ!' or 'My God!' Or, less quaintly pleasant, there are literary Bourbons and die-hard champions of the old order like that cantankerous Irishman, J. W. Croker (1780–1857)—who was yet not without certain merits—bedevilling the new poetry of Keats or Tennyson.

Or again, on a quite different level, there is that true daughter of eighteenth-century good sense, Jane Austen (1775–1817), smiling ironically at current fashions in over-sensibility or hyper-romanticism, which went back, indeed, to Richardson and Sterne, Walpole and Rousseau, but were still mounting to their irrational climax.

There is Sydney Smith (1771–1845), typical of the Enlightenment in that enlightened gaiety which perhaps damaged his career in this more solemn age (he had sunk, he observed by his levity, while—no less contrary to physics—his brother had risen by his gravity); and characteristically wise when, for instance, he takes to task the over-conscientious Lord Grey in the throes of the Reform Bill. 'Do your best with a gay and careless heart. What is it all but the scratching of pismires upon a heap of earth? Rogues are careless and gay, why not honest men? Think of the Bill in the morning, and take your claret in the evening, totally forgetting the Bill.' No wonder Sydney Smith loved Franklin.[1]

Or there is Jeffrey (1773–1850), good-naturedly, but vainly urging a similar balance and proportion on the fanatical and roman-

---

[1] Equally sensible and, I think, admirable is his advice to Lady Morpeth against melancholia (1820). 'Nobody has suffered more from low spirits than I have done' (few would have suspected it)—'so I feel for you'. Remedies: (1) 'Live as well as you dare.' (2) Showerbaths, 75°–80°. (3) 'Amusing books.' (4) 'Short views of human life —not further than dinner or tea.' (5) 'Be as busy as you can.' (6) 'See as much as you can of those friends who respect and like you.' (7) 'And of those acquaintances who amuse you.' (8) Confide low spirits to friends—'they are always worse for dignified concealment'. (9) Watch the effects of tea and coffee. (10) 'Compare your lot with that of other people.' (11) 'Don't expect too much from human life—a sorry business at the best.' (12) Avoid poetry; the theatre (except comedy); music; serious novels; melancholy, sentimental people; and everything emotional not leading to 'active benevolence'. (13) '*Do good*, and endeavour to please everybody of every degree.' (14) A maximum of open air without fatigue. (15) A gay and pleasant room. (16) A struggle, little by little, against idleness. (17) 'Do yourself justice.' (18) 'Keep good blazing fires.' (19) 'Be firm and constant in the exercise of rational religion.' (20) 'Believe me, dear Lady Georgiana, Very truly yours, Sydney Smith.'

tic young Carlyle. Why must he be 'so dreadfully in earnest'? 'You have no *mission* upon earth, whatever you may fancy, half so important as to be innocently happy, and all that is good for you of poetic feeling and sympathy with majestic nature will come of its own accord, without your straining after it.' 'You must have gifts and tasks and duties—and relations with the universe, and strugglings to utter forth the truth—God help you and your vainglorious jargon!' But it was no use. The eighteenth century persuaded in vain. For, like many in this more earnest age, Carlyle 'preferred seriousness to truth'.[1]

There is a similar clash between the rationalism of Peacock (1785–1866) and the romantic idealism of his friend Shelley. For Peacock, though eccentrically romantic in many ways himself, and born so late in the eighteenth century, kept still a good deal of its mentality. For him, as for Sydney Smith, 'the worst thing is good enough to be laughed at, though it be good for nothing else: and the best thing, though it be good for something else, is good for nothing better'. Well may his Mr Hilary observe to Mr Cypress, almost in the words of Walpole to Mme du Deffand[2]: 'You talk like a Rosicrucian, who will love nothing but a sylph, who does not believe in the existence of a sylph, and who yet quarrels with the whole Universe for not containing a sylph.' But there is no reasoning with Mr Cypress— 'Sir, I have quarrelled with my wife; and a man who has quarrelled with his wife is absolved from all duty to his country. I have written an ode to tell the people as much, and they may take it as they list.'

A like division of personality between the old age and the new ran be seen in other figures of the time—in Landor who, with all his comantic quixotries and gasconades, could yet regard with aristocratic disdain 'the hot and uncontrolled harlotry of a flaunting and dishevelled enthusiasm'; in Byron, combining the pageant of his

---

[1] For happiness Carlyle had the fierce contempt of a Nazi. 'There is in man a HIGHER than Love of Happiness' (*Sartor Resartus*); 'Happiness is not only not to be attained on earth, but not even to be desired' (to Goethe); 'Happy, my brother? First of all, what difference is it whether thou art happy or no?' (on Byron). When some poor wretch at Carlyle's house said that the first aim was the happiness of the people, he brought down such a tempest that he had to be escorted from the room by an apologetic Jane, leaving the sage to pace up and down, running his fingers through his hair—'Happiness! Happiness! The fools ought to be chained up!' Heroic, tragic, comical—but not so amusing, in the long run, for the sage's much-tried wife.

[2] P. 123.

bleeding heart with a cynically sharp eye for human folly and affectation, an admiration for Pope, and a contempt for that 'puddle of water-worms', the Lake Poets; in Benjamin Constant, parched with thirst for emotion, yet killing his feelings by that dry dissection he had learnt from Boswell's Zélide, Mme de Charrière; in Stendhal, veering between French logic and Italian passion, between the cold clarity of the Code Napoléon and the abandonment of grand opera, between mathematics, 'comme n'admettant pas l'hypocrisie et le vague, mes deux bêtes d'aversion', and the melodrama of *crimes passionels*; even in Goethe, during those Olympian later years when the author of *The Sorrows of Werther* could yet sum up classicism as health, romanticism as disease.

But perhaps the following passage presents more definitely some of the differences, as seen by ageing eyes, between the Enlightenment, at its best, and the eighteen-twenties. Prejudiced, no doubt; yet, I think, understandable.

> That Age's Dust annoys the Eyes of this;
> Its Verse seems tinkling; its Art, artifice.
> Thin rings its smiling Wisdom in your ears,
> Stunn'd by the Thunder of titanic Years;
> Yet, as those Thunders pass, from far away
> Steal back the Whispers of that vanish'd day—
> Faint as the silken Rustle of a Dress,
> Light as a falling Roseleaf's last Caress.
> I see again dead Faces that once knew
> How to make Life *seem* perfect—yes, a Few;
> Proud without Pomp, graceful without Parade,
> Gay, tolerant, ironic, unafraid,
> They met Life's End, or Love's, Old Age, Disease,
> Undazed by Raptures or by Rhapsodies.
> Mankind might be sad Dogs to contemplate;
> And yet why poison Life, like Swift, with Hate?
> And hate so many Millions? What a Hell!
> Not even Pope could do it. *Vive la bagatelle!*
> Love might be Folly—without it, Life is dead;
> 'What's a Heart for, but to be lost?' we said;
> 'Yet he whose Heart is lost, needs not to lose his Head.
> Castles in Clouds?—though rose and gold they gleam,
> Better clear Vision than the rosiest Dream.

See the harsh Truth; and, seeing, put it by.
Take thought to *live*—it takes no thought to die.'

Your lovers crave a headier Love than we—
Frenzy, and Anguish, and Hyperbole:
Is Love much happier than it used to be?
Your Poets soar upon a wilder Wing:
Does Sense not suffer—sometimes?—when they sing?
Old Eyes grow dim. And yet to mine it seems
Your Wordsworth is a Boor; your Shelley screams;
Byron himself's half vulgar. Froth on muddy Streams.
Your prosing Coleridge, tepid as his Tea,
Of things eternal drawls eternally—
A portly Goldfish in his Highgate Bowl
Mouthing, in Circles, of Reason and the Soul;
A dry-rot Log, a Glow-worm lost in Moss,
Brave Mariner once, and now—dead Albatross.
Ah, for an Hour of Johnson back again,
Rugged as Oak, frank as a Lion, as Sunlight plain!
Or, if you call for what shall stab the Heart,
One cry of Burke, one Love-song of Mozart!
Yes, Gainsborough could paint, and Gibbs could build,
And good old Handel jingle when he willed.

Your Age grows richer—need not count the cost
(So rich its Gains) of some things it has lost—
A Balance, a Sense of Measure, a laughing Grace,
Strange to your noisier Lives, your busier Pace.
Your Forges smoke, your Factories advance—
But *I* hear Voices from a vanish'd France.

This, indeed, is no authentic document. I made it up.[1] But I suspect it is not wholly untrue.

The special attractiveness of the eighteenth century at its best is obviously far more than a matter of mere good sense. Good sense alone, without heart and imagination to balance it, can become a dull and deadly virtue of Philistines. Flaubert's M. Homais the apothecary judged himself a paragon of good sense. But in the type of eighteenth-century character that I mean, there is a whole set of

---

[1] *From Many Times and Lands*, pp. 259–60.

qualities, essentially civilized, which are allied to good sense, but which good sense alone could never give. They need also temperament, training, tradition.

There is, for example, the admirable eighteenth-century tradition of intellectual honesty; because good sense soon discovers that pleasant self-deceptions tend to have anything but pleasant consequences. Whether the period as a whole was intellectually more honest than others, I do not know—it had plenty of pompous rhetoric and cant; but I do not know any period whose outstanding figures stress honesty of mind so forcibly. 'Things and actions are what they are, and the consequences of them will be what they will be: why then should we desire to be deceived?' Easy to say: much less easy to practise. That sentence from Bishop Butler's Sermons has a hard, blunt, steely ring about it, a little startling in a sermon, or a bishop.

There are examples enough of this frank clarity of vision, sometimes even ruthless, bleak, or crude, in characters like Johnson or Chesterfield, Walpole, Hume, or Franklin, Lady Mary Wortley Montagu, Mme du Deffand, or Mme de Charrière. But the same quality can flash out at moments in lesser figures of the time. For example, invited to become president of the Norwich Bible Society, Lord Orford replies: 'I have long been addicted to the Gaming Table. I have lately taken to the Turf. I fear I frequently blaspheme. But I have never distributed religious tracts. All this was known to you and your Society. Notwithstanding which you think me a fit person to be your president. God forgive your hypocrisy!'[1] Or again Sterne, rashly asserting that writers of loose literature should be hanged at their own house-doors, brings on himself the quiet retort of Garrick: 'But, you, I believe, live in lodgings.'

In the age that followed, it became romantic to be swept away by passions; but more respectable than ever to inhibit them—except that passion for work, money, and position, which had long been respectable even for the pious; ever since the seventeenth century when, as has been cleverly said, Calvin became in a sense the Marx of the bourgeoisie. In consequence, the nineteenth-century Roman-

---

[1] Samuel Butler (*Notebooks*, 1951, p. 275) assigns this passage, for which I can no longer trace my source, to 1824. If so, the Lord Orford would be the great-grandson (1783-1858) of Horace Walpole's uncle Horatio.

tics often tended to factitious exaltation; the nineteenth-century respectable to puritanic hypocrisy; and the twentieth century has reacted, sometimes excessively, against the self-deceiving stimulations of the one and the self-deceiving inhibitions of the other. But really to understand the eighteenth century, it is vital to realize that its wisest did not wish to exchange emotion for passionless reason—they merely preferred, like Hume, the calmer emotions, which stimulate the mind, to the more violent emotions, which blind it. It has yet to be shown that they were wrong.

Secondly, with this tradition of honesty towards fact and towards oneself there went, in the eighteenth century at its finest, a tradition of sincerity and simplicity towards others. For good sense must recognize the vanity of pretences in a world where they can, at best, only win an esteem not worth having, for a period not worth considering, from people not worth winning. If one cannot please by being oneself, one is still less likely to please by posing as someone, or something, else. 'Il n'y a que les prétentions qui rendent ridicules.'[1] 'Simplicity and frankness,' wrote Duclos (1704–72), 'can exist in the finest genius, and then they are its most precious and attractive ornament. Little wonder if the vulgar, unworthy to appreciate gifts so rare, admire subtlety of character—often merely the fruit of the fixed, persistent concentration of a mediocre intelligence, animated by self-interest. But such subtlety never goes with a superior intellect, unless combined with a mean heart. A superior intellect disdains petty instruments, it employs only those that are great—that is, simple.' A view perhaps itself over-simple; yet revealing and significant—not least for our own age whose intellectuals have often tended, I think, to attach a quite fantastic value to mere complexity. I once made a collection of last words; it was striking how the men and women of the eighteenth century, even in dying, stood out by their simple directness, humour, or wit. To strut, they knew, is stupid; to preach is tiresome; to lament is weak; the best answer to life's ironies is—irony.

Thirdly, there was that growing tradition of liberty which found a triumphant climax in America, a comic one with Wilkes, a tragic one in France. 'When the eighteenth century,' writes Michelet, 'produces the Regency, the *Lettres Persanes*, and Voltaire, its move-

[1] Mme de Sabran.

ment is simple— it is mounting towards the light, away from the dark Middle Age. Even when it extends itself, through Diderot and the *Encyclopedia*, it still pursues its course. And the apparent divergence of Rousseau leads by a different road towards the same goal.

'All can be summed in a phrase—the escalade of liberty.

'But the nineteenth century, rich and vast, yet heavy, sets its face towards fatality.'

Naïvety there may have been in their failure to realize the inadequacy of political liberty alone, while still coupled with economic slavery. But those, I think, are over-cynical who are no longer stirred by the finest periods of Burke, or the calm majesty of Lord Mansfield pronouncing the freedom of the negro Somersett, because he had breathed of English air. And there is at least something extraordinary in the audacious self-reliance with which Fox could wear the blue and buff of Washington's officers in the House of Commons; or the Duke of Richmond, as Lord Lieutenant of Sussex, sail his yacht through the British fleet, in the King's presence, flying from his masthead the colours of the rebel states. Extravagant or not, here is a defiant individualism none too common in our age of docile masses and tyrannic organization; when even our games can be blamed by an American critic because 'the cheering is quite unorganized'.

Fourthly, there was the remarkable growth of enlightened tolerance—respect for the intellectual liberty of others—in a century that began with burning heretics and witches (backward Poland burnt two witches even in 1793), and ended by laughing over the audacities of Voltaire, to whose statue four crowned heads subscribed. (Imagine Voltaire's expectation of life—or at least of liberty—in the totalitarian states of to-day.) Slowly good sense convinced men of the impossibility of imposing the same certainties on everyone; and convinced a few, like Hume, of the difficulty of finding any certainties at all.[1]

But the battle was long, slow, and hard. Even in 1787 when, 102 years after the Revocation of the Edict of Nantes, civil status in

[1] Cf. Voltaire, *Dictionnaire*, 'Certain': 'Je suis certain; j'ai des amis; ma fortune est sûre; mes parens ne m'abandonneront jamais; on me rendra justice; mon ouvrage est bon, il sera bien reçu; on me doit, on me paiera; mon amant sera fidèle, il l' a juré; le ministre m'avancera, il l'a promis en passant: toutes paroles qu'un homme qui a un peu vécu raye de son dictionnaire.'

France was at last granted to the Protestants, the Church lifted up a disconsolate wail to Louis XVI: 'Ah, Sire, quelle source inépuisable d'amertumes pour l'Église et de séductions pour les enfants, si l'indulgence de la nouvelle législation préparait la voie à un tolérantisme universel!' And even England still penalized Catholics and Dissenters; though, years before, Frederick of Prussia had maintained that his subjects should choose their own routes to Heaven. (Unfortunately by his military genius he sent tens of thousands there himself.)

It was in this field that Voltaire, whatever his faults—mischief, malice, frivolity, superficiality, found at last, as an old man, his finest years. He was sixty-eight when he rose, in 1762, to defend Calas; in 1764-71 it was Sirven; in 1765, La Barre; in 1766, Lally-Tollendal; in 1769, Martin; in 1770, the Montbaillis. 'Affaiblis peu à peu toutes les superstitions anciennes, et n'en introduis aucune nouvelle.' We in our time have introduced enough of them. How well our century of tyrants could have done with that deadly smile and indomitable pen!

Fifthly, there was a growing tradition of civilized humanity and courtesy—a wider form of tolerance. There remained in the men of that age plenty of brutalities that sicken us; but then in other ways we should have sickened them; and it is only fair to consider not only to what point they progressed, but also from what point their progress had to begin. In 1649, after putting 3,000 men to the sword at the storm of Drogheda, Cromwell could write, without a glimmer of irony: 'This hath been a marvellous great mercy. . . . I wish that all honest hearts may give the glory of this to God alone, to whom indeed the praise of this mercy belongs.' But in 1759, it is said, when France was losing battle after battle against Frederick, a jeweller of Grenoble offered the French Minister for War a formula for inextinguishable fire. Tests were successful. But Louis XV (not usually much regarded as a character) thought it would make war too inhuman; and sent the man home with a pension of 2,000 livres to hold his tongue. One can imagine what such minds would have thought of our nuclear weapons.

Now it is true that, only two years before, this same Louis XV had allowed his would-be assassin, the imbecile Damiens, to be executed with tortures at which even the modern Gestapo might have blenched. But legal barbarities seem to have been one of the most backward aspects of the period. Even so, it is striking how little one hears, even during the worst excesses in the French Revolution, of that use of torture which has become revoltingly common in the world to-day; where even the electricity that Franklin beneficently drew from Heaven can be perverted to such infernal purposes.

At times, indeed, the civilized decency of the Enlightenment becomes, by modern standards, astounding. Even in wartime the British Admiralty continued to forward the Voyages which the Abbé Prévost was translating into French. Even in wartime, letters and travellers continued to pass. In 1779, according to Mme du Deffand, English travellers could enter France without passports; though they needed them to return from France to England. In 1778, when Admiral Rodney was detained in Paris by creditors, the old Maréchal Biron thrice pressed on him a loan of 1,000 louis to pay them and return to England. In 1782, when Rodney had defeated de Grasse, the Paris populace grew angry with the old Maréchal for this costly quixotry; but he refused to repent—'he gloried in the man whose liberty he had effected, and in the victory he had so nobly won'. (The French Republic and Napoleon were soon to make an end of such cosmopolitan courtesy in Europe.) Similarly General Eliott, according to d'Allonville, chose to travel by way of France to the Gibraltar he was successfully to defend against France and Spain. 'What!' he was asked. 'In spite of the war?' 'But the English and French are civilized people.' A reply, says d'Allonville, that 'deeply shocked the good Germans'. At the siege of Gibraltar (1779–83), says Mme de Boigne, the Comte d'Artois did not show himself very brave; so the French commander would warn the English when the Comte made his tours of inspection; and they refrained from firing. Reproached for this subterfuge, M. de Maillebois replied: 'Mais cela valait encore mieux que la grimace qu'il faisait le premier jour.' In 1789, besieging Belgrade, the Prince de Ligne characteristically records: 'Je voyais avec un grand plaisir militaire et une grande peine philosophique s'élever dans l'air douze mille bombes que j'ai fait lancer sur ces pauvres infidèles.'[1] We have travelled far here from Cromwell at Drogheda; who would indeed, have regarded the Prince de Ligne as a licentious son of Belial. Their

[1] Cf. pp. 101–2.

moralities were different. 'Je suis,' writes the Prince, 'ni assez moral, moraliste, et moralisateur pour prêcher, et je me moque de ceux qui ne croient pas à ma moralité; mais elle consiste à rendre tout le monde heureux autour de moi.' There have been worse.

Finally, there was in the best of these people an admirable tradition of gaiety; apt, no doubt, to degenerate at times into a dangerous frivolity; yet based on a sane realization that few things are really so important as the solemn assume. And, above all, they kept a tradition of measure and proportion, grace and style, doomed quickly to disappear with the passing of their aristocratic world. 'Rien en relief' was the inscription in the salon of Mme Geoffrin; and very significant, both of that age and of the age to follow, is the reply of the Duchesse de Choiseul to Mme du Deffand, who had been laughed at for using such a strange word as *énergie*—'Assurément je le connais. Je peux même fixer l'époque de sa naissance. C'est depuis qu'on a des convulsions en entendant la musique.' Blake would not have been amused: but Dr Johnson might have given an indulgent smile.

Such, I imagine, were some of the qualities that helped to produce, for the happy few, Talleyrand's *douceur de vivre*. Many of these values, no doubt, can also be found far earlier, in the ancient literature of Greece and Rome—particularly of Greece. For the Greeks too loved sanity, grace, liberty, many-sidedness, and balance; and expressed that love in a literature often richer, more perfect, and vastly more poetic, than that of the eighteenth century. But, for us, the Greeks are remoter. To many, they are accessible only in translation. We cannot know them as intimately as we can know Walpole, Hume, Franklin, and their fellows.

What, one may wonder, would these men have thought, could they have known our age, as we know theirs? Hume, I suppose, might have been gratified to find his philosophy had worn so well; and might see little reason to-day to grow one jot less sceptical. Walpole could observe that he long ago foretold, in the days of Montgolfier's first balloons and of the French Revolution, what might happen to a pugnacious world where increase of knowledge brings so little increase of wisdom, and whose civilization remains only skin-deep. Franklin, more fascinated by the giant progress of his beloved science, might yet shake his wise old head and reflect how right he was to say that men are often devils to one another, and that most of them might be better with a set of healthy instincts than with the so-called 'reason' they seem only able to misuse. Burke's eyes might be fixed even more grimly on Moscow and Pekin than once on Jacobin Paris; horrified to see the Leviathan of Hobbes grown so vast that his nose rests on the Elbe, his tail in the Yellow Sea. And Gibbon might own that perhaps he spoke too soon in saying that civilization could never again be menaced with barbaric destruction, as in the days of Rome.

And what would they do, had they another span of life in our anxious age? Much the same, perhaps, as before. Hume might still cultivate philosophy and friendship; Walpole write endless letters, even if annoyed to be answered so often by telephone; Franklin, finding modern science too specialized for him, turn again to public service, propaganda in the cause of common sense, and gaiety; Burke sharpen his pen once more to better the feeble case that the West seems to make for itself, despite its better cause, against the ceaseless propaganda of the Kremlin; and Gibbon, perhaps, sit down for another twenty years (mistakenly, one hopes) to pen *The Decline and Fall of the Western Empire*. For, after all, they knew that the two most hopeful foundations for happiness are, first, work (and plenty of it); secondly, affection. *Amando, laborando*.

Would they be as effective as once they were? That seems by no means certain. Our world has turned away from their aristocracies, their classics, their passion for the rational. Its writers, instead of trying to be the conscience of mankind, have tended to concern themselves more and more with providing stranger and stranger forms of intoxication. There seems to me much truth in Julien Benda's *Trahison des Clercs*. Orpheus, who once humanized the wolves, now often prefers, instead, to howl with them.

Many years ago I was struck by a passage in Arthur Waley's introduction to *The Analects of Confucius*: 'The downfall of Liberalism has been due to the failure to associate the Middle Way with any strong trend of emotion. The success of Confucianism, its triumph over "all the hundred schools" from the second century B.C. onwards, was due in a large measure to the fact that it contrived to endow compromise with an emotional glamour.'

How on earth did Confucius do it? For though he is said to have died disappointed and disillusioned by his failure (like Plato's) to influence the rulers of his day; though his teaching met violent opposition from other schools, such as Taoists and Realists; though it became, as is the way, garbled and vulgarized by posterity; still its effects endured for century on century—and this although the Master refused to bribe men with hopes or fears of the hereafter,[1] and contented himself with an aristocratic reasonableness that seems at times very eighteenth-century, and must account for some of the congenial attractiveness that the eighteenth century found in China.

Consider some of his utterances.

'The Master said: "The true gentleman is conciliatory, but not pliable. Common people are pliable, but not conciliatory.'

'The Master said: "The true gentleman is easy to serve, yet difficult to please. For if you try to please him in any manner inconsistent with the Way, he refuses to be pleased; but in using the services of others he only expects of them what they are capable of performing. Common people are difficult to serve, but easy to please. Even though you try to please them in a manner inconsistent with the Way, they will still be pleased; but in using the services of others they expect them (irrespective of their capacities) to do any work that comes." '

Now where is the 'emotional glamour' of such things? They seem to me delightful, because admirably wise, admirably clear-cut in thought and word. But what is there in them to capture the feelings of the many?

'The virtue of a gentleman,' Confucius also said, 'is like the wind; and that of common men, like grass. The wind blows; the grass bows the same way.'

Unfortunately, as he seems to have found to his cost, common men can often be much more like stones than grass, and may bow not one millimetre to all such winds of wisdom.

The success of Confucianism remains for me a mystery. I can only suggest that there was in him something that suited the shrewd, wise practicality already characteristic of many Chinese minds. He was perhaps preaching to men by temperament already half converted. He uttered what, after long years of anarchy, they were ready for, though they could not formulate it for themselves. He did

[1] 'While you do not know life, how should you know about death?'

not force—he reinforced—their minds. Even genius may need hearers who are already, by nature, 'congenial'—'les âmes amies'. The rest are indifferent, or even indignant. No matter. It is all in the day's work.

Something of the kind seems suggested at moments by Confucius himself.

'The Master said: "Only one who bursts with eagerness, do I instruct; only one who bubbles with excitement, do I enlighten." '

'The Master said: "Not to talk to one who could be talked to, is to waste a man. To talk to those who cannot be talked to, is to waste one's words. He who is truly wise, never wastes a man; but, on the other hand, he never wastes his words." '

The wisest of the eighteenth century seem to me as well worth listening to as Confucius. My part has been merely that of Scott's Old Mortality, who busied himself in clearing the moss, and bringing back to light the words, on the gravestones of the dead who seemed to him to have served humanity. This needs to be done and redone, generation after generation, in a world where there persists always a strong tendency to read newer writers, not because they are better, but just because they are newer. The moss grows fast, and ceaselessly.

To not a few of these eighteenth-century minds, Reason seemed something to be loved like a mistress: for many in the century and a half since then Reason has become, rather, a boring, nagging wife, hard to get rid of completely, but very hard to endure. Better, they feel, the livelier intoxication of flirting with nonsense, or frenzy.

> You know, my Friends, with what a brave Carouse
> I made a Second Marriage in my house;
>   Divorced old barren Reason from my bed,
> And took the Daughter of the Vine to Spouse.

Yet one may doubt whether that second marriage, and its offspring, have proved after all so happy. I have seen the flower of my generation die of it; and a quarter of the earth become a prison.

Reason need not be the sterile kill-joy that some suppose. She can be on the contrary fascinating, amusing, exciting, consoling, like that Mme Geoffrin of whom Walpole wrote from Paris in 1765: 'I never saw anybody in my days that catches one's faults and vanities and impositions so quick, that explains them to one so clearly, and convinces one so easily. I never liked to be set right before. You cannot imagine how I taste it. I make her both my confessor and director; and begin to think I shall be a reasonable creature at last, which I had never intended to be. The next time I see her, I believe I shall say, "Oh! Common Sense, sit down. I have been thinking so and so; is it not absurd?" '

Such characters as Mme Geoffrin, such ages as hers, are not common. Some will grant that they are very entertaining—but no more. For some resent the idea that they have anything to learn from any-one. How insulting! And how tedious! Yet I doubt if it is possible not to learn from the company one keeps—in books as much as in life. One is moulded, if not by sympathy with them, then by re-action against them; and if not consciously, then unconsciously. If some find these eighteenth-century characters merely amusing, very well. Even that is something gained. But it is my experience—naïve, perhaps—that there are plenty of occasions in life when it is by no means an idle question, either for one's own happiness or for that of those who have to live with one, to ask 'What would John-son or Hume have thought? What would Franklin or Montesquieu have done?'

INDEX

INDEX